Slavophile Thought
and the
Politics of Cultural Nationalism

SUNY series in National Identities

Thomas M. Wilson, editor

Slavophile Thought
and the
Politics of Cultural Nationalism

Susanna Rabow-Edling

State University of New York Press

Published by
State University of New York Press, Albany

For information, address State University of New York Press,
194 Washington Avenue, Suite 305, Albany, NY 12210–2384

Production by Michael Haggett
Marketing by Anne M. Valentine

Library of Congress Cataloging-in-Publication Data

Rabow-Edling, Susanna.
    Slavophile thought and the politics of cultural nationalism / Susanna Rabow-Edling.
        p. cm. — (SUNY series in national identities)
    Includes bibliographical references and index.
    ISBN 0-7914-6693-0 (hardcover : alk. paper)
    ISBN 0-7914-6694-9 (pbk : alk. paper)
    ISBN-13: 978-0-7914-6693-3 (hardcover : alk. paper)
    ISBN-13: 978-0-7914-6694-0 (pbk. : alk. paper)
    1. Russia—Intellectual life—1801–1917. 2. Slavophilism—Russia—History—
19th century. 3. Russians—Ethnic identity. 4. Nationalism—Russia—History—
19th century. I. Title. II. Series.

DK189.2'R333   2006
320.54'0947'09034—dc22
                                                                                2005014016

10 9 8 7 6 5 4 3 2 1

Contents

Acknowledgments

This book has been long in making and I have incurred many debts on the way. It began as a dissertation at Stockholm University and I would like to thank everyone at the Department of Political Science, who contributed to make this a special time both intellectually and socially. Several people read and commented on drafts of my work at different stages and they deserve special mention: Björn Beckman, Henrik Berglund, Birgir Hermansson, Maria Jansson, Bo Lindensjö, Betil Nygren, Jouni Reinikainen, Daniel Tarschys, Maria Wendt Höjer and all the members of *The Beagle Boys* (and Girls). The Institute of Foreign Affairs, the Anna Ahlström and Ellen Terserus Foundation, and Stockholm University provided financial support for my research. A grant from the Swedish Institute gave me the possibility to work at Oxford University for two terms. I am also grateful to a number of specialists on Russian history and political thought and on the politics of nationalism, who read the manuscript either in part or in its entirety. Robin Aizlewood, Catherine Andreyev, Kristian Gerner, Susan McCaffray, Derek Offord, Nicholas Riasanovsky, and Bernard Yack all offered helpful criticism and advice.

John Hutchinson served as "Faculty Opponent" when I defended my dissertation. I am grateful to him for turning this ordeal into an interesting discussion and for his important remarks and suggestions. I am also indebted to Per-Arne Bodin och Lena Jonson, who acted as examiners.

The revision of the dissertation into a book began at Cornell University. I would like to thank the Department of Government and especially Valerie Bunce for inviting me as a visiting scholar and providing a stimulating yet peaceful environment. I am grateful to The Swedish Foundation for International Cooperation in Research and Higher Education (STINT) for funding my stay at Cornell. The final revision of the book was made at the Department of East European Studies, Uppsala University. I would like to thank my colleagues in the department for offering me such a warm welcome and for their keen interest in Russian history.

I owe my greatest debt to Max Edling, who read numerous versions of the manuscript, despite his deep aversion to the Slavophiles. His criticism of Romantic thought has been particularly helpful. Katarina Rehn and Ingegerd Rabow offered comments on grammar and language. I am grateful to them both.

Finally, I wish to acknowledge the kind permission of editors and publishers to use material from: "The Political Significance of Cultural Nationalism: The Slavophiles and Their Notion of a Russian Enlightenment" in *Nationalities Papers*, vol. 32, no. 2, June 2004, *http://www.tandf.co.uk* and "The Role of Europe in Russian Nationalism" Copyright © Edited by Susan P. McCaffray and Michael Melancon. From: *Russia in the European Context, 1789–1914*. By: Edited by Susan P. McCaffray and Michael Melancon. Reprinted with permission of Palgrave Macmillan.

Introduction

The first comprehensive idea of a distinctive Russian national identity was articulated by a small group of intellectuals, the so-called Slavophiles, in the second quarter of the nineteenth century.[1] This original Russian nationalism is commonly seen as a conservative criticism of modern society. Its advent is ascribed to the so-called Westernizers and their promotion of Western liberal values. According to the general view, the Slavophiles reacted against the Westernizers' espousal of Western values by promoting Russian customs and institutions and by taking an interest in Russian history, folklore, and the philosophy of the Eastern doctors of the Church. Their explorations of the Russian soul prepared the ground for subsequent ideas of the distinctive Russian nation. Nevertheless, because of their apparent interest in abstract philosophy, both Westernizers and Slavophiles have been accused of being utopian and of not taking the social realities of contemporary Russia into account. Thus, Andrzej Walicki, one of the leading scholars of Russian thought, writes that it was "a strongly utopian variety of conservatism . . . In fact, it was not so much an ideological defence of an existing tradition, as a utopian attempt to rehabilitate and revive a lost tradition." As a consequence of its "transcenden[ce] in relation to existing social realities," we should understand it as a "conservative utopia." Thus, Slavophilism was "introverted" and did not lead to any activity aimed at changing the world.[2]

Scholars have focused on the philosophical meaning and originality of Slavophile thought, rather than on its historical context. As a consequence, the important question with regards to their ideas has been whether they contributed to a distinctive Russian philosophy, and not why their ideas were formulated in the first place. By shifting the focus from the concepts that have generally been regarded as central to their ideology, to the problems the Slavophiles themselves identified and addressed, this

1

study questions the conventional view of these thinkers as conservative dreamers.[3] It argues instead that Slavophilism was a critical assessment of contemporary Russian society and a project for social change. Slavophilism was formulated as an attempt to solve an identity crisis among Russian intellectuals. Hence, it cannot be treated as an escape from reality. Rather, it should be regarded as a rational confrontation with what contemporaries saw as genuine problems.

This reinterpretation of Slavophile thought is best understood when placed in the context of cultural nationalism, wherein we can make sense of the problems the Slavophiles addressed and the solutions they proposed. Scholars have indeed pointed to links between Slavophilism and cultural nationalism, but this connection has generally rested on a mistaken conception of the cultural idea of the nation, a conception formed by an unjustifiable celebration of the civic or political idea of the nation.

In the early twentieth century, Friedrich Meinecke made a distinction between the political nation, or *Staatsnation*, based on a common political history and a shared constitution, and the cultural nation, *Kulturnation*, based on a shared cultural heritage. The most important distinction between the two is that while membership in the former is voluntary, membership in the cultural nation is not a matter of choice, but of common objective identity. Meinecke maintained that political nationalism derived from the spirit of 1789, i.e. from the idea of the self-determination and sovereignty of the nation. Cultural nationalism, in contrast, strove for national individuality, characteristic of anti-Enlightenment German thought.[4]

Hans Kohn later used this distinction in trying to account for the difference in development between Eastern and Western Europe along with North America. Kohn described the cultural form of Eastern nationalism as an organic, mystical, and often authoritarian nationalism, in contrast to the civic and rational political nationalism of the West. Instead of using Western rationalism and universal standards as its justification, Eastern nationalism looked to the heritage of its own past and extolled the ancient peculiarities of its traditions. Kohn argued that because of the backward state of political and social development, nationalism outside the Western world found its first expression in the cultural field. Here, the nation was the dream and hope of scholars and poets, a venture in education and propaganda rather than in policy-making and government.[5] More recently, Michael Hughes made a similar distinction between what he calls liberal nationalism, inspired by the political ideals of the French Revolution, and

Romantic nationalism. The latter was, in his view, mainly a cultural movement, formed as a reaction against what was perceived as the cold rationalism of the Enlightenment.[6]

Recently, scholars have questioned the dichotomy between a cultural and a political nationalism, but they are mainly interested in criticising the way this dichotomy justifies political nationalism by cleansing it from cultural elements. These scholars claim that a cultural component exists also in political nationalism. Bernard Yack argues that political nationalism is almost always based on ideas of a distinctive cultural identity. The conclusion drawn from this assertion is that "all nationalisms are cultural nationalisms of one kind or another."[7] But the fact that all nationalisms are cultural nationalisms to some degree, does not warrant the rejection of the attempt to distinguish between the basic features of different kinds of nationalisms. After all, there is a fundamental difference between a nationalism based on voluntary allegiance to a constitution and that based on membership in a distinctive people.

Hence, although this recent criticism of the nationalist dichotomy makes important assertions regarding political nationalism, it fails to account for the specific role and character of what is generally referred to as cultural nationalism. In order to make sense of nationalism, both parts of the original dichotomy need to be reconsidered without denying the differences that do exist. Admiration for the political, or civic, idea of the nation has not only neglected the cultural basis of political nationalism, it has also generated distorted images of other forms of nationalism. The contempt or disregard for cultural nationalism has thereby deprived us of a valuable tool for understanding nationalist thought.

Just as political nationalism contains cultural elements, so cultural nationalism can be political, albeit in a way different from political nationalism. This book argues that there is a cultural nationalism with a politics of its own. This form of nationalism has its own specific agenda and its own way of making social changes that does not fit into traditional definitions of politics as having to do with government and the state. In contrast to other forms of nationalism, cultural nationalism does not strive either for a convergence between state and nation, thus realizing the nationality-principle, or for the establishment of political rule based on the principle of popular sovereignty. Instead, it seeks to achieve social change through the moral regeneration of the nation.

This distinctive form of nationalism has received little attention from social scientists because it is seen as nonpolitical in character. Most studies of nationalism have been concerned with the process of nation-building and, consequently, have focused on political movements that are trying to establish an independent nation-state through political means. Given that cultural nationalism is not concerned with political power and control of the state, scholars have regarded it as a marginal and, at the same time, undesirable phenomenon. It has commonly been looked upon as both politically indifferent and as an antimodern, regressive tendency.[8] Since cultural nationalism originally developed as a Romantic critique of the universalistic claims of the French Enlightenment, it has been subjected to the same set of criticism as Romanticism itself. In fact, the common distinction between political and cultural nationalism has its origin in an equally common distinction between Enlightenment and Romantic thought. Thus, whereas Enlightenment thought is seen as politically informed and progressive, Romantic thought is regarded as politically indifferent and regressive. Like cultural nationalists, Romantics have been accused of retreating from an unattractive reality instead of trying to change it.[9]

In a recent study of early German Romanticism, Frederick Beiser challenges the current view of Romantic thought as politically indifferent, arguing that it can, in fact, be seen as a radical political project. The ideas of the early German Romantics, he asserts, were not "harmless abstractions," but powerful weapons used for political struggle. Furthermore, there is a strong continuity with Enlightenment thought; and some Enlightenment ideals, such as education, progress, and universality, are preserved in Romantic thought.[10] For this reason, the use of Romantic concepts and arguments does not make cultural nationalism apolitical and regressive. Indeed, this was a way of thinking and speaking found among many contemporary liberal nationalists.

John Hutchinson makes a case for giving cultural nationalism more scholarly attention by arguing for its significance in shaping the modern political community.[11] He claims that emerging cultural nationalist movements have preceded the struggle for nationhood everywhere in the modern world. Cultural nationalist movements are "historico-cultural revivals" which emerged in nineteenth-century societies. These movements of regeneration subsequently inspired rising social groups to collective political action.[12] Cultural nationalism is based on a historicist view of cultures as unique organisms, "each with its peculiar laws of growth and decay." While the purpose of political nationalism is to gain political power in order to transform the state and make it congruent with the nation, cultural nationalism wishes to transform society in order to realize the nation.

It strives to regenerate the true character of the nation, which is to be manifested in its culture, that is, in its art, thought, and way of life. By reviving the dormant national spirit, cultural nationalism seeks to unite the different aspects of the nation, or rather, of the national culture; the traditional and the modern, the rural and the urban, reason and faith. To cultural nationalists, the glory of a country comes not from its political power but from the culture of its people and the contribution of its thinkers and artists to humanity.[13]

By reformulating Slavophilism in the light of cultural nationalism this study repudiates the prevalent view of the Slavophiles as conservative and utopian. It also questions the image of the origins of Russian nationalism as isolationistic and antagonistic to the West. This view has its foundation in an essentialist conception of Russian culture as fundamentally different from Western culture, which is shared by critics and followers of Russian nationalism alike. Both find explanations for Russia's otherness in her own distinctive culture which, they claim, has been formed in separation from the development of Western culture. In the standard account, there are primarily two historical factors that justify Russia's specific development: the reception of Christianity from Byzantium, and the Mongol invasion. The impact of these events led Russia away from Western individualism toward an acceptance of Eastern absolutism.

Samuel Huntington presents the most provocative argument for cultural difference based on religion. He argues that Russia is the core country of a separate civilization, "carrying and protecting a culture of Eastern Orthodoxy" and that "Europe ends where Western Christianity ends and . . . Orthodoxy begin[s]."[14] In contrast, Richard Pipes employs a political argument for Russia's difference. He claims that what distinguishes Western types of government from non-Western types is the existence of a distinction between political power and private property. In Russia, these institutions were never clearly separated, something Pipes claims accounts for the difficulties in restraining absolutism there. The absence of private property in Russia therefore prevented the development of liberalism and constitutionalism.[15] To the majority of Western scholars, the dichotomy between Russian and Western culture implies not only that the two cultures are fundamentally different, but also that an aversion to the latter is inherent in the former.

According to this view, the lack of what are generally believed to be typically Western values is seen as an expression of a flaw in Russian culture.

Western culture is defined in accordance with positive values, such as civilization, progress, liberty, democracy, openness, and friendliness. Russian culture is regarded as embracing opposite values. It therefore becomes barbarian, backward, intolerant, authoritarian, secluded, and antagonistic.[16] It is this perception of Russian culture that forms the basis for many Western assessments of Russian nationalism. Since this culture is perceived as distinct from Western culture and thereby embodies a string of negative characteristics, it follows that Russian nationalism, basing itself on Russia's national character, must promote these values, which are seen as destructive. Consequently, Russian nationalism has often been described as anti-Western, antagonistic, ethnic, and authoritarian in contrast to the liberal or civic nationalism, which allegedly characterizes most Western countries.[17] Hence, a dichotomy has been created between a good, liberal, rationalistic nationalism in the West and an evil, anti-Western deviation in the East.

As noted, Hans Kohn made the classic and most influential distinction between these two forms, claiming that "[w]hile Western nationalism was, in its origin, connected with the concepts of individual liberty and rational cosmopolitanism current in the eighteenth century, the later nationalism in Central and Eastern Europe and in Asia easily tended towards a contrary development."[18] More recently, the ideology of Russian nationalism has been portrayed as "antagonistic to all the main principles on which modern democracy is based" and seen as a "malignant and monolithic force that is unreformable and tends inexorably towards extreme forms of racism and authoritarianism." Its content is ethnic, collectivist, and authoritarian and infused with anti-Westernism.[19]

To explain this hostility to the West, scholars have long argued that Russians came to dislike the West since it served as the model for its development. "The dependence of the West often wounded the pride of the native educated class, as soon as it began to develop its own nationalism, and ended in an opposition to the 'alien' example and its liberal and rational outlook."[20] Hence, scholars have seen Europe as the Other in relation to which the idea of Russia is defined.[21] Thus, Liah Greenfeld claims that in Russia, *ressentiment* was the single most important factor in determining the terms in which national identity was defined.[22] Pointing to the role of Europe as the Other against which a Russian national identity must be formulated helps to uphold the dichotomy between a Russian and a Western culture. As a result of this thinking, it becomes impossible for Russians to advocate Western values and express a Russian national identity at the same time. When such attempts are made, no effort is spared to prove either that the ideas are not really Western, or else that their aim is not to express a Russian identity.

Following this logic, discovering similarities between the Russian Westernizers and the Slavophiles, Liah Greenfeld claims that the Westernizers were in fact anti-Western nationalists, who, like the Slavophiles, were steeped in *ressentiment*.[23] More common, however, is the perspective which holds that the Westernizers represented the good, liberal, Western-oriented tendency in Russia that had nothing to do with Russian nationalism. According to this view, the Westernizers formulated values diametrically opposed to Slavophilism, which they saw as "a provocative defence of outmoded values."[24] The contention here is that Slavophiles and Westernizers set out with the same anxious concern for the absence of a Russian national culture and its subsequent implications for the future of Russia. The solutions they presented led in different directions, but neither side was steeped in resentment.[25]

In reformulating the common view of Slavophilism, this book questions the Russian-European dichotomy and the view of Russian nationalism as antagonistic to the West. Instead, it seeks to present a more complex image of the role of Europe and the West in shaping a Russian national identity. Martin Malia's conception of Europe as a spectrum of zones graded in level of development from the West to the East is useful to describe the complex position of Russian intellectuals in Europe.[26] Although Russia was located in the extreme periphery, members of the educated elite nevertheless saw themselves as part of Europe. Yet, the country's peripheral location made the question of Russia's relationship to Europe problematic. The Slavophiles wanted Russian culture to assume a leading role in a universal progress of humanity and to make a genuine contribution to the world. The Slavophile project can thus be seen as a desire to claim a position for Russia at the core of Europe.

Despite the great influence Slavophilism has exerted on Russian intellectual life, the ideology was formulated by only four persons. Aleksei Khomiakov (1804–1860) and Ivan Kireevsky (1806–1856), were the older originators; Konstantin Aksakov (1817–1860) and Iurii Samarin (1819–1876) were younger and became Slavophiles only when the core of Slavophile ideas was already articulated. Although the movement was broader, other members did not make any theoretically important contribution to Slavophilism. Since Khomiakov and Kireevsky were the formulators and main contributors to Slavophile thought, this study is primarily based on their writings.[27]

The Slavophiles participated in a public discussion concerning the state of the Russian nation and culture. They were not the only participators, however. The Westernizers, who, as we have seen, are usually considered to have been the Slavophiles' ideological opponents, took part in this discourse as well. Those usually identified as the main figures of the Westernizer group were Vissarion Belinsky (1811–1848), Alexander Herzen (1812–1870), and Mikhail Bakunin (1814–1876), who are commonly referred to as the radical Westernizers, and Timofei Granovsky (1813–1855), Vassilii Botkin (1811–1869), and Pavel Annenkov (1813–1887), who are regarded as more liberal.[28] Like the Slavophiles, the members of this group held diverging ideas and focused on different issues, both individually and as members of the radical or the liberal fraction. The latter differences mainly concerned their attitudes to religion, to the Jacobins of the French Revolution, and to art. But, their differences did not undermine the sense of common political aims.[29] Here, I am concerned only with the radical Westernizers, since their function in this study is to constitute a contrasting reference point to what is usually taken to be the much more conservative ideas of the Slavophiles.

The Westernizers are introduced into this work in order to show that Slavophile ideas were part of a discourse that engaged Russian intellectuals as a group and concerned their own role as both Russians and intellectuals. The contention here is that Slavophilism was formulated as an attempt to create a new identity, which involved both a new role for the nation and for the emerging critical intelligentsia; and that the two roles were intertwined. In formulating their ideas, the Slavophiles were thus trying to find a way out of a dual crisis of identity. Hence, their ideas are perceived as part of a critical discourse in Russia, that involved those who were dissatisfied with the contemporary state of Russian culture. In making this claim, this book challenges the assertion that in contrast to many European countries, nationalism and liberalism did not emerge as part of the same movement in Russia.[30]

The Slavophiles were not only involved in a Russian discourse on the future of their nation but were also part of a general European intellectual discussion, which we know as Romanticism, although more as receivers than as contributors.[31] The discourse about the Russian nation and culture was thus conducted in the idiom of Romanticism. This is seen both in the concepts that the Slavophiles used, the issues they discussed, and the arguments they pursued. It should be noted, however, that in looking at the Slavophiles in the context of Romanticism, I am not concerned with the origins of their Romantic notions, but rather with how the context of the Romantic worldview can further an understanding of the way in which the Slavophiles presented their ideas and what they meant by them. In order to fully understand the formulation of Slavophilism, it is necessary to see it both in the context of the contemporary Russian intellectual criticism and in the context of the Romantic movement.

Official nineteenth-century apologies for the Russian regime were also based on the concept of the nation, but were made in a totally different context. In such accounts, the nation was placed next to orthodoxy and autocracy as the pillars of the state, but it was the state, rather than the nation, that was glorified. The nineteenth-century historian, Alexander Pypin, coined the term "Official Nationality" to describe the nature of these ideas. Although it was supported by a few independent-minded academics, this ideology was never meant to serve anything but the government. By providing an official definition of the Russian nation, the promulgation of this doctrine was intended to put an end to independent thoughts on the matter. Unofficial opinions were proscribed. The Slavophiles, like other independent thinkers in Russia, scorned "Official Nationality."[32]

Neither their concern with the Russian nation, nor the fact that all Slavophiles and most Westernizers belonged to the Russian gentry made them supporters of the regime. Both groups were constituted at a time in Russian history when the educated elite had been separated from the state and an intelligentsia had started to take form. They saw themselves as positioned between the people and the government. Although most of the members of this proto-intelligentsia were of noble origin, what united them was not their class, but their intellect. They believed that being an intellectual was equivalent to being independent-minded, and thus were, in general, critical towards the regime and its apologists. It is true that the Slavophiles at times cooperated with Stepan Shevyrev and Mikhail Pogodin, who have been seen as promoters of the doctrine of Official Nationality. But although the Slavophiles expressed an appreciation of certain aspects of their work, their opinions differed on many matters, most importantly on the role of the state and on their assessment of the reforms of Peter the Great. Furthermore, there was a great difference between these academics and the journalists Nikolai Grech and Faddei Bulgarin, who were considered base flatterers of the regime and the main exponents of "Official Nationality."

The Slavophiles were as repelled by the official doctrine as they were by Western rationalism.[33] They believed in the necessity of freedom of thought and expression and considered censorship, along with the control exercised by the state on intellectual life, as a form of abuse. Not only were the Slavophiles' rejection of Peter the Great and their concept of a limited state displeasing to the tsar, but their emphasis on the village commune could also be considered offensive, since it implied approval of a measure of local self-government and criticism of increasing control by the bureaucracy.[34] Accordingly, the tsar regarded the Slavophiles as a threat and members of both the Slavophile and the Westernizer groups were affected by the strict censorship policy.[35]

The autocratic regime's desire to exercise an absolute monopoly of ideas—expressed in the establishment of the Third Department—deprived these intellectuals of the possibility to discuss their ideas in public.[36] Instead, they were forced into the "semi-private" sphere of salons, private clubs, and circles. Here, essays were read and debated and questions of literature and philosophy were discussed freely. Of course, this stifling situation was bound to have an impact on what was written. Russian intellectuals very likely engaged in self-censorship, and chose to deal with apolitical subjects that did not catch the censors' eye and implied things that could not be stated plainly. Nevertheless, there is also evidence that as long as there were no direct references to the tsar or his government, potentially subversive articles could get past the censor, as illustrated by the publication of Peter Chaadaev's "First Philosophical Letter," and Nikolai Gogol's *Dead Souls*, for even though tsarist censorship was harsh, it was ineffective and not strictly enforced. At least until 1848, the tsar seems to have allowed writers some latitude and was halfhearted in his hostility towards unofficial opinions.[37] It is indeed difficult to know whether the Slavophiles would have been more critical of the regime had there been no censorship, but it is nevertheless safe to say that they would not have been less critical.

Certain methodological assumptions have guided this investigation of Slavophile thought. Treating the Slavophiles as self-conscious critics of Russian culture and society, their ideas are seen as the result of conscious action. Thus, I deliberately reject the idea that a key to understanding the Slavophiles, is to determine in what respect their ideas were the outcome of structural change in Russia. Such a perspective has made scholars present Slavophilism as the expression of the decline of the educated nobility, of the conflict between city and country, or of the specific character of Russian culture.[38] This book's aim has not been to find signs of economic, social, or cultural determination in Slavophile ideas. Neither has the intention been to identify the ideological origin of Slavophile thought in order to establish whether it emanated principally from German Romanticism or from Eastern philosophy, a point that has generated considerable scholarly controversy.[39] Nor, finally, am I interested in Slavophilism as philosophy, that is as contributions to perennial questions without reference to the historical context in which they originated. Rather, I have treated Slavophile writings as interventions in a debate about Russian culture and society.

My interest is in the way ideas were used in a certain historical situation, involving specific actors. This approach to the study of intellectual history is associated with the methodological writings of Quentin Skinner, John Dunn, and John Pocock. These, and other historians of ideas reacted against the traditional study of political thought as a study of ideas about eternal questions, the answers to which were of immediate relevance to present-day reflections on society and politics. Instead, Skinner, Dunn, and Pocock argued that the aim of the history of ideas was to understand ideas in their historical context. Thus, Skinner argued that in order to reach a proper historical understanding of a text, we need to know what the writer intended to mean in writing a certain work. It is therefore necessary to be acquainted with the political, social, and, especially, the intellectual context, in which a writer wrote a text. Most importantly, we need to know what audience the writer was addressing and which works, actions, or phenomena he or she intended his or her writings to comment on.[40]

A consequence of my approach employed in this book is that the problems and issues the Slavophiles themselves address are taken seriously, even when these ideas seem superficial and repetitive. Therefore, this treatment of the Slavophiles is not concerned with the philosophical meaning and origin of the concept of *sobornost* (the orthodox principle of free unity in multiplicity), the notion of the "integrated personality," or the idea of communalism institutionalised in the *obshchina* (the village commune)—which usually make up the core of studies of the Slavophiles—but rather with the ideas that made the articulation of these well-known concepts essential in the first place. This does not mean that Slavophile thought can be defined in its entirety by the fundamental ideas presented here. Rather, it entails a new way of looking at the Slavophiles. While scholars have seen them as representatives of a distinctive Russian mind and therefore focused on concepts that can be seen as original to their thinking, or at least as a contribution to philosophy, this book aims to show what they hoped to achieve by developing and presenting their ideas.

Even though individual Slavophiles held diverging opinions in some cases, I refer to the cluster of their ideas as Slavophilism, as do most other students of Russian thought.[41] This is not only done for the purpose of simplicity, but also to emphasize their agreement concerning fundamental issues. They were indeed seen as a group that represented one specific way of thinking, both by themselves and their contemporaries. Nonetheless, when individual differences are apparent, they are taken into account. In addition to individual differences, there is a transformation, over time, that has to be considered. However, because I am interested in the original formulation of Slavophilism, i.e. its constituting phase, this is not a study of later alterations of the original ideas. Even so, I recognise both that the original Slavophiles developed their ideas over time and that other thinkers transformed these ideas at a later stage.

The book begins with an attempt to identify the most fruitful way of interpreting Slavophilism, as a form of nationalism, by looking at different theories of nationalism and Slavophilism. Chapter 1 emphasises the importance of the cultural identity crisis experienced by members of the educated elite in the second quarter of the nineteenth century and discusses the political, social, and intellectual context that contributed to its outbreak. Chapter 2 deals with the way this crisis was expressed by both Slavophiles and Westernizers—as a problem of imitation. It is argued that the issue of imitation had to do with Russia's standing as a nation among other nations and that this role was related to the identity of Russian intellectuals. Therefore, Slavophilism has to be seen in the light of the idea of the nation. In chapter 3, different concepts of the nation are discussed. I conclude that the notion which tells us something about Slavophilism, is the Romantic idea, that forms the basis of cultural nationalism. It is in terms of the Romantic notion of the nation, according to which the national culture is to be regenerated and the intellectuals are to act as its interpreters, that the Slavophiles are best understood. Hence, Slavophilism should be seen as a cultural nationalism, which I define in a way that distinguishes it from political nationalism on the grounds of its different aims and strategies, although both movements are equally concerned with social change and may use identical foundations for mobilization. Chapter 3 ends with an account of the meaning and context of cultural nationalism.

In chapters 4 and 5, I argue that the realization of Russia's cultural backwardness, due to the practice of imitation, led to different solutions in the form of new identities for Russian intellectuals connected to their nation. The Slavophiles and the Westernizers both believed that the notion of a Russian enlightenment was the answer for Russia, but they differed in their interpretations of this concept. Chapter 4 deals with the Westernizers' view and chapter 5 with the Slavophiles' ideas concerning a Russian enlightenment. Coming to the conclusion that the Slavophiles' notion of a Russian enlightenment encompasses a complex mix of ideas which concerns social change, chapter 6 is devoted to an analysis of the social vision of cultural nationalism and an attempt to characterize its project for change. Chapter 6 also serves as a background to chapter 7, where the social project of Slavophilism as a cultural nationalism is examined. Here, I argue that Slavophilism can be seen in the context of Russian intellectual criticism, but that it involved a change in focus from the law and the state to the nation, the community, and the intellectuals. In my conclusions, I consider whether or not the Slavophile project should be seen as a failure or a success.

Chapter 1

A Dual Crisis of Identity

This book interprets Slavophilism as an attempt to deal with the question of Russia's national identity. The aim of this chapter is to furnish ground for understanding Slavophilism as a form of nationalism. It begins with a discussion of the literature on the rise of nationalism and the attempts that have been made to explain the emergence of Slavophilism. From this discussion two insights are derived. First, that a national identity originated in Russia not as a broadly shared sentiment among the people at large, or as a popular movement, but in a discourse on Russia's future among the educated elite. Second, that this discourse was the result, as well as the expression, of an identity crisis experienced by members of the educated class. The reasons for this crisis can be found in the social and political conditions of the educated class in Russia in the early nineteenth century and so the chapter proceeds to an account of these circumstances. The latter part of the chapter addresses the influence of Romanticism on Slavophilism. It establishes that Romanticism shaped the intellectual agenda at the time so as to bring certain issues to the forefront of debate. Yet, even more important, Romantic ideas, concepts, and language provided the material out of which a Russian national identity took form.

THE EDUCATED ELITE AND THE
RISE OF NATIONAL CONSCIOUSNESS

Nationalism and Modernisation

Scholars have long emphasized the importance of the process of modernisation for the understanding of nationalism. Economic growth, industrialization, urbanization, democratization, the development of capitalism, the invention of the printing press, the process of vernacularization, and a growing and increasingly powerful middle class are factors, which have been described as crucial to the rise of nationalism.[1] However, because writers have different understandings of what nationalism is, they also have different theories of its emergence.

Ernest Gellner describes nationalism as a principle of congruence between the political and the national unit. Nationalism is rooted in the division of labour characteristic of industrial society. It is a consequence of a new form of social organisation, based on a literate high culture, which is co-extensive with an entire political unit and its population. According to Gellner, nationalism is really about participation in such a high culture. Historical contingencies determine which actors are central in promoting nationalism, but the principle is inherent in a certain set of social conditions and is part of the modernization process.[2] Gellner's interest lies in the structural conditions of nationalism, or rather, in the way nationalism structures society. For this reason, the ideology of nationalism, or the ways that social, political, or ethnic groups put nationalism to use, is of limited interest to him.

Benedict Anderson introduces more variables than Gellner into his theory of the rise of nationalism. Both social phenomena, such as capitalism and print technology, and cultural phenomena, such as the diversity of language and the erosion of religious truths, were central factors in the shaping of a national consciousness according to Anderson. Without capitalism, which assembled related vernaculars and created print-languages the new national communities would have been unimaginable.[3] Anderson's account, therefore, makes capitalists, and the bourgeoisie in general, the foremost promoters of nationalism.

When it comes to applying Gellner's and Anderson's theories to the origins of Slavophilism, two problems present themselves. The first is obvious: Some of the elements of modernity were already present in Russia under Peter I, or at least under Catherine II, such as the erosion of religious truths, print technology, a literate high-culture, and the emergence of a national consciousness. Yet, other indications, such as a strong middle class, economic growth, and democratization, were still to be seen. Serfdom and widespread illiteracy characterised the economy and society. A rapid and, at the same time, quantitatively significant industrial growth began in Russia only after 1855, while commercial institutions remained backward at least until 1860 and business institutions were poorly developed until the last decade of the nineteenth century.[4] The second problem with Gellner's and Anderson's theories concerns the definition of nationalism. Had Russian nationalism focused on the nationality principle, it would logically have been an ideology that turned against the tsarist empire. Yet, anti-imperialism did not dominate the ideas of nationalists. Other things did.

Even if a direct link between modernization and the rise of nationalism is difficult to establish in the case of Russia, it is undeniable that a novel and distinct national identity arose among some elements of Russian society in the second quarter of the nineteenth century. To understand this development it is necessary to turn to theories of nationalism, which place greater stress on the importance of specific actors in the rise of nationalism.

Nationalism and Feelings of Backwardness

Many writers stress that the emergence of nationalism is linked not so much to modernity as to a discrepancy between modernity and traditional society, and to the feeling of backwardness this discrepancy often fosters. They use a socio-psychological explanation, where nationalism is said to be an outcome of a crisis of identity resulting from the exposure of traditional society to modernity. In such studies the focus is on the intellectuals, or, alternatively, on the middle class.

Eric Hobsbawm talks about a need for nationalism among intellectuals due to social changes. In his work on the invention of tradition, Hobsbawm argues that because of social change, new traditions were needed which could express social cohesion and identity when old traditions were no longer adaptable to the new social patterns. These new traditions were founded on the nation as the unifying element rather than a national church, a royal family, or other cohesive traditions or collective group-identities. Nationalism became a new secular religion, and the class that most needed this mode of cohesion, was the growing middle-class, which lacked other forms of cohesion.[5]

Liah Greenfeld argues in a similar way. She distinguishes three phases in the formation of specific nationalisms: structural, cultural, and psychological.

To begin with, the adoption of a national identity is necessarily preceded by a dissatisfaction with the existing identity of the concerned groups. The reason for this dissatisfaction is that the definition of the social order expressed by the traditional identity is inconsistent with the experience of the group members. Because of a change in the position and roles of influential social groups, a crisis of identity occurs. The inadequacy of the traditional identity of the involved groups creates an incentive to search for a replacement. A national identity is imported and adopted, partly due to its availability, partly because of its ability to solve this crisis. However, the imported idea has to be adjusted to the situational constraints of the actors and be reinterpreted to fit indigenous traditions. This explains variations between individual nationalisms.[6]

Greenfeld further argues that the importation of the national identity fosters envy and hatred (*ressentiment*) towards the source of the imported model, since the model is considered superior to the imitation. These feelings are based on the assumption of equality between model and imitator that is inconsistent with the actual inequality. *Ressentiment* can lead to "a transvaluation of values, whereby the originally supreme values are denigrated and replaced with notions which are unimportant, external, or antithetical to the original values." However, Greenfeld argues, the new system of values is not a direct reversal of the original model. "The matrix of national identity evolves out of the transvaluation of values, which together with the original principles, modified according to the specific structural and cultural context, results in the unique character of any one nationalism." Nevertheless, *ressentiment* felt by the group who imported the idea of the nation usually results in an emphasis on elements of indigenous traditions hostile to the principles of the original nationalism when they articulate the national consciousness of their particular society.

Applying her theory to Russia Greenfeld maintains that there, indigenous cultural resources were absent, or insufficient, so that *ressentiment* was the single most important factor in determining the terms in which national identity was defined.[7] This explains why the Slavophiles gave much more attention to refuting Western values than presenting Russian ones, and why those values, which actually were presented, were portrayed as directly opposed to Western ones.

Anthony D. Smith also regards nationalism as a solution to a crisis of identity. But to Smith it is the model imported from the West, the scientific state, that creates the crisis. Yet, even if ideas rather than the social constraints of the actors, as in Greenfeld's theory, instigate a crisis of identity, these ideas are part of the modernization process and it is the confrontation between, on the one hand, the traditional and cosmic world view and, on the other, the modern and rational world view, which gives the intellectuals a "double loyalty." Both systems demand absolute loyalty, since there cannot be two truths—one religious and one scientific. According to Smith there are three logical solutions to this dilemma. First, to preserve the traditional world view; second, to transfer loyalty to the scientific state, and third, to combine the traditional and the modern order in a new synthesis through reforming the religious culture and tradition of the society. It is the third solution that can best respond to the needs of the upper middle-class.[8]

Nationalism as the Solution to a Crisis of Identity

Historians and social scientists who have investigated the reasons for the appearance of Slavophilism have all employed the concept, if not the terminology, of an identity crisis. A common argument is that the Slavophiles formed their ideas as a reaction against the decline of the Russian nobility and the emergence of a middle-class. The Slavophiles belonged to noble families and so, the argument goes, their social position best explains their ideas and actions. They were simply afraid of losing their privileges and therefore presented a conservative, reactionary program to defend their class interests. In doing this, they were part of the same counterrevolutionary tendency that had tried to retain noble privileges in Western Europe. As Russian aristocrats, the Slavophiles were afraid that the bourgeois revolution would come to their country. This argument has been presented both as a purely Marxist one, and lately as a more loosely held socio-economic, structural argument related to the fixed position of social groups in different stages of the modernization process.[9] Andrzej Walicki uses a long-established argument of a time lag between Russia and Europe, claiming that if a certain delay is taken into account, the social and political situation in Russia can be compared to Germany's during the counterrevolution, so that the Slavophile movement can be seen as part of the European counterrevolutionary movement.[10]

The major difficulty with this argument is that the Russian economy had not developed very far by the early nineteenth century. Consequently, it is doubtful to what extent class tension served as the catalyst of Slavophile ideas. To any attempt, such as this book, to take the Slavophiles' own words seriously, there is an additional problem; there is little in Slavophile writings that support the claim that their ideas were a reaction to the threat posed by the growing middle-class.

Another way to look at Slavophilism is to see it as a reaction, not to class tension, but to the bureaucratic state and the artificial culture of the Petersburg court. Slavophilism, then, becomes an expression of the "court and country" divide within Russia's upper classes. Dominic Lieven writes that Slavophile thought reflected the alienation of part of the nobility from the bureaucratic regime, which they regarded as tyrannical, and un-Russian. In contrast, the Slavophiles presented a vision of the true Russia, which was based on the nation, the people, and the land. Although they accepted the monarchy, the Slavophiles' emphasis on the nation made them hostile to the state.[11]

In a similar way, Abbott Gleason points to the "ruralism" of the second part of the eighteenth century as an important factor behind the development of Slavophilism. This was a nostalgia for the safety and harmony of Russian country life, brought about by the loss of status and influence at court. It was a desire, expressed by members of the gentry, to escape the control and power of the state, and be released from the formal, superficial life at the Petersburg court. Gleason claims that a yearning for some kind of "spiritual wholeness" in opposition to the culture of St. Petersburg, is clearly evident in eighteenth-century Russian Freemasonry. But this yearning was not formulated in a coherent theory until the educated elite had separated themselves from the autocratic state, after the brutal crushing of the Decembrist uprising in 1825. Furthermore, an intellectual transformation was needed. The rural nostalgia could not be formed into Slavophile ideas until Romantic and counterrevolutionary concepts were available to members of the gentry.[12]

Lieven's and Gleason's presentation of Slavophilism, as a reaction to the Russian state and the social life of the court, captures an important development of the gentry's self-perception. Slavophilism was in part an attempt to impose a distance between the educated elite and the government. Yet, what is lacking in this treatment of the Slavophiles is an explanation of the frequent comparisons of Russia with nations in the West, which is such a dominant theme in the work of the Slavophiles. Indeed, their writings are marked by nothing as much as an anxious assessment of Russia's achievements as a nation. A definition of Slavophilism that restricts it to a country opposition against the Russian state does not explain why the Slavophiles paid so much attention to the problem of cultural and artistic imitation, and to the need for Russia to make a national contribution to humanity.

The Slavophiles' concern with Russia's standing compared to other nations has commonly been approached through an investigation of the anti-Westernism, which forms a strong and persistent aspect of their writings. The Slavophiles reacted fiercely against Western rationalism and against the formalism, legalism, individualism, and atomism it was supposed to cultivate. In their view, the extolling of reason in the West had destroyed the harmony and integrity of the human personality. As a consequence, the unity of social life was destroyed by individualism and fragmentation.[13] Kireevsky stated that "the distinctive character of Western culture in all its aspects [was] a fundamental striving toward personal and self-contained rationalism in thought, in life, in society, and in the motivating forces and forms of human life."[14] Industry was described as "the apotheosis of rationalism in action." Since this form of rationalism was abstract and had nothing to do with the actual way of life, it gave rise to violence and oppression, sometimes disguised by formal democratic processes.[15] Democracy was, Kireevsky held, founded on paper constitutions and regulations. It was an institution of formally reconciled interests, but it was deprived of brotherly spirit and love.[16] Hence, its social order was damaged by a constant struggle of contending parties. The reign of the majority was the reign of the powerful, the "lawful dominion of a party preponderant in quantity of force."[17]

The Slavophiles were certainly aware of the negative effects of modern industrialism and capitalism.[18] Yet their critique of European conditions did not mean that they turned their backs on Europe. Indeed, by the 1840s, both socialists and conservatives in Russia believed it was their task to help Europe solve its social and political problems, and that a social consciousness had to be developed in order to curb unrestrained individualism, cultivated by unbridled liberalism.[19] The Slavophiles presented the Russian peasant commune, the *obshchina*, as an alternative social and moral organisation, destined to save humanity from the proletarization they had seen developing in the West.[20] Through its principle of land redistribution and the social obligation to help other members, the commune would eliminate poverty. According to Khomiakov, mutual help was much more effective if it was based on common benefit, instead of on involuntary contributions, as in the West.[21] It was precisely the emphasis on the social character of human interactions, as opposed to the individual, which made the *obshchina* so popular among Russian social critics, who yearned for alternatives to egoistic individualism. And yet, it was crucial that the stress on communality should not restrict the freedom of the individual, who was described as "a part of, not apart from, the community." Through the notion of the *obshchina* the Slavophiles applied the Christian belief in the brotherhood of man to social and economic conditions.[22]

This sense of brotherhood was expressed in Russia's traditional system of customary law and in the practice of unanimous decision-making in the commune "with its judgement based on the voice of conscience, and on the truth of heart."[23] According to Khomiakov the custom of counting votes wrongly implied that "wisdom and truth always belonged to the greater number of votes, when actually very often a majority depends on chance." In contrast, the communal meeting was described as "a school for the people," which disseminated a healthy notion of legality and justice to its participants so that they could develop intelligent judgement.[24]

Although the Slavophile critique of the West may seem to corroborate Greenfeld's claim about the importance of *ressentiment* in the formulation of a national identity, the idea that Russia had a mission to solve Europe's problems shows that anti-Westernism does not exhaust the contents of the Slavophile ideology or the national identity it proposed. Too much stress on anti-Westernism makes Slavophilism appear one-sided and antagonistic. In fact, a close reading of Slavophile writings, as is undertaken in this book, shows that their ideas about Russia's relationship to the West were far more complex than merely an expression of *ressentiment*.

The Identity Crisis of the Educated Elite in Nineteenth-Century Russia

The preceding discussion of the origins of nationalism suggests that the development of a national identity is the result of an identity crisis experienced by a key social group. Accounts of the origins of Slavophilism also stress that these ideas were the result of an identity crisis, whether it was due to a confrontation with the middle class, the Russian state, or the Western model of social development. In the following, Slavophilism is presented as an expression of an identity crisis within the educated elite, which was due to certain social and political developments in late eighteenth- and early nineteenth-century Russia.

The backward state of the Russian economy resulted in a uniformity that naturally had an impact on the social organisation of Russia. The majority of hereditary nobles were not clearly delineated from other groups in society. Comparing the Russian with the Prussian gentry, Lieven notes that, unlike Prussian gentry, the Russian court and service aristocracy did not have deep local and provincial loyalties, or old traditions of public service in corporate institutions. Although the social consolidation of a landed nobility increased during the eighteenth and nineteenth centuries, it was not institutionalized in autonomous corporate structures until the early twentieth century, and until the late nineteenth century, privileges and social mobility resulted almost exclusively from service. Since education, merit, and performance were the formal criteria for advancement, both newcomers and nobles of ancient lineage were in a similarly insecure social position.[25] As we shall see, these criteria, and the importance of service in defining the relationship of the nobility to official society, were important factors in the shaping of a specific elite identity.

If the nobility was not clearly delineated as a social group, the definition of the middle strata was extremely vague. Distinct middle-classes were virtually nonexistent until the late nineteenth century and the emergence of professional classes resulted primarily from state-directed occupational training and specialisation. The undifferentiated character of Russian society, lacking in autonomous corporate structures, economic security and local independence, can thus explain why there was no independent public sphere, separated from the state, in the beginning of the eighteenth century, and why a "political bourgeoisie," associated with a civil society, was absent.[26] "If the *philosophes* wanted to reform early modern European societies along certain lines," Nicholas Riasanovsky writes, "in Russia such a society had to be formed in the first place."[27]

The formation of Slavophilism coincided with the particularly oppressive regime of Nicholas I (1825–1855). Marquis de Custine, who visited Russia in 1839, described its government as "military discipline in place of civil order, a state of siege which has become the normal state of society."[28] Others have portrayed Nicholas's regime as a gendarmerie. Not even the nobility enjoyed security of person and property. The earliest guarantees against arbitrary search and arrest did not come to Russia until the judicial reform of 1864. The political and social life was more similar to the French eighteenth-century experience than to the situation in the contemporary West. There was absolutely no freedom of expression. In the absence of parliamentary government, a free press, or political parties, people met in salons, private clubs, and societies to participate in public discussion. Hence, independent public communication was located in the private sphere.[29] The lasting dependence on the state and the lack of any economic, political, or institutional base, provided the gentry with a weak sense of a distinct social identity. In its place, a feeling of cultural affinity emerged.

Already by the mid-eighteenth century, Russia possessed a socially diverse, self-conscious reading public. Both men and women, came together in theatres, libraries, social clubs, literary societies, private salons, and Masonic lodges. They defined themselves not by noble birth, nor by economic or political power, but by culture, morality, civility, and virtue.[30] Through the universities, which also served as meeting-places for the reading public, the sons of the gentry and the middle classes, such as professionals and merchants, were subsequently brought together, joined in their taste for literature and philosophy.[31] Calling attention to the existence of an educated public in early nineteenth-century Russia, it must be emphasised that this group constituted a small minority. Although it grew rapidly, the reading public remained a tiny minority of the Russian people. Lieven writes that by 1800, Westernized aristocrats lived as "islands in a noble world still often uncultured and obsessed with the traditional pursuit of rank and imperial favour."[32]

The educated public was a product of the cultural Westernization of Russia, introduced by Peter the Great. These Western innovations affected only the noble service class and neither the peasantry, the clergy, merchants nor artisans associated themselves with cultural Westernization. As a consequence, the noble service class came to distinguish itself from the masses by education, way of life, cultural values, and an affinity with the Western cultural community. Since titles meant little to the Russian nobility, social status was enhanced by skills in foreign languages and knowledge of Western literature and culture. Compared to their English or Prussian counterparts, Russian aristocrats were more culturally insecure and isolated. Through association with Western culture, they were given a sense of individual worth and dignity, but this also provided them with common values and roles. Hence, Westernization had a significant impact on the formation of a public identity for the educated elite, and this identity rested on the two ideas that brought them together—public service and culture. Members of the educated elite felt an obligation to serve their country by acting as its cultural leaders, disseminating Western culture and enlightenment.[33]

However, the transformation of Russia, according to Western models, only stimulated the development of intellectual and cultural life and ignored all other aspects of social life. This one-sided process of modernisation led to frustration among the educated elite. The government wanted Russia to be regarded as a modern European state but such a state could not be created without an educated elite to carry out the tasks of modernization and to act as leaders of Russia's cultural progress. While this image of a modern Russian power included a sophisticated cultural life, it definitely excluded any political transformation. As Raeff notes: "Unfettering civil society and promoting its progress was not part of the state's programme, though it was a necessary consequence of its goals of Europeanization and modernization."[34] The liberation of civil society gave rise to demands for social and political changes, compatible with the modernization of cultural and intellectual life. These demands were increasingly raised following the Napoleonic wars, when the discrepancy between cultural and sociopolitical modernization became even more evident.

Taking part in the wars, Russian officers encountered the modern West and could therefore make direct comparisons with their own country. Filled with pride over Russia's victory and her role as the liberator of Europe, they could not help noticing that the conquered nations were in fact better off than their own. Many young officers were struck by the contrast between Russia's military and diplomatic achievements abroad and the apparent backwardness at home and it produced a feeling of embarrassment among them. Furthermore, sharing the experiences of war with ordinary peasants made officers aware that the lower classes were as loyal and devoted to their country as they were. Altogether, this heightened their consciousness of the need to reform Russian institutions and they felt obliged as an educated elite to improve the living conditions of the people.[35]

This newly awakened social consciousness produced an enthusiasm for reform among members of the educated elite, which was emphasized by the tsar's repeated promises to make social changes. When Alexander I subsequently failed to fulfil his promises, reform-minded Russians were greatly disappointed. The tsar's reluctance, or inability, to introduce reforms eventually led some officers to conspire against the tsar in the Decembrist revolt of 1825.

All hopes for reform were shattered when the revolt against the autocracy was brutally crushed. After the defeat of the Decembrists, the educated elite became even more alienated and frustrated. They found themselves isolated from both the people and the state.[36] The new tsar, Nicholas I, excluded the gentry from participation in government, since they could no longer be trusted. At the same time, many members of the gentry turned away from service by choice. Whereas in the Napoleonic Wars "the highest form of idealism had been to serve in the army," after 1825 it was regarded as "a betrayal of all idealism and humanity." As a result of this change of attitude, young noblemen enrolled in the universities instead of choosing a military or bureaucratic career in the service of the state. Accordingly, Russia's cultural elite was no longer integrated into, but rather separated from, and, most importantly, in opposition to, official society. The notables of Russian culture were now associated with the universities, instead of the court.[37]

Although consciously separated from the people, late eighteenth-century educated society had not distinguished itself from official society, i.e., from the court and government. This was partly due to their dependence on the state, partly to the widespread belief in enlightened despotism. Riasanovsky argues that not even the Decembrists could entirely free themselves of the image of the enlightened ruler and state. By contrast, in the second quarter of the nineteenth-century, being a member of educated society implied being separated from the state and government.[38] The tsarist state, Lieven argues, alienated educated society by denying it the rights and freedoms to which it felt entitled as a group of civilized Europeans.[39] But the feelings of alienation had a deeper sociopsychological foundation as well. The process of Westernization had created an educated elite, a reading public with a common identity based on shared values and roles. Following the defeat of the Decembrist revolt, this identity and the roles it entailed were no longer in agreement with their perception of Russian reality; this naturally led to feelings of alienation and, in some cases, to a crisis of identity.

The gentry-intellectuals of the 1820s had inherited the concepts of public service and cultural leadership from the eighteenth-century Russian nobility.[40] These deep-rooted concepts, established in the Petrine era, implied not only service to the state, but also service to the people, and to the community as a whole.[41] The Decembrist generation still saw their role as serving both the state and Russia. After the defeat of the revolt, most members of the educated public realized that serving the one meant working against the other. Their role of social criticism and commitment to the welfare of the people turned out to be incompatible with service to the state.[42] Totally alienated from the state, these educated Russians "were left with ideas alone." This was further aggravated by what Martin Malia calls "a qualitative overproduction of 'humanism'" in Russia. Through the new civilian educational establishments, which were not in full operation until the 1830s, "free individuals" were created in a society based on "unreflective obedience," where the possibilities for individual initiatives were very limited. The world of ideas thus became the only free sphere of activity. Using the arguments of German idealism to exalt this activity, gentry-intellectuals began to think of themselves as the embodied consciousness of the nation. Hence, the universities led the young westernized gentry into "a rootless 'internal emigration' with no home but its ideal visions."[43]

To conclude, the identity crisis of the educated elite was not caused by a clash between traditional identities and a modern state, proposed by some scholars as a common motivation behind nationalist feelings, but rather by a conflict between modern identities and a traditional state; between modern culture and traditional society; between an ideal and reality;

and between the educated elite and the mass of the people.[44] In short, the "honorable public" or "educated society" was westernized, while their country was not. As a consequence, the cultural and intellectual life of Russia stood in glaring contrast to its social, economic, and political life. That was why educated Russians came to devote themselves entirely to the world of culture and ideas. It was in the fields of philosophy and the arts that a contribution to public life was still possible. As cultural leaders, they hoped to find a role of public service that was separated from the state, but related to the nation, to Russia. When this possibility too was closed, due to a change in the intellectual context, their identity crisis became acute.

THE TRANSFORMATION OF THE INTELLECTUAL AGENDA

The educated elite in early nineteenth-century Russia experienced an identity crisis. So far I have dealt with the social and political reasons for this crisis. This account, however, provides no reason why the lack of cultural achievements was so disturbing to educated Russians. To do so, it is necessary to address the question of the influence of ideas on the origins of Slavophilism. Below, I argue that the transformation of the intellectual agenda was a very important factor in shaping the form of Slavophilism and the national identity it presented.

Culture and Ideas

Some cultural and intellectual historians explain the nation's intellectual and cultural life with reference to certain perpetual characteristics of Russian culture and society. They describe Russia as having a special character, which is static and homogenous. In stressing cultural continuity, these arguments refute the modernization theories presented above. Commonly, scholars point to the impact of Eastern monastic thought and literature on the formation of an independent Russian culture. The fact that the rise of this new Russian culture coincided with the fall of Constantinople, the second Rome and the centre of the "true religion", to the Turks in 1453, gave this new culture a unique character. Now Russia was isolated as "the sole repository" of the Orthodox Christian religion and the legitimate successor to Constantinople. Moscow was now considered as the Third Rome. According to Edie et al, all these events helped create a sense of distinctive national identity in Russia.

Being culturally isolated, Russia did not go through the reformation that produced the Protestant churches in the West. Hence, it never experienced the religious criticism necessary for the emergence of a secular culture independent of the Church. A strictly secular culture did not develop until the nineteenth century. What is more, Russia did not experience the Renaissance until the late seventeenth and early eighteenth century, at least two centuries after Western Europe. Not until Peter the Great "cut a window into Europe" was Russian society introduced to Western culture on a wide scale. Therefore, Edie et al conclude, an understanding of the earliest attempts at formulating a genuine Russian philosophy requires that the specific characteristics of Russian spirituality are taken into account. One has to consider the Byzantine origin of Russian thought together with its religious soul. Two central features dominate Russian thinking, both deriving from Eastern Christianity and its monastic tradition: a theocratic conception of religion that focus on the mystery of liturgical worship rather than political activism, and an ascetic world-denying tendency.[45]

Peter Christoff also points to specific characteristics of Russian culture as crucial to our understanding of Russian thought. This culture prevented bourgeois liberalism, the dominant ideology in mid-nineteenth-century Western Europe, to make any progress in Russia. Christoff claims that in Russia, a rural country with a weak, embryonic middle-class, the prerequisites for liberal arguments did not exist. "Western, particularly Anglo-Saxon individualism, deeply rooted in the Protestant ethic and eighteenth-century rationalism, was alien to the Russian historical heritage intellectually, morally, and culturally." The characteristic social consciousness of the Russian was wholly incompatible with Western individualism and the principle of private property.[46]

The most elaborated of the cultural explanations is probably Boris Uspenskii's and Iurii Lotman's semiotic approach.[47] These authors assert that there is a dualism in Russian culture. They argue that in Western thought there is a three-fold-system with a neutral sphere in the middle, while in Russia there is only black and white. This dualism, or binary model, is manifested in the fact that in the Orthodox Church, there is no purgatory. This left Russians with two opposite poles—one good and one evil. It has characterized Russian culture since the Christianization of Kiev in 988 until today. This dualism leads to a continuous struggle between the two poles, so that every new period in the history of Russian culture is oriented toward a break with what preceded it. Following this theory, Slavophilism can be seen as a reaction against the Russian eighteenth-century elite with its pronounced admiration for Western Enlightenment thought, and for everything Western in general. If admiration and imitation constituted one pole, rejection and distinctiveness was the basis of the other.[48]

There is no denying the importance of Russian cultural history for understanding Russian ideas. Indeed, the Slavophiles themselves referred to it as the basis of Russian nationality. But the specific character of Russian culture cannot explain why the Slavophiles formulated their ideas at the particular time they did, nor why they assumed a specific form.

However, not all intellectual and cultural historians see Slavophilism and the Russian national identity as expressions of permanent cultural features. Many argue that the intellectual agenda had been transformed in the early nineteenth century so as to make it possible for a coherent theory of Russian nationality to emerge in the form of Slavophilism. In the literature on Slavophilism and Russian intellectual history, two influences on Slavophile thought have been stressed. First, certain ideas which originated in Russia in the late eighteenth century, and second, ideas which originated in the Romantic movement and in German idealism.

Native Sources

It is sometimes claimed that a Russian national consciousness was already developed in the eighteenth century. The main argument is that much of eighteenth-century thought was concerned with issues of national identity and values. Hans Rogger argues that on occasion Catherine II had been forced to "claim otherness as a value." The publicist N. I. Novikov provides another example. At the end of the eighteenth century, he wrote that it was no disadvantage for Russia to be less enlightened, or technically advanced, than the West. On the contrary, the very backwardness of Russia, in this formal sense, prevented the negative aspects of progress from destroying valuable human virtues. These qualities would ensure that "when the time came and the need arose, Russia would prove her equality in every way."[49] But it was Denis Fonvizin's letters from Europe which, according to Rogger, constituted the first significant attempt made by an educated Russian to address the problem of Russia's relationship with Europe. Although it did not question Western culture as such, Fonvizin's comparison between the two cultures was, nonetheless, a critical assessment of certain aspects and phenomena of Western society. It was not until critical questions about life in the West were posed that a reassessment of Russian culture was made possible. In 1778, Fonvizin proclaimed a thesis based on such a reappraisal. His point was that the very backwardness of Russia was a possible indication of her ultimate superiority over the rest of Europe. Russia had the ability to develop, avoiding the mistakes made by the more advanced countries.[50]

Fonvizin and Novikov instigated a search for a Russian national character that could prove Russia was not inferior to other nations. By the end of the century, the question of what the features of this character were was posed with greater urgency. However, Rogger emphasizes that, not until the formulation of Slavophilism and Westernism, was an attempt made to determine the essence of Russia and the West. The isolated comments of Fonvizin and Novikov should not be interpreted as "a fully developed nationalist theory" or as "a Slavophilism *avant le mot.*" His point is that, while the prevailing mood of the century was decidedly cosmopolitan, there were other statements of "the antithesis between mind and heart, form and substance, Russia and Europe," which seem to anticipate later contrasts made between Russia and the West. Hence, one might assume there was a certain continuity in the Russian intellectual environment and that Russian nationalism had native sources to rely on. Rogger points to striking similarities in the thinking of the eighteenth and nineteenth centuries to confirm this argument.[51] Iurii Stennik makes an even stronger case, arguing that the imitation of everything Western provoked a reaction among the Russian nobility in the eighteenth century and that Slavophilism was a continuation of these thoughts.[52] A national consciousness might have existed in Russia already in the eighteenth century, but the fact remains that a coherent theory about the identity of the Russian nation was yet to be worked out.

The ideas of Romantic nationalism were not introduced into the Russian cultural debate until Admiral Alexander Shishkov did so in the first quarter of the nineteenth century. Scholars have called him the spiritual ancestor of the Slavophiles and have argued that there are numerous parallels to Shishkov's works in their linguistic studies.[53] In line with Romantic thought, Shishkov held that the distinctive genius of a people could be discovered in its language, which, therefore, had to develop organically. Hence, he was opposed to dominant French influences in the Russian language. But he did not confine his criticism to linguistics. Like the Slavophiles, Shishkov was also critical of the foundations of Western culture, which he found barren and unimpressive. Reason had ruined mankind through the selfishness and ambition it fostered. Fortunately, the peasants had preserved the language and values that had once been common to all layers of Russian society and the duty of the Russian writer was to develop this national culture. Alexander Martin argues that, despite his criticism of Western culture, Shishkov cannot be considered a xenophobe.

Like the Slavophiles, he expressed his respect for foreign cultures, but wanted Russia to be her original self. Although many of Shishkov's ideas are similar to those of the Slavophiles, he differed from them in his admiration for both Peter I and Catherine II. Shishkov did not believe that Russia's national identity had been sacrificed when they had transferred European practices to Russia.[54]

A more contemporary source of native influence on the Slavophiles was that of Peter Chaadaev, who himself was under the sway of the new Romantic philosophy. Nicolas Zernov maintains that Chaadaev was the first one to realize the humiliation of Russia's imitation of the West which, in his view, was due to the total insignificance of her national culture.[55] Gleason attributes Kireevsky's evolution towards Slavophilism to the influence of Chaadaev. Given that the very purpose of Slavophilism was to refute the notion of Russia as culturally bankrupt, it seems likely, he argues, that Kireevsky was impressed by Chaadaev's general line of argumentation, amounting to a description of Russia as free from all tradition and from a past.[56] Nikolai Lossky presents some of Chaadaev's ideas that are close to those of the Slavophiles, though expressed by him before the latter had elaborated their theory. They concern imitation, Russia's national mission and contribution to mankind: "If only Russia understood her mission, she ought to take the initiative in putting all generous ideas into practice, for she is free from Europe's ties, passions, ideas and interests. Russia is too great to pursue a national policy; her task in the world is the politics of mankind."[57]

Chaadaev is only one example of a Russian intellectual, who became fascinated by the world of Romanticism at the time of the formulation of Slavophilism. In fact, Romantic and Idealistic thought completely dominated intellectual life in Russia between the 1820s and the 1840s.[58]

German Romanticism and Idealism

In the previous section, we learned that the Russian educated elite experienced a crisis of identity as a result of the uneven modernisation of their country, and that Slavophilism was a response to this identity crisis. However, this account does not provide us with the full picture of the formulation of Slavophile thought. By looking at the influence of Romantic ideas on Russian intellectuals, it is possible to find out why the identity crisis took the form of a cultural crisis, and why certain issues were brought to the forefront of debate. It was the transformation of the intellectual agenda instigated by Romanticism, which intensified the identity crisis of the educated elite. With the critique of cosmopolitanism, launched by the Romanticists, Russia's educated public lost its *raison d'être*. What gave them purpose as Westernized, educated Russians was their role as cultural leaders. Hence, questioning the basis of this culture, indeed the outright denial of its existence, affected them badly. Moreover, by looking at Romantic thought we are also able to understand how the formulation of Slavophilism could solve this crisis, since Romantic ideas and concepts constituted the main source out of which a Russian national identity was formed.

Many scholars have pointed at the Romantic influence on Slavophilism. Riasanovsky even argues that it is wrong to talk about the influence of Romantic ideas on the Slavophiles. Rather, "spiritually the Slavophiles were a part of the Romantic movement" and should, accordingly, be treated as one of the groups of Romantic intellectuals that spread all over nineteenth-century Europe. Slavophile thought represented a Russian version of the Romantic ideology of the age. An analysis of their ideas establishes beyond any doubt their Romantic origin. The central Romantic concept of organism, for example, permeates their thought.[59] It is of course ironic that the Slavophiles used Western Romanticism to criticize the West. The reason for this was that Russia borrowed ideas from the West with a certain time lag. At the point when Romantic ideas were adopted by Russian thinkers, they had already been replaced by new ideas in the West, at odds with the old ones.[60]

The main arguments concerning the impact of Romanticism deals with the originality of Slavophile thought. Some scholars try to trace Slavophile ideas back to their German origins in order to define them properly. Others stress the Russian, or Eastern uniqueness of their ideas. Christoff is one of the few scholars who argues for the patristic influence on Slavophilism. He claims that Kireevsky was attracted to the hesychastic tradition and that St. Isaacus Syrus was one of the principal Orthodox sources of Kireevsky's doctrine of the wholeness of the spirit. Christoff's main point is that the focus on Western Romanticism misses other, perhaps more important, influences. He suggests that what made Slavophilism original, indeed what made it into a new intellectual current, was not its attachment to Romanticism, found in Kireevsky's early writings, but rather the Christian philosophical meaning, into which this Romanticism was eventually transformed. Furthermore, the fact that both Kireevsky and Khomiakov developed their Russian philosophy in contrast to Western thought is a strong indication of their determination to elaborate their own Russian Orthodox philosophy rather than trying to adapt Western ideas.[61]

The determination not to adapt foreign ideas was of course in itself a foreign, Western idea, and Christoff does not altogether disregard Romantic influences. He writes that although Khomiakov's theology and ideas about the nature and structure of the Church were inspired by the early Church Fathers, his social thought was encouraged by the theory of organism and by Western Romanticism in general. Furthermore, the concept of an old, decaying West, which played a central role in Slavophile thought, was actually a prominent feature of Western Romanticism.[62] There are a few scholars, who deny the influence of German thought altogether. Henry Lanz claims that Slavophilism was not "a Russian distortion of German idealism." To him it was not even a reaction against modern European rationalism. It was merely "a modern continuation of a religious tradition which has been dominating Russian life since the time of Saint Vladimir." According to Lossky the philosophy of Kireevsky and Khomiakov was indeed a response to German rationalistic thought. But the attempt to overcome this philosophy was not formed by Western Romanticism, but by a Russian interpretation of Christianity based upon the works of the Eastern Church Fathers.[63]

I agree with the scholars who attach importance to German Romanticism in order to understand Slavophilism, but establishing the origin of ideas does not tell us anything about what the Slavophiles tried to say with these concepts. The sole existence of ideas, original or not, does not make us understand why they were used in a certain place, at a certain time, and in a certain way. What I am concerned with here is how the Slavophiles themselves presented their ideas and the context they tried to relate to in doing so. It is my contention that Slavophile thinking was formed by the predominant "language," or "ideology," of the day and that this language to a great extent was made up of German Romanticism and idealism. The Slavophiles did not formulate their ideas in isolation, but saw their work as a contribution to thinking both in Russia and in the West. Hence, they had to relate to the intellectual world educated Russians lived in, which was very much a European Romantic world. Consequently, an in-depth understanding of Romanticism is essential, not in order to find similarities or differences in concepts, but to follow the Slavophile arguments and to figure out why they were presented in a certain way. In this way, we can better understand what they said with their ideas, and so make sense of them.

Romanticism did not only have an intellectual impact. It had a psychological impact as well. It both created and filled a need among Russian intellectuals for a role and a function connected to their nation. Romanticism made them realize that the long-lasting practice of imitation had led to an acute lack of a national cultural contribution.[64] But it also provided them with the task of being interpreters of their nation. Hence, the same set of ideas served to formulate the problem and provide the solution at the same time. The transformation of the intellectual agenda meant that the question of the nation's cultural achievements and its stature in relation to other nations became of primary importance. Slavophilism originated in a discussion of these questions.

Chapter 2

The Problem of Imitation

If an enlightened European . . . asks us: Where is your literature? Which works can you be proud of before Europe? What are we to answer him?[1]

The previous chapter discussed signs of a reaction against imitation that began to emerge in Russia at the end of the eighteenth century. However, in the second quarter of the nineteenth century, the practice of imitation became unacceptable and there was an outburst of criticism against the idolization of everything Western. The Slavophiles did not distinguish themselves from other articulate Russians in focusing on the problem of cultural imitation. Imitation was on everybody's mind, although, subsequently, different ideas of how to deal with it were developed. Peter Chaadaev offered the most pessimistic assessment, claiming that Russian culture was "based wholly on borrowing and imitation." "[W]here are our wise men, where are our thinkers," he asked. "We have nothing that is ours on which to base our thinking."[2] The literary critic and Westernizer Vissarion Belinsky declared that what was known as Russian literature was an imitative product without historical continuity or internal organic development. "Literary phenomena were not engendered by the national spirit."[3] Imitation, which earlier had been a means to modernize Russia and to put her at the forefront, now caused her to lag behind Europe, since progress at this point depended on the development of the nation. Russian intellectuals of different opinions shared the concern for the lack of an original Russian culture and they agreed that without such a culture they would never be recognized as Europeans. However, to be of value to Europeans they had also to leave their mark on European culture. A Russian culture could not be separated or stand on its own in solid isolation. It would then be of no significance to Europe. It had to contribute to the progress of history and mankind. In other words, it had to be part of something greater and make an original impress in the same way as other cultures had done. Belinsky characterized the common feeling of uncertainty and backwardness among Russian intellectuals in the following words:

> We seem to have taken alarm for our life, for our significance, for our past and future, and are in a hurry to solve the great problem of to be or not to be? . . . we are now anxious to know whether any living organic idea runs through our history, and if it does, what exactly is it, what is our relation to our past from which we seem to have been sundered and to the West with which we seem to be related.[4]

Demands for a unique Russian contribution to European culture were raised in the first Russian philosophical circle, *The Society of Lovers of Wisdom*, 1824–1825. The society's president, prince Vladimir Odoevsky, described Russia's predicament in his novel, *Russian Nights*, through the main character, Faust:

> Every day we talk about German philosophy, about English industrialism, about European enlightenment, about the progress of reason, about the movement of humanity, and so on; but we have not yet thought of asking . . . : what kind of a wheel are we in this strange machine? . . . In a word: what are we?[5]

Dmitry Venevitinov, a fellow member, was also concerned with the insignificance of Russian culture. He argued that it was not possible to build a national culture with external forms imported from the West. Without a genuine foundation, there could only be an illusory culture. Russian intellectuals had to ask themselves "which level of the movement or performance common to everyone [Russia] had attained in comparison with other nations?"[6]

Ivan Kireevsky continued in the vein of the *Society of the Lovers of Wisdom*, where he himself had been a member. In an early article, he claimed that Russian works could be of no interest to the rest of the world solely as reflections of European literature, except perhaps in terms of quantity. Russian literature had to be regarded in relation to the literature of other nations, and in order to be of any significance to them, it had to reflect the Russian way of life. To Kireevsky, it was a cause of embarrassment not to have a literature of one's own, to possess no "works to be proud of before Europe."[7] The reason for the insignificance of Russian literature, Kireevsky wrote, was the Russian practice of imitation, which separated the educated elite and its specific culture from the inner source of the Russian way of life, the "Russian enlightenment."[8] In place of a Russian literature, there was "a strange chaos of undeveloped views and contradictory yearnings, there were discordant echoes of every possible movement in German, French, English, Italian, Polish, and Swedish literature, and a diverse imitation of every possible and impossible European tendency."[9] It was not only writers who were accused of imitation. The critics were no less guilty. Their views were totally dependent on the influence of foreign literature. "One judges us according to the laws of French literature, the other takes German literature as his model, yet another takes English literature and praises everything that looks like this ideal."[10] According to Kireevsky, the members of the educated Russian elite did nothing other than translate, imitate, and study alien literature, following the slightest foreign movement.[11]

Slavophilism was concerned with solving the problem of imitation, and this involved both the role of the Russian nation and that of Russian intellectuals. In the following I will try to show that 1) imitation constituted a serious problem to both Slavophiles and Westernizers; 2) that they used Romantic arguments to define this predicament; 3) that imitation was closely linked to the question of Russia's role as a nation; and 4) that this role or identity was interwoven with the identity of the Russian intellectuals. Imitation was a problem only in connection with Russian culture. In other areas, such as the applied and abstract sciences, borrowing from the West was not considered an impediment to Russian development.[12] The importance of culture in this respect was of course due to its prominent position in Romantic thought, but was perhaps underlined by its specific role in Russian society, as the only sphere where the intellectuals were allowed some independence. The cultural fields most affected by imitation, or at least the ones most frequently referred to, were literature, philosophy, and history. The principal arguments, used by the Slavophiles to present this problem, were based on the Romantic concepts of organism, and of the "degenerate West." But the intention of their critique was to counter the feeling of backwardness among Russian intellectuals by promoting the development of a genuine Russian culture.

THE ORGANIC ARGUMENT

Just as the German Romantics, the Slavophiles employed organic metaphors to justify their arguments. They compared the import of European ideas to the implantation of alien, or inorganic, elements into the body of Russia. On the surface of Russian life, Kireevsky stated, a borrowed culture prevailed, grown from another root.[13] Khomiakov described the state of Russian literature as "colourless words and colourless ideas," which revealed the foreign origin of the "engrafted plant."[14]

The Westernizers used a similar language. Belinsky, for example, maintained that an alien, borrowed content could never compensate, either in literature or in life, for the absence of a national content, although it might, in time, be transformed into it.[15] He described the "genius of a nation" as timid and subdued when it did not act originally and independently, maintaining that its produce in such cases would resemble artificial flowers.[16] We have come to take for granted that Europe should produce every truth and discovery by the sweat of her brow, Herzen argued. But there was one thing that had been overlooked: "the child [European culture] is not of our flesh and blood and there are no organic ties between it and us . . . Science can grow anywhere, but it will never produce a harvest where it has not been sown." According to Herzen it must germinate and mature in every nation.[17] "Science," used here in the broad sense of knowledge and learning, was a "living organism" and could thus not develop without an organic, i.e. a national content. "Guided by the letter of science alone, the formalists had reached a point of complete indifference to everything human."[18]

Metaphors alluding to the dichotomy between life and death were also common, as in the descriptions of the westernized Russian culture as expressing "lifelessness of science" and "immobility of life," or in the westernized intellectuals' alleged lack of "living consciousness" and "living fellow-feeling."[19] In fact, Khomiakov believed that it was natural for the intellectual to reject everything living on behalf of the dead.[20] Both Khomiakov and Kireevsky complained about the "emptiness of life" in Moscow society, where everything was imitated. People lost their intellectual and spiritual way of life in "the snobbish rigidness" of the salons.[21] The metaphor of death is also connected to the concept of formalism, i.e., empty form without content, which the Slavophiles held to be an outcome of imitation. Since the imports were ready-made models, or forms, without any living content, formalism would spread in all spheres of society with its "lifelessness" and "petrifaction."[22]

Hence, imported ideas, models, and systems were denounced because their foundations were derived from a culture and a history alien to Russian life. Whatever Russia acquired from the outside world had to be in harmony with the character and history of her own culture. It had to be the fruit of an inner organic development, based on Russia's own experiences. Consequently, the Romantic concept of organism turns imitation into a problem. In the article "Russians' opinions of foreigners," Khomiakov wrote that imported models or systems from foreign countries should not be understood as ready-made solutions, independent of "the spiritual historical movement" that had generated them. On the contrary, every system and institution in the West contained a solution to questions posed during earlier centuries. Khomiakov believed that transferring these systems to another people was dangerous and harmful, since the problems to which these systems constituted solutions had not had the possibility to arise under the conditions of the importing society. If these problems could not reasonably have appeared in the receiving society, the whole process, according to Khomiakov, came to resemble that of trying to introduce inorganic elements into an organic body.[23]

This was also the view of Chaadaev, who held that Russia could not simply take over Western institutions or the Western way of life, since she did not enjoy the conditions out of which these institutions and this lifestyle developed.[24] In his view, the problem of imitation had to do with the absence of a natural, inward development in Russia. Thus, new ideas replaced old ones, instead of growing out of them. The fact that the Russian people were unable to connect their thinking with any succession of ideas, which had been progressively developed in society, influenced the mind of every individual. As a consequence, the best ideas were no more than "sterile visions," which remained "paralysed in our brains" owing to precisely this lack of connection with earlier ideas.[25]

In nations that develop independently, Khomiakov held, the "richness of content" precedes the "perfection of form," but in Russia it was the other way around.[26] Kireevsky agreed, claiming that literature in Russia was only Western form without any real, in other words, Russian, content. Therefore, it was lifeless. In the Western nations, on the contrary, every movement in literature sprang from the inner movement of the culture, of which literature was a reflection. And in case this literature was subjected to foreign influence, it accepted this influence only when it corresponded to the requirements of the inner development of the nation's own culture and adopted it only in so far as it was in harmony with the character of its enlightenment, based on the nation's cultural foundations.[27] Commenting on the same theme, Khomiakov stated that all noteworthy artistic phenomena carried a clear imprint of the nation or people in which they occurred. They were all full of that life which gave them a foundation and a content.[28] In Russia, on the other hand, the arts were not yet in harmony with Russian culture. They had, in Khomiakov's words, yet to become an expression of her contemporary soul. But in order to be so, both form and content had to be national. Forms taken from the outside world could not serve as expressions of the Russian soul. The spiritual personality of the nation could only be expressed in forms created by itself.[29] Lacking national forms of art meant lacking a national culture, the existence of which was a measure of enlightenment and progress.

The same argument was applied to philosophy. A specific Russian philosophy was needed in order to build a foundation for a Russian culture and way of life. "A philosophy is essential for us," Kireevsky wrote in 1830.[30] He criticized the universal claims of Western rationalism, or, as the Slavophiles frequently called it, the "Western enlightenment." According to Kireevsky, its principles were not valid for the spiritual life of all human beings and of every people. Western thinking did not by itself give common meaning and truth to all external forms and individual ideas. If there was something essential in these forms and ideas, Russia could only incorporate it when it grew out of her roots, when it was a result of her own development and did not "descend on us from the outside in the form of a contradiction to the whole structure of our conscious and customary way of living."[31] Khomiakov described the current state of the Russian imitated culture as "a ripe fruit, transferred as a formula from alien clime." The problem here was that this imported culture, which in itself was seen as a living force, had no connection to the life from which it arose, and on which it depended. Being cut off from its living foundation, it could not "feel sympathy" for any life or for anything living.[32]

Kireevsky argued that the foundation of Western thought and science had developed from the history of Western culture. The character of European culture was, in his view, purely rational, not founded on the recognition of the highest truth, derived from faith, but on the concentration of individual opinions, on the predominance of logic over all other sources of knowledge, while in the character of Russian culture the logical development only constituted a dependent part of the spiritual conviction.[33] This meant that in those states that shared a common European culture, the new rationalistic philosophy was not a fragment, but a continuation of the spiritual life of humanity. It built on the inheritance from earlier thinking. In those states, all elements of universal thought were joined with their nationalities, without any contradictions.[34] In Russia, on the other hand, the imitated culture was not joined with the original development of the historical Russian culture. It had been separated from its inner source.[35] The solution lay in the development of a Russian philosophy, where the highest development of thinking, or "true science," was in harmony with Russian life.

Khomiakov tried to point out the limitations in the project of transferring to Russia not only certain positive elements of Western knowledge, but the whole system of its thinking He asserted that Russia's spiritual basis embodied both freedom and unity, in contrast to Western culture, characterized by freedom or unity. As a consequence, Russia's national foundation, which had the capacity to adopt and preserve such a spiritual basis as a result of its inner unity, could never be subjected to conclusions historically arisen from "Western duality," or adopt this duality in itself. It would be impossible.[36]

According to Khomiakov, analytical thinking always had to be accompanied by a "concealed synthesis," which was completely dependent on people's inner life. Philosophy had a certain meaning and character of its own, which only grew from the roots of living human intercourse.[37] It was the foundation for society and social science, and could therefore not arise from the arbitrariness of individual thinking. It needed a spiritual and social basis. In other words, analytical thinking could never completely free itself from the nation in which it was developed and from the faith that formed its basis. Philosophy had to be rooted in faith for its existence and in the historical foundation of society for its expression.[38]

Khomiakov's views on the requirements of philosophy naturally influenced his theory of knowledge in line with the organic idea of the nation. Accordingly, he argued that, since Russian and Western culture had different foundations, the historical basis of Russian culture could not be found in Western historiography. Even if this basis was indeed found by Western historians, they could never understand it. To Khomiakov, the nation was an organic being and, just like humans, it had a consciousness. However, in the same way as human beings were not conscious of themselves through logical reasoning, neither was the nation. This consciousness was broader and stronger than the formal and logical consciousness. It was a "living consciousness," which lay in the unity of habits, in the identity of the moral or spiritual motivation, in the continual organic exchange of ideas, in the founding of the people and its inner history. It belonged to the personality of the people and its way of life. It was incomprehensible both to the foreigner and to such members who had isolated themselves from the rest of society.[39]

According to Khomiakov, philosophy was an outcome of the human spirit's strivings for knowledge. In other words, it was a fruit of life. Consequently it needed a "living basis," something abstract logic did not provide.

Russia's dilemma was that imitation had prevented scientific thinking from being a product of its local, historical life. Knowledge had become separated from the Russian way of life and was therefore weak and impotent. In fact, philosophical development had become almost impossible due to this inner division in Russian society.[40]

The theory of organism, presented here by the Slavophiles, leads to a view of cultural development as unique and national. An imitative culture becomes a sign of backwardness, both with regard to the culture itself and to its articulators, since it was considered their duty to interpret and express the basis of the true national culture. To find a way out of this predicament a national literature and philosophy had to be developed. However, there was more to the Slavophile critique of imitation. It was not just that the practice of imitation had become outmoded; the model that was being imitated was in itself deficient. It was only logical, as Liah Greenfeld claims in her theory of nationalism, that in order to demonstrate the nation's unique foundations, the earlier model had to be rejected, although it is not correct to suggest that Slavophile criticism of the West was marked by *ressentiment*.[41]

Another reason for turning against the Western model was that its founding ideas, such as rationalism, universalism, positivism, and materialism, were incompatible with the ideas of originality, uniqueness, sensitivity, and spontaneity, which were upheld by all Romantics regardless of nationality. Hence, the Slavophiles' anti-Western arguments were part of a Western critique of European culture and were not intended to separate Russia from Europe. Rather, the use of the concept of the degenerate West in Russian discourse reflects the intellectuals' involvement in and adherence to European culture.

THE DEGENERATE WEST

The Slavophiles declared that the West had degenerated both morally and philosophically. They argued that with Hegel not only German philosophy, but the whole Western philosophical tradition, had reached its impasse. The completeness of Hegel's system, providing a rationalistic explanation of all spheres of human life and understanding, was unsatisfactory to the deeply religious Slavophiles. German philosophy, represented by Kant and followed by Hegel, was considered the forefront of the rationalistic tradition of thought starting with Descartes. Therefore, its fall had vast implications for the whole of Western thinking. According to

Khomiakov, German philosophy had long been standing at a spiritual abyss without knowing it, but it was not until "the decay" of Hegelianism that this became clear.[42] He claimed that German philosophy, by virtue of its one-sidedness, in Hegel reached its final result: self-invalidation.[43]

The result of Hegel's thinking was the decomposition of the whole development of "European reason" down to its last basis. There was nothing left to do. Reason had reached its limit and thus showed its inadequacy for philosophical development.[44] In Kireevsky's view, the whole development of Western thought from Descartes to Schelling was joined in this Hegelian last system and in it found its final development and justification. Now, it seemed, the destiny of philosophy was determined, its goal was found and its limits stretched to the impossible. For, as Kireevsky expressed it:

> When the essence of reason and the laws for its necessary activity is understood, when the equivalent of these laws is determined as the laws for an unconditioned existence, when the same eternal reason recurs according to the same grounds for eternal necessity, whereto could the inquiring thought of human beings yet strive?[45]

Not even Schelling's attempt to transcend logical reason was accepted by the Slavophiles. Kireevsky argued that, although aspiring to a new basis for science beyond logical reason, this philosophy nevertheless pursued the development of laws of intellectual necessity and thus could not transcend reason.[46]

Hegel revealed the disastrous conclusion of Western thought, which in its turn exposed the plight of Western culture as it was based on this rationalistic thinking. Indeed, Kireevsky declared that the distinctive character of Western culture in all its aspects, and as a whole, was a fundamental urge toward personal and self-contained rationalism in thought, life, society, and in the motivating forces and forms of human life. As a consequence, the inadequacy of European culture was more and more strikingly exposed.[47] The Slavophiles were aware that Western Europe was considered degenerate and doomed even by Westerners, which of course did not make it a useful model for Russia. Khomiakov wrote that "we ought to be ashamed of ourselves chasing after the West. The English, French, or Germans do not have anything good for themselves. The further they look around, the worse and the more immoral their society appears to them."[48] Instead, the "inner wavering" and "spiritual petrifaction" of the Western world should serve as a bad example for Russia.[49] Having lost belief in its earlier foundations, Western thinkers tried to create new ones analytically, by way of logic. But this practice only led to relativism, "this constant change of ideas, where old ideas were recurrently condemned as lies and new ones promoted as truths."[50]

Clearly influenced by Romantic thought, it was the Slavophiles' contention that the dominance of England and Germany, currently at the forefront of the European enlightenment, could not continue, for their inner life had already come to a close, making their culture suitable solely to them. It had lost its common significance and could therefore not contribute to universal progress. As a result, Europe, marked by its old culture, appeared petrified. Khomiakov asserted that the poor state of Western culture, characterized by division and struggle, had now gone to the extreme. The life of the people had reached a final weakness, which was reflected in the unlimited dominance of the egoistic personality governed by reason. Kireevsky noted that the prominent thinkers of Europe all complained about the contemporary situation of moral apathy, a lack of convictions, and a general egoism. According to him, these thinkers demanded a new spiritual force outside of reason. They demanded a new source of life independent of material advantage. In other words, they searched for faith and could not find it at home, for Christianity in the West was perverted by individualism.[51] Only two nations did not take part in the general degeneration: the United States and Russia. However, due to "the one-sidedness of the United States' English culture," Russia was Europe's only hope.[52] Compared to the stale Western social life, Russia's spiritual forces were still vigorous. Her potential was great, because the development of her culture had been halted before it could yield any fruit.[53]

The West obviously constituted a poor model for Russia. Instead, Russia should turn to her indigenous foundations, which were not tainted by Western rationalism, and use those as a basis for her culture and society. However, Western thought was not to be totally discarded. Instead, it should be used as a seed to something new. What was needed was a Russian philosophy that encompassed the whole human spirit and thus united Western knowledge and Christian faith. In this way, the development of a specific Russian philosophy would save Russia from falling into the same abyss as the West, and at the same time, save the West from its own degeneration and decay. To the Slavophiles, at least, that was an inevitable outcome of the logic of Western thought. Based on different foundations and developed by way of different paths, Russia had an important role to play in solving the predicament of Western philosophy.

Seen in the context of Romantic organicism, the idea of the degenerate West helped Russia to define her place in the progress of history. According to this thinking, all cultures in the world are organisms tied together in a process of universal progress. Cultures live and grow old just like every other organic being; this allows new cultures to replace the old and decaying ones. The concept of a decaying Western culture thus becomes not an argument for separation from the West, but for allowing Russia to make a genuine contribution to universal progress. Combining the legacy of Western culture with her special way of life, Russia could save Europe. By declaring that Russian culture had a special role in universal history, the Slavophiles suggested a way out of the feeling of backwardness felt by members of the educated elite in their relation to the West.

RUSSIAN BACKWARDNESS AND THE ABSENCE OF A NATIONAL CONTRIBUTION

Because Western rationalism, as we have seen above, had reached an impasse it could no longer make any universal contribution; Russia now had a chance to revise its status as a culturally backward nation. The problem with imitation was that it hampered the development of a national culture, thus preventing Russia from being part of the universal progress of humanity. Many Russian intellectuals felt that Russia had nothing to give to the world, since all it had was imitated and borrowed. Chaadaev had come to the devastating conclusion that Russia was so culturally underdeveloped that indigenous sources would never allow the development of a civilised, enlightened nation with an original national culture.[54] This lack of a national culture was considered a sign of backwardness. It showed that there was no progress in the Russian nation. Hence, the Slavophiles were critical of imitation because it led to cultural backwardness, which implied national backwardness.

In the eighteenth century and beginning of the nineteenth century, the educated Russian elite saw themselves as European intellectuals, imitating and adopting the main tenets of European culture. Many of them spoke foreign languages fluently, were instructed by French, German, or English tutors and travelled in Europe. They were familiar with the latest Western literary currents and philosophical ideas, which they discussed in salons, clubs and circles.[55] These educated Russians saw it as their role to study, absorb and disseminate European culture. Imitation was seen as a means to enlighten Russia. However, with the introduction of Romanticism in Russia in the early nineteenth century, this practice became unacceptable. Educated Russians realised that in order to be full members of a common European culture they had to possess a culture of their own, which they did not. This realization brought about an identity crisis. Russian intellectuals now came to believe that the West despised Russia for her imitation and want of a national culture when, as Belinsky expressed it, "the national spirit of European nations was so sharply and originally expressed" in their culture.[56] This was the reason Kireevsky so urgently asked what Russia had to show to Europe. Hence, it was the attachment to European culture and its prevailing ideas of Romanticism and Idealism that forced Russian intellectuals to develop a culture of their own and to formulate a specific Russian national character.

The Slavophiles realized that if they were to counter the feeling of backwardness among educated Russians, it would not suffice to denounce imitation as such, or to attack the Western model. The only way for Russian intellectuals to come to terms with their identity crisis was to present a national culture that could make a genuine contribution to the common cause of universal human enlightenment. The Slavophiles believed that enlightened Westerners were prepared to respect Russian thought when it was genuine and not just an imitation of foreign ideas.[57] But any work of art, however great, which did not bear "the sharp imprint of nationality," would lose its chief merit in the eyes of Europeans.[58] Therefore, the central aim of the Slavophile critique of imitation was to show how Russia could contribute to universal progress.

An example of the importance that the Slavophiles attached to the role of Russian culture in the European context is the way they expressed appreciation for the open lectures of Stepan Shevyrev on the history of the Russian literature and language. In a letter to a friend, Khomiakov wrote that the great interest in Shevyrev's lectures showed the heights of enlightenment to which Russia had arisen and how originally the nation could already think and speak.[59] The national contribution to, and participation in, a universal development was thus closely connected to the nation's originality and uniqueness. Russia had to be original precisely in order to make a contribution to humanity, and in order to be part of universal progress. This also meant that the national culture had to be of universal significance. Without a genuine, national culture, Russia was left on the outside of universal history and of the progress of mankind. This was why Chaadaev's assertion that Russia had given nothing to the world was so devastating to the educated elite. Claiming that Russia had "not added a single idea to the mass of human ideas" nor contributed anything "to the progress of the human spirit" and that "nothing has emanated from us for the common good of men," he pointed precisely at the root of the problem.[60] Kireevsky stressed how important it was not to lose the universal meaning of Russian culture. "We have to be part of the common life of mankind or else the basis of our culture becomes one-sided, instead of being the basis of a complete, true, living enlightenment," he wrote.[61]

Imitation separated the educated elite from the inner source of the Russian culture, thereby making its principles useless for the common cause of universal progress. For this reason, Kireevsky felt that it was very important for literature to emerge from its "artificial state" and become relevant. Literature had to be an expression of Russian culture and, at the same time, a source from which this culture might evolve. Because the state of the arts, and especially literature, measured the state of a nation's culture, or the level of its enlightenment, the absence of a national literature indicated the absence of a national culture.[62] But the Slavophiles went even further and claimed that a nation's culture characterized its whole social and political life. This made the need for a national literature all the more acute. In practice, the want of a national literature meant that Russia was backward in all areas; politically, economically, and culturally. It had no history and no future, as Chaadaev so gloomily remarked.[63]

However, to the Slavophiles, imitation was not only an expression of underdevelopment, but also its cause. The practice of imitation hid any possible national characteristics under alien forms and prevented the "free" development of a Russian culture. It made Russian science and art incapable of generating a creative development of its own, thereby preventing Russia from making an original contribution to the world. According to the Slavophiles the seeds of the native enlightenment had been suppressed by the knowledge taken from abroad, and so the ancient Russian Orthodox culture had been arrested in its development before it could "yield to life its lasting fruits or reveal its thriving potential for the mind." That was the reason for the poverty and lack of character in the contemporary Russian arts.[64]

To place all the blame for the poor state of the Russian arts on imitation helped Russian intellectuals to explain their sense of backwardness. The argument pursued by the Slavophiles was that imitation had created an inner division in Russia between the genuine national life and an imitated life. It was this division that prevented "the good" in Russia to develop fully and made Russia's "living consciousness," i.e. her national spirit, inaccessible to the intellectuals. "We have lost our national personality, i.e. ourselves," Khomiakov exclaimed. He argued that without a national identity, Russian intellectuals were just as helpless as the nation and that this was why the conditions for a national literature, philosophy, and history were deficient. The solution was for Russians to cease measuring everything in their society by a standard not suited to their way of life. In order for them to give a fair judgement of Russian culture, or "a clear and sensible understanding of many, and perhaps the most important phenomena in her history," Russian intellectuals had to use a different national standard when making judgements of their national culture. This would lead to the development of what Khomiakov called "the good in ourselves" and make Russia's "living consciousness" accessible.[65]

What Khomiakov proposed, then, was the promotion of a Russian enlightenment through the regeneration of the national culture. It was Kireevsky who most clearly formulated this idea. According to him, imitation of alien forms prevented the development of a Russian culture, and the growth of a genuine enlightenment. Now it was high time for Russia to develop her own culture, which had grown out of her history, and to a certain extent, had been preserved by the people. But the development of a Russian enlightenment was not possible until Russian intellectuals concentrated on expressing and developing their own national culture.[66] In other words, the educated elite should "replace their contemporary submission before everything foreign with a reasonable veneration for Russia's old foundations."[67] If the core principles of the Orthodox-Slavic culture were true, Kireevsky declared, then they should serve as a necessary complement to European culture, "cleaning it from its exclusive rationalistic character and penetrating it with new meaning." To continue borrowing from the West, on the other hand, would make Russia useless for the common cause of universal human enlightenment.[68]

History could be used to find the specific foundations of Russian culture. It could explain why Europe and Russia had developed in different ways and why these two geographical entities now were found at different stages of development.[69] For this reason, it was of great importance that Russian historians studied the basis of their country on its own premises. They should no longer believe what foreigners said or wrote about their country.[70] The concepts of organism and the degenerate West, made it possible for the Slavophiles to argue that there was a future for Russian culture, a calling. According to this thinking, each nation had a specific role in history, assigned to it by universal history. The time would come when Russia would be a cultural leader, because universal history would judge the "one-sided spiritual grounds," i.e., the rationalistic principles that governed Western thinking, as irrevocable. As a consequence, looking for new principles to carry humanity forward, universal history would rouse to life and activity "the more complete and living foundations" contained in Russia.

Since Russian culture was born when other countries had already finished the cycle of their spiritual development, it was Russia's task to begin where they had stopped. European culture could be seen as "the ripe fruit" of human development to be used as a stimulating means for the evolution of Russian intellectual and spiritual activity. The crown of the European enlightenment served as a cradle for Russian culture. Kireevsky compared the contemporary character of the European enlightenment with that of Roman-Greek culture, which, after having been developed to its own antithesis, was forced to adopt another new basis that had been preserved in another people and which, before that time, did not have any universal-historical meaning. This historical analogy allowed Kireevsky to argue that Russia, in the communal customs of the people and in the Orthodox faith, had a firm basis for a national culture of universal significance. What was now inaccessible to the West was accessible to the Russian people, Khomiakov argued.[71] Only the Russian people could revive the foundations of life itself, since they alone had preserved true Christianity, while the West had decided on a heretical path leading to rationalism and atheism. This made it possible for Russia to contribute to universal progress.

Contrasting the dead end reached by Western thought with the possibilities of the Russian culture, Kireevsky argued that the new demands of the European mind and Russian fundamental convictions in fact had the same meaning. At the root of European culture, there was one essential question about the relationship of the West to the hitherto undiscovered foundation of life, thought, and culture that lay at the basis of the Slavic-Orthodox world.[72] Hence, the possibility for saving Europe lay in the "living enlightenment" of the Russian culture. In creating a specifically Russian philosophy, Russia could make an original contribution to universal knowledge, to enlightenment; and at the same time save both the West and itself from ruin. But in order for Russia to rise above other nations, her faith, which contained the basis of true social ideas, must penetrate social life. To do so, it had to be combined with reason and made universal. It had "to pass through science, i. e. through the consciousness of all history and all the results of human intellectual activity" in order to be of common relevance.[73] That was the task the Slavophiles urged the educated Russian elite to take on.

Pointing to the problem of imitation, the Slavophiles wished to demonstrate to the members of the educated elite that the reason for Russia's cultural backwardness was to be found in the members of the educated elite themselves, in their Westernization and alienation from their own nation. This establishes a direct link between the crisis of identity among Russian intellectuals and the crisis of Russia's national identity. The Slavophile critique of imitation was directed towards the educated reading public. The formulation of Slavophilism constituted, in effect, an attempt to overcome the division in Russian life, brought about by the adoption of foreign models and systems. The alienation of the Westernized elite from the genuine Russian way of life separated the educated elite from the people, in whom this life was preserved. "It ruined the bond of community and life between them," as Khomiakov wrote.[74] A rift appeared between these intellectuals and the people, or nation. In order to develop an original Russian culture of universal significance and thereby gain the respect of Europeans, harmony had to be restored.

THE CRISIS OF IDENTITY AND THE GAP BETWEEN ELITE AND PEOPLE

The practice of imitation had created a gulf between the educated elite and the people. For this reason, intellectuals had not fulfilled their role as interpreters of the nation. Most of them had not even realised that this was their task. Belinsky wrote that he could not but "half-agree" with the Slavophile assertion that there was a sort of duality in Russian life and consequently a lack of moral unity; and that this deprived the Russian people of a clearly defined national character such as distinguished all the European nations; "that this makes a sort of nonesuches out of us, well able to think in French, German and English, but unable to think in Russian."[75] The imitation of everything Western involved both a depreciation of and an alienation from Russia's national character. It was only natural that the adoption of the Enlightenment from the West should lead to a depreciation of what was specifically Russian, since this was a system of ideas that neglected everything specific, or national. The important point to be made here, according to Khomiakov, was that the disapproval of the Russian life by the Westernized elite was not due to malevolence but to "a sin of ignorance," for "we do not know Russia." Besides, contemporary Russian intellectuals could not be held responsible for their alienation from the life of the people and its "higher grounds." This alienation was inherited from an earlier generation who came to believe in the incomparable supremacy of the Western world.[76] The contemporary division in the Russian nationality was a historical accident and lay neither in her spiritual basis, nor in the character of her social structure as in Europe. It was a consequence of being unacquainted with this nation's "wealth of knowledge" and would disap-

pear when the educated strata became familiar with it. Europe's other nations, on the other hand, would only find division and struggle when they
returned to their past.[77]

What worried Khomiakov, though, was that Russian intellectuals had
lately expressed more contempt for, and a more complete denial of, everything national than previously. The reason he gives for this change was not
that the practice of imitation had turned into a campaign against everything national, but simply that the question of national character was not
an issue for the earlier generation. However, the transformation of the intellectual agenda brought about by the rise of Romantic thought in Russia
put the nation in focus, and forced everybody to relate to it. What Khomiakov referred to was thus only different standpoints in a common discussion of Russia's national character and contribution, taken part in by
diverse intellectuals. He criticized those who could not see the future of a
Russian nation in the people for not being able to value the special character of their nation. This made them unable to see that the solution to Russia's predicament might be found precisely there, in the development of
Russia's national character. Khomiakov described these Westernized intellectuals as travellers. They were like "alien observers, living by themselves
according to themselves. They wander about in society, but are not members of it. They travel among peoples, but do not belong to any of them."

This lack of contact with the people and its culture naturally implied a
lack of understanding of it. It was the "proud contempt" of the educated for
the people and their inability to understand organic national phenomena
on the whole that made the Russian way of life inaccessible to them. In the
absence of "facts" that could be made objects of an analytical investigation,
these Westernized intellectuals were at a loss. The facts of Russian life could
not be understood with minds brought up on foreign ideas, caught in foreign systems, without having anything in common with the foundations of
their nation's old spiritual life and ancient culture. As a consequence of their
ignorance, Westernized intellectuals not only recognized the weakness of
their people, a humble act in Khomiakov's view. They had to assert that the
moral or spiritual law, which lay at the basis of the people's life, was weak
and incomplete. That was not humility, but denial. Khomiakov declared
that not to honour the spiritual law of the people inevitably belittled the nation in the eyes of other people. It also carried with it a sense of inferiority
in relation to other peoples.[78] It was this denial of the Russian way of life
that led to a gap between the educated elite and the people in a sociological,
historical, philosophical, and psychological sense. In their effort to overcome this division and make Westernized intellectuals conscious of their

duty as organs of the nation, the Slavophiles used the concept of the gap in different ways.

One of the many functions of the concept of the gap was to point at the different frames of reference of the people and the educated public, which made it difficult for them to understand each other. On the one side, were the educated, Westernized, artificial, and not very religious aristocrats. On the other, were the uneducated, genuine, Orthodox, Russian people, living in serfdom. The wish to bridge this division was not only a nationalist objective. In fact, it was a primary objective for both Westernizers and Slavophiles.[79] Belinsky wrote of a prevailing spirit of disunity in the Russian society, where each of the social estates possessed specific traits of its own—its dress and its manners, its way of life and customs, and even its language. He believed that the spirit of disunity was hostile to society, which, in his view, should be organic—a multitude of people internally linked together.[80]

Kireevsky argued that before the dispersion of Western culture, founded on scientific rationalism, all Russian enlightenment, the thinking of all social classes, came from a common source: the teaching of the Russian church. Now, the relationship between the lowest and highest classes had changed. The understanding of the higher strata, formed by Western science, was separated from those of the people.[81] Khomiakov agreed, stating that the Westernized Russian elite was separated from the life of the people and thereby from the "true enlightenment." In another article, Khomiakov accused the educated elite of isolating themselves in their pride of their "insignificant knowledge of the people," as a "colony of eclectics, abandoned in a country of savages." Naturally, the existence of a gulf between the Russian educated elite and the people made the development of an original Russian culture difficult. In fact, Khomiakov claimed that "true enlightenment" was only possible in countries whose inner structure was founded on unity. Indeed, Russia's inner division made it impossible for the national spirit to develop fully, because her "living consciousness" which, according to Khomiakov, constituted a necessary, and perhaps the most important, focus of the enlightenment of the people, was incomprehensible to the educated elite.[82]

Another meaning given to "the gap" was that of a rift between the educated elite and its past, involving an alienation from the moral and spiritual grounds of the nation. The Slavophiles argued that imitation made the educated elite uninterested in Russia's past. Hence, they did not acquire any knowledge of Russian history.[83] Here, knowledge does not only denote objective learning, but it also, and to a higher extent, indicates a subjective understanding of Russia and its past. It is subjective in the sense that only those who live a Russian life can have this understanding. Therefore the Westernized intellectuals, having alienated themselves from their roots, could not understand Russia's past. They looked at Russian history with Western eyes, using Western scientific standards, which made them incapable of discerning the foundations of Russia.[84] Due to this rift, "it was impossible for the members of the educated elite to have a clear understanding of many, and perhaps the most essential, phenomena in Russian history." Most importantly, these individuals were ignorant of the ancient sources of their nation's life and thus could not develop them. "We do not know Russia," Khomiakov maintained, "if we do not acknowledge the moral and spiritual law that shows itself in the historical development of the people."

The Slavophiles criticised Russian historians for not treating the Russian way of life as Russia's history. Despite the importance of Russian history for the development of a national culture, contemporary historiography disregarded legends and the essential human insights of uneducated people. "With all the force of our reason," Khomiakov wrote, "we have separated ourselves from the history of our Fatherland and from its spiritual essence." Hence, in depriving the educated elite of a past, this gap had at the same time deprived them of their Fatherland.[85] For man was intimately associated with his country and people. Each person had a dual identity as an individual and as part of a people. Belinsky expressed this argument in the organic language of the day:

> Every man, in existing for himself, at the same time exists for the society into which he was born; . . . he is related to society as a part to the whole, as a limb to the body, as a plant to the soil . . . Hence every man lives in the spirit of that society, mirroring in himself its virtues and failings, sharing with it its truths and errors. We see that society, as a vast agglomeration of human beings who, despite their individual distinctions, have something in common in mentality, sensations and creeds, is a united, organic whole, in short, that society is an ideal individuality.[86]

The ephemeral existence of an individual detached from the species created an unpredictable life without any memory of the past, Chaadaev wrote.[87] Khomiakov argued that in denying his moral or spiritual grounds, man severed all bonds with his earlier life and ceased to be himself since this was such a fundamental part of his identity. Furthermore, if he did so while speaking in the name of the people, he thereby separated himself from the nation, which was even worse. Without this national identity, this identification with his people and history, man was alienated, atomized, an incongruity without contents. "The traveller is forever alone in the weakness of his personal arbitrariness," as Khomiakov put it.[88] Chaadaev agreed with this Romantic standpoint and argued that nations, like individuals, could not advance without a profound sense of their individuality, or awareness of their selves. But, taking Russia as proof, he maintained that nations could nevertheless exist without a nationality.[89] As expected, the Slavophiles did not agree with Chaadaev on this point. In their view, Russia had a nationality that could be found in the people, because they had preserved the specific Russian character, undistorted by Western influence.[90] For this reason only, Khomiakov asserted, we should be grateful for the emergence of a gap between the educated elite and the people, allowing the latter to remain unaffected by Western thinking,"thereby saving us from a complete break with the whole of our historical life."[91]

The separation between the imported Western ideas and the historical life of Russia leads to the third use of the concept of the gap. Here, it refers to a division between knowledge and life, where the educated elite naturally represents knowledge and the people represents life. In the highest layers, there was "knowledge completely cut off from life"; while in the lowest, there was "life, never rising to consciousness." This was a gap between the spiritual and intellectual essence of Russia, expressed in two opposite yearnings: on the one hand for originality and on the other for imitation. However, imitation was not the only negative consequence of the gap between knowledge and life. To the Slavophiles, it also had epistemological implications. Because "where knowledge has been separated from life, where the society [i. e., the educated elite] that keeps this knowledge has been disconnected from its own basis, only reason can develop and dominate." And reason, in Khomiakov's view, was an isolated and divided force, since it could only use external facts. The wholeness of the mind, that is all its faculties taken together, demanded wholeness in life.[92] It demanded facts from within, facts from life. Thus, a complete understanding of the Russian way of life was impossible as long as there was a gap between knowledge and life in Russia.

It is interesting to note that Herzen too was concerned about this rift. Science, he wrote, could not participate as a living element in the current of practical life as long as it rested in the hands of the "caste of scientists." Only those who belonged to life could introduce it into life. The scientists who lived an artificial life forgot all living interests and departed from the contemporary world and the people. Therefore, science must strive to descend from its throne into the "thick of life." Herzen idealized ancient Greece, where, in his words, "thinkers, poets, historians, were citizens above all, were people who belonged to life, to the civic council, to the square." To Herzen, an actual unity of science and life, where scientists acted in their place and time, was an ideal.[93]

In its third sense, the gap was all the more problematic since it was in the fusion of knowledge and life that a Russian national identity was to be formulated, and this in turn was to constitute the point of departure for the development of a Russian enlightenment. On the other hand, to explain the absence of a national culture and the backwardness of society in terms of a gap, which was supposed to have paralysed the "forces of life," implied that there was a future for Russia if this gap was bridged.[94] The Slavophiles could not, or would not, close the gap between the modern culture of the educated elite and traditional society, because this demanded political action. The gap to the West, however, could be closed by uniting the educated elite with the Russian people or nation, i. e. through a cultural transformation. In this sense, Slavophilism can be seen as a project for change. The people or nation could only be made to speak through the intellectuals. Articulate Russians therefore had an explicit role to fulfil in raising the Russian life to consciousness. To the extent that Russia's national character or identity was regarded as something articulated and not merely as a way of life, it had to be formulated by artists and intellectuals in order to exist.

The continuing practice of imitation had negative consequences for the way the Slavophiles saw the role of the intellectual and the artist. When all you could do was imitate, there was no room left for artistic creation, for making a real contribution to the world of art and science, or for that matter, promoting a Russian enlightenment. Khomiakov described this situation as intellectual slavery and it was presented as a formidable challenge.[95] The Slavophiles were anxious to make social changes and, like the German Romantics, they believed literature and philosophy were the means to do so. "Our aim," Kireevsky wrote to Koshelev, "is the well-being of our country and the common means is literature."[96]

Although the Slavophiles stressed the negative effects of the alienation of the educated elite from everything Russian, the existence of an unrealized national basis nonetheless held a promise for the future. There was a belief among the Slavophiles that the universal development of history demanded of Russia that she now expressed her national foundations which were "more complete and comprehensive" as compared to the foundations of the West. By articulating these foundations, and thereby creating a genuine national culture, Russia could make an imprint on universal history.

The problem was that the educated elite had no knowledge of their nation and its past, and so there were no organs to express its founding principles. Therefore, the Slavophiles urged Russian intellectuals and artists to get out of the state of "non-national abstraction" and participate fully in the original life of the people. A return to the national, or what the Slavophiles called "the foundations of life," was necessary.[97] Indeed, the thought and life of the people could only be expressed and manifested by someone who completely lived this life and thought these thoughts.[98] Khomiakov even asserted that the artist did not create of his own will, but that the spiritual force of the people created through the artist. Art was not the work of one individual soul, but the work of the national soul in one person.[99] The artist's task was to articulate what already existed, but was yet to be expressed. Literature should be an expression of the inner life and culture of the nation. It should not only reflect intellectual and artistic culture, but the whole completeness in the people's way of life.[100]

The consequences of not taking on this national project were severe both with regards to the role of the Russian nation and the role of the Russian intellectuals. When the living foundation of Russia ultimately flourished, which the Slavophiles were convinced would eventually happen, the "articulate Russians" would perhaps only become "withered and unfruitful twigs."[101] The prospect of being useless, or superfluous, was a matter of real concern to the Slavophiles, as it was to other Russian intellectuals of their time. This is also the reason why they were so critical of what they referred to as the imitative, superficial, and indifferent Moscow high-society. Kireevsky emphasised that the decline of Russian culture did not come about without the "inner guilt" of Russia's educated elite.[102] It was their duty to work for a common cause and to instil compassion for fellow countrymen. Instead, they enjoyed all that was comfortable, good, and beautiful. They were indifferent to moral questions, and did not have any opinions of their own.[103] It was this alienated attitude among educated Russians that was put forward as the reason for the absence of a national culture.[104]

Then again, the Slavophiles were often ambiguous when it came to causal relations. Sometimes they argued in a way that made the alienation and the ensuing gap a consequence of the practice of imitation, sometimes it was the alienation and the gap that caused imitation. What is important to note is that the Slavophiles took the matter one step further, to what they believed would be the consequences of this alienation for the regeneration of the national culture and ultimately for Russia's standing as a nation. Whether imitation had created a division in Russian society, or whether the division had caused imitation, the importance attached to this issue illustrates the crisis of identity felt by many Russian intellectuals at the time.[105] Even if Russians had been conscious of the gap between the elite and the people as early as the eighteenth century, this did not constitute an urgent predicament until the need for a national culture emerged, brought on by the new intellectual agenda of the Romantic movement. Now, the question was not how to build an educated society, but how to form a national culture, how to express the nation.

The main objective of the Slavophiles' critique of imitation was to counter the feeling of cultural backwardness among Russian intellectuals, triggered by the Romantic demands for a genuine contribution to the advancement of humanity. Obviously, neither isolationism, nor an antagonistic posture towards the West would remove these feelings. The only way Russian culture could be appreciated by others was for it to make an original contribution to universal progress. Hence, the Slavophiles used the Romantic concepts of organism and the decaying West to claim a future place for Russia in universal history and to present Russian intellectuals with a new public role as articulators of their nation.

Chapter 3

Conceptions of the Nation

The previous chapter showed that the Slavophiles were concerned with the Russian practice of imitation and the absence of a genuine national culture. In this chapter, I argue that Slavophilism is best understood in the context of nationalism. But nationalism existed and exists in a variety of forms and in order for the idea of the nation to cast light on Slavophile theory, it has to be properly characterized and defined. Nationalism is usually seen as a two-edged phenomenon, resting on one of two different concepts of the nation, historically following each other in time. Here, they are referred to as the idea of the sovereign people and the idea of the unique people. In Greenfeld's words, these two concepts are "grounded in different values and develop for different reasons."[1] For present purposes, their different criteria for membership in the nation and the consequences this has for the realization of a national community are of primary importance. The concept of a sovereign people is commonly seen as the basis of political nationalism, while the concept of the unique people lies at the heart of cultural nationalism.[2] This dichotomy can and will be questioned below, but will nevertheless be used here since there are fundamental differences between these two ideas of the nation which have to be understood in order to comprehend Slavophilism as a nationalism.

THE SOVEREIGN PEOPLE

What is often referred to as the first idea of the nation began to be used systematically during the Age of Revolution, when an explicit idea of the nation was clearly formulated in political discourse. This concept is best characterized as a democratic idea of the sovereign people. As the French Declaration of Rights of 1795 stated: "Each people is independent and sovereign, whatever the number of individuals who compose it and the extent of the territory it occupies."[3] For the first time in history, popular sovereignty was the source of legitimacy for political rule. In the French Revolution, popular sovereignty was taken to mean "the nation," while in the American Revolution it was referred to as "the people." The primary meaning of the nation was thus political, in the sense of equating the people and the state in the manner of the French and American revolutions.[4]

In this "imagined political community,"[5] the people were "the bearer of sovereignty, the central object of loyalty and the basis of collective solidarity."[6] As a consequence of the revolutionary transformations, people ceased to be subjects of a king and became citizens of a nation. Civil rights were granted to all citizens equally, not only to certain privileged categories. What characterized the nation of the citizen-people was that it represented the public good against particular interests and privileges. Abbé Sieyès wrote that a nation was a body of associates, living under common laws and represented by the same legislative assembly.[7] However, it was not only the case that the members of the nation should be ruled by the same government. It was to be a government by the people or its representatives.[8] Moreover, in Continental Europe the will of the nation was not restricted by a constitution. According to Sieyès, the crucial issue was the right of the nation to devise the constitution for itself rather than being ruled by it. In sum, mass participation and citizenship were closely related to the nation. In this sense, nationalism and democracy were inherently linked. As Greenfeld observes, originally nationalism developed as democracy, since fundamental equality among members of a nation was recognized by investing sovereignty in the people. She argues that the word "nation" was applied to the population of the country and made synonymous with the word "people" and that the populace was thereby elevated to the position of a political elite and the supreme object of loyalty.[9] This contention is not altogether unproblematic. The right to political participation was determined by citizenship, and not every member of the population had the right to be a citizen.

Just as the primary meaning of this idea of the nation was political, the central criterion for being a member of the nation was political in the sense of resting ultimately on a social contract. The nation rested on an act of will; a person was a citizen by wanting to be one. In this way, a body of individuals would become a nation. "The existence of a nation," as Ernest Renan wrote "is an everyday plebiscite, just as the existence of the individual is a perpetual affirmation of life." It renews itself by the clearly expressed desire to continue the communal life.[10] Membership of the nation was not natural or organic, but voluntaristic. It was a matter of choice, which is clearly expressed in the oath of allegiance that members of the new nations in America and in France had to take. The fact that large groups of people resisted the creation of these nation-states and, when their resistance failed, chose to leave them, demonstrates the same point. So does the willingness to award citizenship to persons alien to a nation's language, culture, and history. One case in point is Thomas Paine, who, an Englishman by birth and a subject of the British monarch, held both American and French citizenship. This is not to say that there were no collective identities based on notions of a common culture, ethnicity, history, or language both before and after the appearance of the political, voluntaristic nation. However, such notions did not define the formal membership. This was determined by citizenship. There was a moral and economic criterion as well, which required that a citizen contributed to the well-being and maintenance of the nation. Sieyès for example asserted that the third estate in fact represented the whole nation, since it represented all those who worked, all those who contributed.[11] But the essential criterion was political-volitional. One became a member of the nation, not by belonging to a culture, but by belonging to a state, since the nation was defined as a union of the people and the state.

Naturally, the goal of political nationalists, who promoted the political idea of the nation, was the congruence of the political unit, that is the state, and the national unit, that is the people.[12] In autonomous states, political nationalists tried to reform the state in order for the people to gain political power.[13] Nations that lacked political autonomy aimed for national self-determination through the creation of a nation-state and the destruction of the *ancien régime*.[14] It is clear that the latter form of nationalism had to be based on another definition of the nation in order to justify the claim for national independence. In this case, it was the political aim of the nationalists to achieve an autonomous state, which gives reason for calling them political nationalists. John Hutchinson argues that the ideal of political nationalists is a civic polity of educated citizens united by common laws and mores. Such nationalists have a cosmopolitan rationalist conception of the nation, aiming for a common humanity transcending cultural differences. The principle of nationality is important as a necessary means to secure a representative state for a community, thereby allowing it to participate as an equal in the developing cosmopolitan rationalist civilization.[15]

The obvious link between popular sovereignty and nationalism has led theorists to treat the concept of the nation as an idea, the foremost importance of which lies in its contribution to the formation of modern nation-states; and so nationalism has often been studied in terms of nation-building.[16] However, the fact that the formation of modern, democratic nation-states and nationalism coincided in time does not mean that all forms of nationalism are connected to this process and can be understood by referring to it.

TWO FORMS OF NATIONALISM

By the late eighteenth century, another form of nationalism appeared, connected to Romanticism rather than to democracy. This form must be differentiated from the political nationalism discussed above. Its basic ideas were drawn from the late eighteenth-century counter-Enlightenment and from the philosophy of Herder in particular. It can be understood as a reaction to the European intellectual hegemony based on the cultural predominance of the French Enlightenment, as well as to the imperialist tendencies of the Jacobins and Napoleon. This nationalism was directed against the looming threat of European uniformity.[17]

The equation between nation and people still applied, but the people now constituted a unique people, instead of a sovereign citizen-people. Historical and cultural distinctiveness was emphasized as opposed to the French civic or political nation. The French revolution had stifled originality; now, diversity was promoted in place of uniformity. The concepts of distinctiveness, uniqueness, and individuality, in a corporate sense, were central to this thinking. Nationality was a means to awaken from selfish individualism, although individuality was to be transcended, rather than removed. According to this ideology, the meaning of the nation was cultural, not political. The nation was defined as the people and the culture, rather than the people and the state. The criterion for membership in the nation, accordingly, changed from a political one to a cultural. A person became a member of the nation, not through being part of the state, by way of citizenship granted by a constitution, but through belonging to a culture defined as a common way of living and thinking.

This form of nationalism, commonly referred to as cultural nationalism, takes the expression of a national culture as its point of departure. It is based on the conviction that a culture is formed by the nation, as a manifestation of the spirit of the people or the national character.[18] The purpose of cultural nationalism is not to transform the state or to gain political power, but to transform society in order to realise the nation and regenerate its true character.[19] As we have seen above, this shift of focus, away from the state and the centre of political power to the moral regeneration of the nation, caused cultural nationalism to be dismissed as a regressive, utopian movement, of absolutely no significance for the shaping of modern nation-states or the development of popular sovereignty, that is democracy.

Although there has been an awareness in the recent literature of the significance of cultural nationalism for the shaping of modern nations, most studies of nationalism still focus on state-oriented nationalist movements as the only meaningful objects of study.[20] In the case cultural nationalism has been taken into account, scholars have either asserted that its basic idea converged with the political notion into a demand for an independent nation-state for the people or, acknowledging the different aims of these forms of nationalism, maintained that they nevertheless produced the same effect, that is, the establishment of a modern autonomous state.[21] In short, all nationalist movements of any significance are seen as state-oriented, striving for the same goal: the establishment of an independent nation-state. Anthony Smith's notion of the common aim of nationalist movements around the world is a case in point. He argues that nationalism reveals the same basic pattern in twentieth-century Africa as in nineteenth-century Europe. It exhibits almost identical aspirations in both cases, that is, the attainment of self-rule and independence.[22] Common to all these writers is that they regard nationalism as primarily about power and control over the state. John Breuilly, for example, uses the term nationalism only to refer to political movements seeking or exercising state power and justifying such action with nationalist arguments. From this standpoint, it clearly becomes difficult to assert that Slavophilism should be seen as a nationalism.[23]

This book questions the common dichotomy between political and cultural nationalism, without seeking to disregard the differences that do exist. The fact that political nationalists may use ideas from cultural nationalism to mobilize support for their movements has made scholars treat these types of nationalism as one and the same. As a consequence, they have regarded the differences in their ideology merely as separate strategies for the realization of the same goal. But, it is exactly with regard to the important differences in the focus and aims of nationalist projects that the distinction ought to be upheld. Although, as Bernard Yack holds, political nationalism might in fact always be based on ideas of a distinctive cultural identity, there is also a cultural nationalism, which does not have any political ambitions in the traditional sense of striving to reform or control the state.[24] This does not mean that there is no wish for social change in cultural nationalism. Neither does it prevent political actors from using the cultural definition of the nation to legitimize their political project. But it does suggest that we cannot uphold a distinction between political and cultural nationalism, based on the definition of the former as liberal, hence good; and the latter as conservative, hence bad.[25] Instead, to the extent that one is interested in the aims of nationalist projects, it is necessary to uphold a distinction between a state-oriented nationalism striving for an autonomous nation-state, and a culture-oriented nationalism, striving for a moral regeneration of the national community. Here, cultural nationalism will be used in the latter sense.

CULTURAL NATIONALISM

If political nationalists try to secure a representative nation-state that will guarantee its members uniform citizenship rights, cultural nationalists perceive the state as accidental. To them, the essence of a nation is its distinctive character, which is the product of its unique culture, history, and geography. Nations are not just artificial creations, but organic beings. The nation is therefore not founded on consent or law, but on the passions implanted by nature and history. Cultural nationalism is based on a historicist view of cultures as unique organisms, "each with its peculiar laws of growth and decay."[26] While political nationalism was originally based upon a legal, abstract concept of society, cultural nationalism found its justification in the notion of a natural community, which was held together not by the will of its members, nor by any obligations of contract, but by common traditions, customs, and way of life. Cultural nationalism substituted for the legal and rational concept of citizenship the much vaguer concept of "the people," which could only be understood intuitively.[27] This view of the unarticulated nation, expressed as "the people," explains why its proponents are above all historical scholars and artists, who try to recover the "creative force" of the nation. In contrast, the central actors of political nationalism are the agitators, the politicians, the representatives and the legislators. To cultural nationalists, creativity and spontaneity are important concepts. The nation needs to be created, it is a potentiality rather than a reality and the people is the source of creativity. Every true member of the nation is an "artist-creator." The inspiration for their artistic creations is found in the life of the people, where the peculiar character of the nation has been preserved.[28]

The set of ideas which forms the basis of cultural nationalism is deeply connected to the cluster of ideas that we refer to as Romanticism. However, it was Herder, who was not himself a Romantic albeit an important source for Romantic thought, who formulated the idea of cultural uniqueness most clearly, and who has been the source of inspiration for all subsequent cultural nationalism. In order to understand the way of thinking, the language, and the logic of this form of nationalism, it has to be seen against the background of Herder's thought.

THE ROLE OF THE NATION

Central to Herder's view of the nation is the concept of organism. The notion that the world consists of interrelated and interacting organisms, each of which is necessary to the whole, is the principal notion of his theory of organism. Herder rejected the notion of the state as a mere artefact established to serve limited ends and maintained that lasting political and social associations were products of natural growth, that they were based on forces of social cohesion.[29] For a state to be a natural political association that would persist in time, it had to be the result of spontaneous growth out of a specific cultural environment in which language and literary traditions were the determinate characteristics.

The German Romantics adopted Herder's organic view of society and history. In their view, society was based on a common culture: the religion, traditions, and language of a people. Hence it was not held together by laws or external force of any kind, but by the national spirit of the people. In line with Herder, they maintained that society should be the product of a gradual historical evolution, and that social development should grow from within rather than being imposed by external force or rational plan.[30] The organic metaphor made the nation inimical to imitation. As Herder vividly expressed it: "transplanted flowers decay in unsympathetic climates;

so do human beings." Imitation meant artificiality, which was destructive to the historical continuity of a *Volk*, in the sense of a conscious transmission of its social culture. In particular, imitation was destructive to the life and art of the people or nation.[31]

The concept of life was central to Herder's idea of the nation, just as it was to the Slavophiles. Herder used it in two senses: The first refers to the nation as organic and living, in opposition to the artificial state based on constructed bonds and formed by reason rather than by feelings. In this way, life and feeling are contrasted against artificiality and reasoning. The second meaning of the concept of life refers to the way of life of the people or nation, that is, to its habits, traditions, art and thinking. "Life," in this sense, can be translated both as the spirit of the people and the national culture. What is important to emphasize is that in both senses, the concept of life is linked to the community, which is why Herder makes the claim that life can only be found in action with or against others. Man is shaped by his association with others.[32] He is born into society and it is not possible to think of the individual as something outside society. Social life is formed out of natural need, that is to say, human interdependence. A social contract is therefore not required.[33]

The Romantics also stressed the social nature of human beings in their philosophical anthropology. Just as the parts of an organism are interdependent, each having its identity only within the whole, so people should be interdependent in a community. In other words, individuals realized and developed their unique individuality only through interaction with others. According to the Romantics, it was the need for love that made people live together and because love was the deepest impulse of our nature, social life was natural.[34]

The natural basis of political association was the *Volk*, defined as a people with its own peculiar national character. National character constituted the essence of social and political organisation. To Herder a state without national character was a political machine without life. Language was singled out as the most determinative characteristic of a *Volk*, since it expressed a particular historical tradition shared by them; other characteristics were particular habits and modes of thinking.[35] The concept of interaction, which was part of the organic metaphor, emphasized the negative consequences of cultural imitation. According to this theory, foisting a set of alien values on another nation would be harmful, because it would cut off the people from their "texture," it would tear them from their "living centre," from the only conditions to which they naturally belonged and in which it was possible for them to live full lives. It would dehumanize and degrade them. Without membership in a group, human goals could not be realized and true creation was stifled.[36]

But the doctrine of diversity, also stemming from the theory of organism, dealt the hardest blow to imitation. According to this concept, human nature is not identical in different parts of the world. To be ourselves, we have to be characteristic of our nation. This idea of diversity, or uniqueness, gave the concept of the nation a relativistic character. If all cultures were incommensurable, genuine translation from one way of life to another was impossible.[37] Therefore, in Herder's words, "each nation must be considered on its own merits, with regard to its situation and its own distinctive features."[38] But not only was human nature unique in different parts of the world, each age and civilization was unique and incomparable as well. The principle of incommensurability implied that to understand a culture, one must enter the time and place of a people and fully immerse oneself in their situation. An experience could only be understood by trying to grasp what this experience meant to those who expressed it. Therefore, to Herder, all understanding was necessarily historical.[39] The principles of one age were not automatically valid for another. Herder stressed the value of historical understanding to defend national cultures against claims to universality, which he believed could be used to curb the development of other cultures.[40] Assimilation to a single universal standard or social structure would destroy what was most living and valuable in art and life because it implied imitation and artificiality, which were incompatible with the idea of the unique organic nation.[41]

The principle of incommensurability allowed Herder to disregard criticism in the name of universal laws or values. "Let us follow our own path," he exhorted the Germans. "Let men speak well or ill of our nation, our literature, our language: they are ours, they are ourselves, and let that be enough."[42] While the Slavophiles made good use of this argument, it is important to note that neither they, nor Herder, promoted national isolation. It was an argument for cultural diversity, stressing national originality instead of eternal universal values.

THE ROLE OF THE INTELLECTUALS AND ARTISTS

In order to follow a unique national path, one had first to identify it. In other words, the national character had to be determined, as seen in Herder's appeal to the Germans to get to know themselves and to understand their role in time and in space.[43] One way of identifying a culture's national character was to develop a literature and a philosophy that could express its unique values, beliefs, and traditions.[44] This was precisely what the Slavophiles tried to accomplish. The problem was that, according to Herder and the Romantics, national character was really not explicable in abstract terms or through scientific methods. It was only open "to the eye of imaginative intuition."[45] All this formed a need for interpreters: artists, who articulated the people's collective individuality, its life and art, and historical scholars, who tried to discover the social customs, folklore, and literary traditions of a people.[46]

Both the principle of interaction and the Romantic idea of unity of the mind had bearing on the artist and his or her interpretation. According to the first principle, everything a person says expresses the collective identity, outside of which all individuals are inconceivable. Equivalent to this argument is the doctrine of the unity of mind, which suggests that everything a person says and does conveys his, or her, whole personality. Since the individual is a member of a group, everything he or she does must express the aspirations of this group. The true artist creates only out of the total experience of his whole society. Thus, to understand any creator is to understand his age and nation. A poet is at the same time a creator of a people and created by it. He, or she, is the highest expression of the spirit of the age and national enlightenment.[47] The artist was the creator and the people the creative source. This is why imitation in the arts and life of the people, and in creation in general, was inconceivable. Imitated cultural products neither express, nor create, anything.

In order to establish a link between the past and the future, national traditions had to be transmitted and assimilated. Here education, or enlightenment, had an important function. It re-appraised and re-evaluated the cultural heritage. Herder believed that through education the individual became aware of his relationship to the past and the future and learned what he could receive from, or add to, his cultural traditions. Hence, it involved both opposition to and acceptance of the value patterns and modes of thought that constituted his national heritage. Through education, the individual acquired the capacity for conscious and creative development, i.e., for *Bildung*. In this way, education constituted the most determinate factor in shaping a community's social consciousness, making its members aware of their common identity and specific character.[48] Moreover, education provided the means of furthering *Humanität*, the purpose of all human endeavours. Education, in the form of conscious moral development, or *Bildung*, should aim for *Humanität*, without which we would "sink back, higher and lower classes alike, to crude bestiality." Herder believed that all individuals had the capacity for *Humanität*, but it could only be developed through commitment and effort.[49]

As Herder assumed that knowledge of what a person can do involved knowledge of what a person ought to do, the educated class had a moral calling, a social obligation unique in time and place. Each generation, he argued, had to interpret its specific goals towards self-development in light of the circumstances prevailing at any given time and place.[50] As a consequence, education could not concern itself solely with enlightenment of the mind. That practice would only lead to the formulation of universal laws. In order to express the particular, philosophers had to take an active part in everyday life. Philosophy could only play a constructive role if it had something to say about the life of the people and was expressed in a way that made it accessible to them. The people would be educated by stimulating them to think for themselves, not by forcing dogmas on them. Hence, the true purpose of education was the development of the power of autonomy and self-government in the people themselves.[51]

Herder held that intellectual and cultural activity had its source in the middle-classes, which was also the habitat of the *Volk*. His idea of the *Volk*, as the creative source of a nation's culture, was quite revolutionary at the time, but it was not an all-inclusive concept. Herder drew a sharp distinction between the rabble, or the *Pöbel*, and the *Volk*. The aristocracy was also excluded. The burghers, who he believed were least affected by the impact of civilization, were the ones who best embodied the *Volk* characteristics of spontaneity and simplicity.[52] "In order to re-vitalise the whole of the people," Herder wrote, "the middle class would need to become diffused in both the upward and the downward direction."[53] The solution lay in the emergence of popular leaders, who would spread the gospel of education and guide the rest of the nation. It is not clear whether these leaders were to come from the people, or were merely to lead them. What is clear is that in a period of transition "men of learning" or so-called "aristo-democrats," would provide for education.[54]

The German Romantics inherited the humanist idea of *Bildung* from Herder. Their common journal and organ, the *Athenäum*, was devoted to the world of *Bildung* and art.[55] Romantic art, Schlegel wrote in the *Athenäum*, would overcome the gap between reason and life by making people conscious of, and inspiring them to achieve, the kingdom of God on earth. The chief aim of the Romantics was the rebirth of German culture and public life through the magical powers of art. The artist was seen as the reproducer of the magic, beauty, and mystery of the natural and social world.[56] Hence, the role of the artist was crucial to Romantic thought, but the intellectuals in general had an important function in educating the people, promoting the development of *Bildung and Humanität*. Therefore, educated individuals had to have power over the uneducated.[57] Novalis wrote that "[t]hankfully we must shake hand with the intellectuals and philosophers, for their conceits must be exploited for the best of posterity."[58] Their task as intellectuals was to define the standards of morality and taste, so that the public would be given a cultural norm, and a model of virtue.

Later religion took the place of art as the key to cultural revival and the foundation of *Bildung*. Although the means was another, the goal was still the same. The main task of religion was to bridge the gap between theory and practice.[59] Hölderlin and Schelling believed that it was the role of the spiritual elite, to which they both belonged, to be the vanguard of a new class of free men. As members of the clergy they felt they had a responsibility to formulate and disseminate the values of their society and they were committed to creating a sense of identity and vocation for the people. In fact, they aimed at revising the consciousness of the entire middle-class in their community. A new philosophy, religion, and art would liberate the consciousness of the citizenry and make them capable of true freedom.[60] However, as Schiller had argued, philosophers could preach the first principles of morality, but only artists could make people act according to them. Thus, it was the artist who played the major role in the moral education of the citizen.[61]

In short, both Herder and the early Romantics saw themselves and fellow intellectuals as educators of the people, a task formulated already by the *Aufklärer*. This self-assumed role forms an interesting link between the cultural and the political concept of the nation, to which I will return. An important question in this connection is, who exactly constituted the people? Was it the entire population, the burghers, the middle-class, or was it the nation as a collective individuality, as a culture? There is a strong case for arguing that the people, as a whole, were not to be enlightened. This argument will not be pursued here, however. Instead, I will return to this question when discussing the Slavophile notion of enlightenment, which is clearly related to and illuminated by the notion of *Bildung* and *Humanität* considered here.

To conclude, Slavophilism can be characterized as a cultural nationalism, a conscious intellectual project striving for the moral regeneration of the national community.[62] Because the Slavophiles take the idea of cultural uniqueness as their point of reference in developing their theory, it can shed light on their thought. It is in terms of this idea that they argue against imitation. Indeed, the idea of the unique, organic nation, as formulated by

Herder and developed by the early Romantics, makes imitation problematical from the start. In addition, the concept of interaction gave rise to the impression that only those who share a common language and cultural tradition are worthy of recognition as a nation. This changed the agenda for all cultures with pretensions to be nations.[63] However, the cultural idea of the nation did not only create problems for culturally backward countries, it also offered a solution through resuscitation of national culture and national spirit. As a consequence, the educated elite in general, and the artists in particular, acquired a central function in cultural nationalism as articulators, or organs, of the nation's life and art. In this way, cultural nationalism satisfied both the quest for a role or identity on behalf of the nation, and for a public identity on behalf of the educated elite.

We have seen that the discussion of imitation in Russia concerned precisely the role of the nation and of the educated elite. It is now time to examine the Slavophile solution to this predicament in the form of a specific Russian enlightenment, and look at how this notion was connected to the Romantic concept of the nation and the role of the educated elite.

Chapter 4

The Russian Enlightenment and the Westernizers

Chapter 2 demonstrates that Slavophiles, Westernizers, and many educated Russians were deeply troubled by the Russian practice of imitation because of the negative consequences it had for the development of a genuine Russian culture. In this chapter, I argue that, although the Westernizers' formula for solving Russia's predicament differed from the Slavophiles', it rested on similar assumptions about the significance of a national culture. Russia's greatness and cultural contribution were central to the thinking of both groups, as was the role of the intellectuals in expressing their national culture.

Not only did Westernizers and Slavophiles agree on where the root of the problem was found, their views as to possible solutions coincided as well. Both groups were equally convinced that the promotion of a specific Russian enlightenment constituted the answer to the problem of their nation's cultural backwardness. Although Slavophiles and Westernizers held diverging views of the meaning and implementation of such an enlightenment, both solutions took the form of a new public identity for Russian intellectuals which was connected to their nation. The fact that the Slavophiles did not act in isolation, but that Russian intellectuals of conflicting camps originally shared the same problems, the same language, and the same arguments, i.e. were part of the same discourse, shows that the Slavophiles did not represent a peripheral extremism.

The principal issue addressed here is the sense in which the Westernizers presented the notion of a national enlightenment as a solution to what they saw as Russia's cultural backwardness. Related to this concern is the question of how the concept of a Russian enlightenment could solve the identity crisis among members of the Russian educated elite. To answer that question, this chapter will analyse the precise nature of the relationship between the nation, the people, and the educated elite in the ideas of the Westernizers.

THE NATION, THE PEOPLE, AND THE EDUCATED ELITE

Referring to the literature of the 1830s, Vissarion Belinsky wrote that nationality was "the alpha and omega of the new period." To be meaningful, i.e. to be genuine and original, literature had to express the national spirit. Regardless of whether or not this spirit was manifest in the people or educated society, literature had to be the expression and symbol of its inner life, which also was the life of the nation. This did not exhaust the meaning of literature, but was one of its most essential attributes and conditions.[1] A national literature should be:

> the collective body of such artistic literary productions as are the fruits of the free inspiration and concerted . . . efforts of men, born for art, living for art alone, and ceasing to exist outside of it, fully expressing and reproducing in their elegant creations the spirit of the people in whose midst they have been born and educated, whose life they live and spirit they breathe, expressing in their creative productions its intimate life to its innermost depths and pulsation. In the history of such a literature there are not, nor can there be, any leaps . . . Such a literature cannot be at one and the same time both French and German, English and Italian.[2]

To Belinsky, the originality of a nation consisted of a specific mentality and outlook. It was visible in its religion, language, and above all, the customs peculiar to that specific nation. Selecting rustic words, or copying songs and tales was not enough to make a literary work national. Nationality was found in the workings of the mind and in the way of seeing things. To be national, literature should express a nation's character, spirit, and way of life. The problem was that in Russia of the 1830s, nationality in literature resided in faithful representations of scenes from Russian life, not in any particular spirit or trend, manifest in all creations, irrespective of their subject and their content.

This led Belinsky to declare that Russia did not yet have a national literature, i.e. a literature that expressed genuine nationality, a mode of thinking and feeling peculiar to a given nation. The reason for this was that

Russian society was too young. It was still in the process of formation, not yet freed from European tutelage; its features had not yet taken form. That is, Russian nationality was not sufficiently fashioned for the Russian poet to express it. There would come a time, though, when enlightenment would spread throughout Russia. Then "the intellectual countenance of the nation" would stand out clearly, and the creations of artists and writers would be permeated with the Russian spirit.

This view of nationality, including its universal aspirations, was quite similar to that held by the Slavophiles. However, there is a difference in the emphasis on a necessary attachment to reality in literature. Thus, to Belinsky, it was not enough for a writer to be a faithful echo of the national spirit; he also had to be the true reflection of his time. In order to become original and national, literature had to reflect real life.[3] Herzen stressed this point in relation to philosophy, which he believed had to develop close to reality, to life.[4] The Slavophiles also urged artists and intellectuals to get closer to "life," but real life to them was the genuine life of the nation in a more timeless sense. It was eternal but not static.

What separated Belinsky most clearly from the Slavophiles on the one hand, and from Bakunin and Herzen on the other, was the negative view of the people he entertained in relation to the nation and its enlightenment. In Belinsky's mature thinking, the Russian people epitomized the backwardness of the country.[5] They were described as coarse, uncivilized, and uneducated. It is interesting to note that Marxist historians saw the negative view of the people among some Westernizers as a reaction against the government's use of this concept in its conservative propaganda. But there is really nothing in Belinsky's writings that supports this claim. Clearly he had no confidence in the capability of the Russian people to change their situation. He was well aware that modernization in Russia had always come from above. What was different in Belinsky's own time was that a public life had emerged through the formation of an educated society, which had gained the initiative from the court. Therefore, the future lay in the hands of the educated elite. Because Belinsky came from a simple background, it is likely that he reacted against the idealized picture of the people entertained by other intellectuals, nearly all of them noblemen. Herzen's position was quite the opposite. He saw hope for Russia's future in the peasants and their communalism.[6] Like the Slavophiles, Herzen accused the educated elite of disregarding all that was good and promising in the common life of the Russian people.

According to the dominant German philosophy, the expression of a national spirit was a sign of progress: Without nationality, progress was not possible. Chapter 2 shows that while this theory created problems for Russia it also pointed to a national enlightenment as a solution to the feeling of backwardness. There were diverging views among Russian intellectuals as to where the basis for the development of a genuine enlightenment was found. As we have seen, to Belinsky, the common people epitomized backwardness. Hence, nationality, as an indication of progress, could not reside among them. He strongly disagreed with the opinion that a true Russian nationality in literature was found in works dealing with the life of the lower and uneducated classes. Neither did he support the view that everything developed and refined in Russia was un-Russian. This view, Belinsky argued, was a result of a common Russian confusion between form and substance.

Nationality had been confused with commonality. The secret of nationality in every nation, Belinsky claimed, lay not in its traditional dress and cuisine, but in its way of seeing things. It dwelled in the very spirit of the people. A poet may be national even when describing an entirely alien world, which:

> he regards through the eyes of his national element, the eyes of the whole nation, when he feels and speaks in a way which makes his countrymen believe that it is they themselves who are thus feeling and speaking.

To render a faithful picture of any society, one first had to comprehend its particular essence. This could be accomplished only by actually learning, and evaluating philosophically, the sum of the rules on which that society rested.[7]

In his early writings, Belinsky agreed with the Slavophiles that the Russian national character was mainly preserved among the lower-classes, but he subsequently claimed that the nation was solely made up of the middle- and upper-classes. In their mode of life and customs, the middle- and upper-classes were representative of progress and intellectual movement. They were educated, enlightened, and the only group with at least some amount of consciousness, which Belinsky saw as a prerequisite for intellectual and moral interests. Such common interest was, in turn, a precondition for progress. Since the national spirit of Russia resided where progress and public life were located, it had to be found in the collective consciousness of educated society. Belinsky argued that if nationality constituted one of the highest merits of poetical works, genuine national works would be found among poetical compositions whose subject matter had been taken from the life of this estate. It was "an estate that adopted for itself the forms of cultivated life." It was created as a result of the reforms of

Peter the Great and thus was part of the modernization of Russia. Before the emergence of this estate, public life, in the sense of a common life with a common purpose, did not exist.

The concept of public life had much in common with the Slavophile notion of enlightenment. It indicated culture and civilization, but also referred to intellectual life and common, moral interest. Educated society, the carrier of public life, was not a constant and material entity, but spiritual and moving; it was organic and progressive. According to Belinsky, the only movement in Russian life occurred in the educated class, not in the people. It represented the cultured, or civilized, aspect of Russian life and, if Russia indeed had a culture that was original and independent, i.e. national, it would be found in educated society. In 1844, he wrote that it was time to realize that a Russian poet could reveal himself as a genuinely national poet only by depicting the life of educated society.[8] Hence, to Belinsky, the artist's mission was to describe his nation by depicting his own class.

The role of the educated elite was thus intimately connected with the role and identity of the nation, but in an almost converse relationship to the one invoked by the Slavophiles. While both the Slavophiles, and the Westernizers Bakunin and Herzen, thought of the people and their commune as the pillars of a future Russia, Belinsky maintained that the people had nothing to give to the educated class in terms of national enlightenment and progress. It followed from this conviction that he did not propagate for the enlightenment of the people. Rather, and more in line with the Slavophiles, Belinsky stressed the importance of further educating the upper classes, so its members could express the national character of Russia. He accused writers of failing to understand the obligations imposed on true men of letters. Instead of cooperating to the best of their ability to realize the common cause, they were "sowing the sand by singing to the moon, the maid and champagne and relating stories of fiction, which, although very entertaining, were devoid of all idea."[9]

Like Belinsky, Herzen believed intellectuals and artists were under an obligation, but in his case their obligation was intimately connected to the people. He attacked philosophers, who allegedly wrote only for the benefit of philosophers. Philosophy should become accessible to the people. Man's vocation was not logic alone, but also the socio-historical world of "moral freedom" and "positive action." Spirit and ideas were the results of matter and history, not of pure reason. Thus, man could not evade the reality around him.[10] Herzen wrote that the set of educated people, who had grown to accept "a living comprehension of mankind and the contemporary age, was a mighty, living medium, which absorbed the life-giving fluids through different fibres and transformed them into beautiful corolla." An intellectual, or an artist was essentially a teacher and advisor to the people, who had previously received their knowledge directly from life. He should not alienate himself from the world and the people, but instead make learning accessible to them. Bakunin came to hold a similar position.[11] Thus, contrary to Belinsky, both Herzen, Bakunin, and the Slavophiles believed that the key to Russia's enlightenment and progress was found in the way of life of the people.

It is important to emphasize that Belinsky did not oppose the education of the people. Rather, he assumed education and enlightenment would come as a result of progress. For that reason, the educated Russians, who were the leaders of progress, had to be (re)educated. Belinsky held that literature had a crucial role to play in the advancement of enlightenment. He claimed Russia's literature was moving towards "the attainment of eternal and hallowed truth, the realisation on earth of the ideal, which imperceptibly contributed to the progress of public enlightenment." Belinsky also maintained that literature served as the connecting link between people who were divided in all other respects. In drawing people from different classes closer together in bonds of taste and aspirations towards a noble enjoyment of life, literature transformed these classes into a society of letters. "Our literature," he wrote in 1846, "has paved the way for the inner rapprochement of the estates, has formed a species of public opinion and produced a sort of special class in society which differs from the middle estate in that it consists of people of all estates who have been drawn together through education, centred exclusively in a love of literature." Hence, literature played a crucial role for the progress and enlightenment of society. In fact, the education of society was a direct effect of literature upon the ideas and morals of society. According to Belinsky, all moral interest and spiritual life was concentrated in literature. "Literature is the vital spring from which all human sentiments and conceptions percolate into society."[12] Thus, apparent in Belinsky's conception of the nation, expressed in an artificially created community held together by education, is a mix of Enlightenment and Romantic thinking.

It is difficult to assess what the Westernizers thought about the relationship between the people and the educated elite, not only because they changed their views quite radically between the early 1830s and the late 1840s, but also because they did not constitute a tightly knit ideological group. While Bakunin and Herzen, just as the Slavophiles, came to idealize the peasants and the village commune and believed that the educated elite had much to learn from them, they differed from the latter in their views on the need for the people to be actively educated. Belinsky, on the other hand, was opposed to the idealization of the peasants, but did not specifically stress the need to educate them. All of them, however, argued for the enlightenment of the educated strata. The question is what the enlightenment the Westernizers wanted for Russia would consist in.

A National Enlightenment of Universal Significance

Following Belinsky's argument, enlightenment had to come from what he thought of as the progressive class, i.e. from educated society. But this did not mean that it had to come from the West. In fact, Belinsky wrote that Russia needed an enlightenment "created by our own efforts, cultivated on our own native soil." In this sense, he advocated a specific Russian enlightenment, even though his view of the content or basis of this enlightenment was quite different from that of the Slavophiles. Nevertheless, the aim of Belinsky's Russian enlightenment was not altogether different from the Slavophile counterpart. To begin with, paying tribute to Romantic idealism, both Slavophiles and Westernizers regarded consciousness as the "life-aim," not only of each individual, but also of every nation and, ultimately, of the whole of humanity.[13] According to this thinking, life, or the spirit of life, was seen as moving towards ever higher stages of consciousness. Every person and nation was considered part of humanity and of its universal progress. The attainment of self-consciousness, of understanding ourselves as individuals, peoples, or nations, constituted the highest aim in human life. Without knowledge, without full consciousness, there could be no action that was truly free.[14] According to Belinsky, the need for Russian literature to depict Russian life expressed the strivings of Russian society towards self-awareness, and consequently, its awakening to "moral interests" and intellectual life. This was a prerequisite for the advancement of Russia. At the same time, these ideas gave the intellectuals a new role as subjects striving for self-cognizance in cooperation with their nation. Still, without an independent national culture, expressing the national spirit, Russian intellectuals could not be promoters of their country's progress along the path of enlightenment.[15] Therefore, the Slavophiles and the Westernizers mutually agreed on Russia's need for an enlightenment that would make her part of the movement of mankind towards perfection. Thus, arguing for the importance of a national culture and a national enlightenment did not prevent either Westernizers or Slavophiles from wanting Russia to be part of universal progress.

Like the Slavophiles, Belinsky argued that the nation, in line with its character, played its own specific role in the great family of mankind, as assigned by Providence, and contributed its share to mankind's common treasure of achievements in the field of self-improvement. In other words, every nation was the expression of some single aspect of the life of mankind. Otherwise that nation did not live, but vegetated, and its existence served no purpose.[16] It was only by living its original life that each nation could contribute its share to the common riches of mankind. Belinsky described this relationship in a Romantic manner:

> We see that every society . . . in living its own life, like an individual, at the same time lives for humanity and is related to it as a part to the whole, as a limb to the body, as a plant to the soil . . . Just as the diversity of characters, abilities and wills of a multitude of men . . . forms an organic, united body politic—a nation or a state, so does the diversity of characters in nations form the unity of mankind . . . Every nation is more or less distinguished from other nations precisely because it must contribute its share to the common treasury of mankind.[17]

Herzen depicted nations as grand characters of the world drama, each performing the role of mankind in its own way. He claimed that every nation was part of a great society of humanity and that both Europe and Russia strove to develop its general culture.[18] Like man, a nation was a personality, but of a higher order and like a nation, humanity was a personality, but of a still higher order.[19] Once a people had entered into the broad stream of history, they belonged to humanity and all the past of humanity belonged to them.[20] But in order to benefit from Europe's past, Herzen argued, it was not enough simply to be Russian,

> one must also attain the zenith of human development; be not exclusively Russian, that is to say, consider oneself not as opposite to Western Europe, but as fraternally bound to it. The conception of fraternity does not erase the distinctive traits of each brother, yet these traits must not make enemies of them, for then their bonds of brotherhood would be destroyed.[21]

Applied to literature, this idea led Belinsky to claim that to a poet who wished to see his genius acknowledged by everyone, everywhere, nationality was the primary, but not the sole requirement. In addition to being national his art had to be universal. In Belinsky's words, "the nationality of his creations had to be the form, body and character of the spiritual and incorporeal world of ideas common to all mankind." The Russian poet had to be able to express the national spirit in his works in a way that showed its connection to the common ideas of mankind. Hence, the national poet must be of great historical significance not only to his country, but also to the world. However, poetry could be of such significance only if it appeared in nations that were called upon to play a global historical role in the destiny of mankind. Belinsky maintained that the national life of certain nations was destined to influence the trend and progress of all mankind. Only in nations possessing such worldwide historical significance could national poets appear. Since the poet received his substance from the life of his nation, the merits, depth, scope and importance of that substance depended directly and immediately upon the historical importance of his nation's life and not upon the poet himself or his talent.[22] It was the artist's task to depict this substance in a truthful way.

This view of the role of the artist in relation to the nation bears a close resemblance to the Slavophiles' concept of the artist, discussed in chapter 2. On the whole, the conception of the universal significance of nationality, and the professed need for Russia to make a contribution to humanity through a national enlightenment, was obviously something the Westernizers and the Slavophiles had in common.

THE WESTERNIZERS' CONCEPT OF ENLIGHTENMENT IN COMPARISON

When the Westernizers' concept of enlightenment is compared to that of the Slavophiles, one finds that the difference between them lies less in their motivations and objectives than in their focus. Whether Russian intellectuals stressed the progressive character of the educated elite or of the uneducated peasants; change, enlightenment, and progress were the common goals for both Slavophiles and Westernizers, although they interpreted them in somewhat different ways. One might argue that these differences were much greater than the similarities. But even so, members of Russia's educated elite were fairly united in their original proposition that the role and identity of the Russian nation and its intellectuals were equally problematic. Both sides formulated their arguments in relation to Romantic and idealistic ideas and values of their time, and tried to create a future role for themselves and for Russia in this context.

The similar assumption behind Herzen's description of the acceptance of ancient learning by Europe and the Slavophile account of the adoption of European enlightenment by Peter I can illustrate this common ground. Classical education, Herzen argued, was an education for the aristocracy. The peasants and the "plain people of the cities" not only failed to take any part in the introduction in Europe of a classical curriculum, but were separated from the well-educated sections by a broader and deeper gulf than before. The change plunged the masses into the starkest ignorance. In a way similar to Ivan Kireevsky's idealization of medieval Russia, Herzen described the European world before its adoption of ancient learning as one where the people had their minstrels and legends, where the priests had preached to them, and local friars had visited them. Formerly, he asserted, there had been a link between the common people and higher education. Subsequently, however, the talented and the educated absorbed elements that were alien to the people and did not appeal to them. The new civilization had not had time to work itself into the inner life of those who had embraced it to the extent where they were able to express themselves freely, i. e., in their own way. "The people had been deprived of their singers, of legends and sagas which had stirred their hearts with familiar sounds and kindred images."[23] In other words, learning and enlightenment should be in harmony with the inner life of the people, so that it would not inflict a gap between the educated strata and the people. This argument constitutes a fundamental critique of the Enlightenment as a civilizing project, and it is very similar to the Slavophiles' criticism of the Westernized, Russian, educated elite.

Belinsky explicitly agreed with the Slavophiles in asserting that the reforms of Peter the Great had deprived the Russian people of their nationality and made them "nonesuches." It was true, he stated, that the reforms had fulfilled their intentions and that the time had come for Russia to develop independently, from her own roots. But, and here the agreement ends, to Belinsky, the Slavophiles were wrong in maintaining that original development consisted in rejecting the epoch of reform, in order to revert to the period that preceded it. Addressing the educated elite as a whole, Belinsky stated that the solution did not lie in changing what Peter the Great had done without the Russian people's knowledge and perhaps in defiance of their will, but in changing themselves, on the basis of "the path foreordained by a will higher than their own." "We ourselves, in ourselves and around ourselves—that is where we should seek both the problems and their solution," he wrote.[24]

Herzen's criticism of Neoplatonic conservatism can also be seen as an attack against Slavophilism. For example, he claims that the bankruptcy of the positive world led the Neoplatonics to scorn everything temporal and to seek another world within themselves. This was a common critique against the Slavophiles. Another argument levelled against the Neoplatonics, but which was really directed against the Slavophiles, was the claim that the force and charm of memories sometimes overcame the temptation of hope, and that some people longed for the past whatever the cost, because they saw the future in it. The pagan world, which Herzen described as exclusively national and spontaneous, always lived under the seductive spell of memories. Not only did it seem theoretically possible to resurrect the past but also to develop and enlighten it. Herzen stated that by a species of nationalism, the Neoplatonics arrived at an allegorical justification of paganism and imagined themselves to believe in it. They wanted to resurrect the past order in a certain philosophic-literary manner. "They saw in the past their future ideal but clad in the vestments of the past. . . . But this life represented an environment quite different from that which the contemporary man needed."[25] Clearly, Herzen's references to the idea of the past as the future and the basis for a national enlightenment are directed against the Slavophiles.

If Russia did not need an enlightenment based on the past, nor one imported from the West, what then did she need? In a letter from 1833, Chaadaev suggested that Russia's future should be established on a profound evaluation of the nation's present position in contemporary Europe, and not on a past that was nothing other than nothingness. "We have to understand ourselves as we are," he wrote.[26] Herzen agreed. In his view, it was destructive to retreat from the world to find comfort in a vision of the past, because only he can be fully at ease with himself who finds the contemporary external world in accordance with his inner convictions. This view made it impossible for Herzen to accept the Slavophile view that conservatism was a progressive force. "Conservatism . . . expresses a most emphatic approval of the existing, a recognition of its right. The urge forward, on the contrary, expresses dissatisfaction with the existing, and seeks for a form better adapted to the new stage of the development of reason."[27]

Compared to the Slavophiles' solution to Russia's predicament, the version presented by the Westernizers' was somewhat more practical, action-oriented and explicitly related to the contemporary social and political situation. The values promulgated were more humanistic than Christian, although they sometimes overlap. Russia's salvation was to be found in the achievements of civilization, enlightenment, and humanism, not in mysticism, asceticism, or pietism. In Belinsky's words, Russia needed neither sermons nor prayers, but "an awakening in her people of the sense of human dignity, which has been trampled down in the mud and manure for so many centuries; she needs rights and laws conforming not to Church doctrine but to common sense and justice, and she needs to have them rigorously enforced."[28] What bound people together in the organic society of Belinsky was not a common faith, or popular custom, but common moral interests, similarity of views and equality of education, combined with a mutual regard for each other's human dignity. Then again, as we have seen above, Belinsky did not envision an enlightenment realized through commerce, industry and shipping. Like the Slavophiles Belinsky held that a society, where "material forces" constituted the principal, instead of merely the auxiliary, means towards education and civilization, would not be held in high esteem. This meant that Russia was not in a bad position after all, since her public enlightenment and education originated from the "noble" source of learning and literature.[29]

Yet, although this position had a cultural basis, it was social in orientation. Belinsky argued that Russia could not continue as a country without any guarantees for personal safety, honour, and property; a country that could not even maintain internal order, and had "nothing to show but vast corporations of office-holding thieves and robbers." The worst aspect of Russia, however, was that it was a country where men traded in men. Together with the repeal of corporal punishment, the abolition of serfdom was the most vital social question in contemporary Russia.[30] "It is better for us to die suspected of human dignity," Herzen maintained, "than to live with the shameful brand of slavery on our brow, and hear the reproach that we are slaves by choice." He argued that a nation could only achieve its true freedom by personal freedom.[31] The main purpose of enlightenment common to most of the Westernizers was the progress of humanity towards freedom.

We have now seen that the Westernizers related to the same Romantic concepts as the Slavophiles in trying to address the problem of cultural backwardness in Russia, and that they did this by assigning a specific role for the Russian intellectuals in relation to the nation. It is now time to return to the Slavophiles and their solution to Russia's predicament.

Chapter 5

The Slavophile Notion of a Russian Enlightenment

The concept of a specific Russian enlightenment (*prosveshchenie*) was presented by the Slavophiles as a solution to the feeling of cultural backwardness in relation to the West among members of the Russian educated elite. The low level of independent, genuine cultural production in Russia in the second quarter of the nineteenth century constituted an acute problem for all Russian intellectuals, even though imitating the arts and culture of more advanced countries had not been considered a problem in the previous century. In the nineteenth century, however, this practice was no longer acceptable. What mattered in the intellectual context of Romanticism and nationalism was not the form of cultural products, but the original content in terms of nationality. Before the Decembrist revolt of 1825, the members of *The Philosophical Society* had already expressed a need for a Russian philosophy and literature, but it was the Slavophiles who formulated a comprehensive theory of a specific Russian enlightenment. The Slavophiles did not want Russia to be enlightened in the French eighteenth-century sense, but rather in a specifically Russian sense. They believed Enlightenment was not useful when acquired in a spirit of imitation, but only if attained in a spirit of independence.[1]

Because the Slavophiles are commonly described as Romantic nationalists, one would assume that they wanted to distance themselves from any enlightenment.[2] Instead, their aim, which they shared with the Westernizers, was to develop Russian culture and learning to a level where it could

contribute to a universal enlightenment. Both Slavophiles and Westernizers agreed that it was only by making a specific contribution to the common cause of progress that a national culture could be of any significance.
The character Faust conveys this view in Vladimir Odoevsky's *Russian
Nights*, claiming "we [the Russians] have not yet understood the sound we
ought to make our own in a universal harmony."[3] The Russian enlightenment that would evolve as a result of national regeneration would reveal
Russia's role in universal history, and thereby furnish her distinctiveness
with common meaning. The "blessings" it would bring to Russia would
ultimately be "shared with the rest of Europe." The Slavophiles believed
that by making this contribution, the debt to Europe that Russia had ac-
cumulated during her cultural education, would finally be paid. This is
why Kireevsky maintained that the destiny of Russia depended on her enlightenment. Its realization was in fact a condition for Russia's standing as
a nation on a par with other European nations.[4]

In what way was the Slavophiles' notion of a Russian enlightenment
going to solve Russia's predicament, i. e. the insignificance of her national
culture and the feelings of backwardness it generated? In this chapter, I assess this issue by addressing three basic questions: First, what was the
meaning of the national enlightenment; second, how would it be carried
out, and third, who would be enlightened? These questions concern the
concepts of the nation, the people, and the educated elite. Therefore, I also
briefly discuss the implications of the Slavophile idea of a Russian enlightenment for our understanding of Slavophilism as a nationalism.

THE MEANING OF THE RUSSIAN ENLIGHTENMENT

The Russian word "*prosveshchenie*," used by the Slavophiles, is sometimes
translated as culture, but the literal translation is "enlightenment," which is
clearly what they had in mind. The question of translation, however, is of limited importance since, to them, as to other Russian intellectuals at the time,
culture was in fact equivalent to enlightenment and the one was not possible
without the other. The concept of enlightenment was used to describe cultural progress or intellectual and spiritual activity. It expressed fundamental
principles underlying a specific civilization. Sometimes it simply meant education and learning; sometimes it was applied to public life, which was
thought to be the habitat of intellectual and cultural progress.[5] Regardless of
how the term was used, it was always thought of as something progressive that
was constantly moving forward. Although, the view of enlightenment as a

process that moved towards higher stages of consciousness might seem strange today, it was completely in accordance with Romantic and Idealistic ideas that dominated European intellectual life at that time.

The concept of a Russian enlightenment was developed largely in discussions of the negative aspects of Western rationalism, and was an attempt to convince the educated elite of the need for a national alternative to an enlightenment based on the "harmful" culture of the West. For this reason, the Slavophiles devoted much more time to attack Western Enlightenment than to promote the Russian version. But this preoccupation with the Western Enlightenment does not mean the Russian enlightenment was discussed merely in negative terms, that is in contrast to its Western counterpart. It also entailed a positive message: It presented a solution to the sense of backwardness felt by educated Russians since it allowed for Russia to make the necessary original contributions to humanity. While the Western Enlightenment, both in its philosophical and empirical form, was founded on the strength of reason, the Russian enlightenment was a spiritual enlightenment, striving towards inner spiritual perfection. This made it special.[6] True enlightenment, Khomiakov argued, was not only "a catalogue of positive knowledge." It was an enlightenment of the whole spiritual structure both in individuals and in peoples.[7] Having transcended the limits of reason, this enlightenment elevated the mind from mechanical reasoning to the highest realms of independent moral reflection.[8]

According to Khomiakov, a national enlightenment should be formed by the national personality that embodied the national idea. The essence of the national idea that formed the Russian enlightenment was the spiritual foundation of what the Slavophiles saw as "true Christianity," expressed in the teachings of the Fathers of the Orthodox Church.[9] The authentic Russian way of thinking, which became the foundation of the national style of life, was formed under the guidance of spiritual leaders. According to the Slavophiles, the spiritual philosophy of the Eastern Church Fathers remained the pure Christian philosophy. It had preserved the basic Christian doctrine after the "defection" of Rome. This philosophy remained pure because the Russian Church had preserved its unity by subjecting the power of individual opinions to the "highest truths" and had therefore, contrary to the Western Church, never changed its teaching.[10] After the fall of Constantinople, Russia was the sole repository of the true Orthodox faith. Hence, religious identity and nationality coincided in Russia.

In having both a spiritual and a national character, the Russian enlightenment was closely connected to the moral condition of both man and people; in fact it was the very life of the Russian soul.[11] Western Enlightenment, on the other hand, had no essential connection to the moral condition of man. In Kireevsky's words, "once adopted, it remained forever independent of the state of its soul."[12] Having no connection to the spiritual life of man or people, the Western Enlightenment was "dead knowledge." It made all the higher demands of the soul automatically yield to individualistic arbitrariness and egoistic calculating. This made it not only lifeless, but beyond salvation.[13] Here, organic metaphors are used to point to the specific character of the Russian enlightenment. In this way, the Slavophile concept of a Russian enlightenment could both explain the cultural backwardness of the nation and indicate the means for the development of a national culture.

According to the new intellectual agenda brought about by Romanticism, nations should make contributions to the advancement of humanity. So, in line with the prevailing ideas of their time, the Slavophiles presented the Russian enlightenment not only as a national enlightenment but as a universal enlightenment. Hence, Russia's national belief was described as a universal, basic Christianity.

But the contribution to mankind could not lie in faith alone. Rather, it was in the combination of faith and reason, the Russian enlightenment could claim to contribute to European culture. In order to be of any significance, the Russian enlightenment had to be compatible with the dominant ideas and values of educated society both at home and abroad. Since the purpose of resuscitating the national culture was to pull Russia out of cultural backwardness, an isolated Russian enlightenment, without any connection to the philosophical ideas of Europe, was of no use to the Slavophiles. Kireevsky emphasized the limited impact of a separate enlightenment: "There is no life in it, no blessings, since there is no progress, nothing of the success which is attained solely through the combined forces of humankind."

It was not possible to evaluate the enlightenment of a people according to the sum of its knowledge, the development of its national character, or the level of civilization. It could only be measured according to its contribution to the enlightenment of all men and its position in the universal process of human development.[14]

One of the challenges of European philosophy at this time was to combine reason and faith. Acting as participants in this European philosophical discourse, the Slavophiles made use of these ideas to form a national culture and philosophy. Consequently, it was by combining faith with reason, and soul with mind that the Russian enlightenment made a general contribution. Faith resided in the Russian culture, while reason resided in Western culture. Mixing the two would create a union between

Russian nationality and the Western universal results of science. As a result of this fusion the Russian enlightenment would develop and express what the Slavophiles called "living knowledge." It was seen as the root from which both culture and learning developed. Knowledge, in its Western rationalistic sense, was weak and unimportant without it.[15]

Even though the Slavophiles made a point of demonstrating the differences between Western and Russian enlightenment, they regarded them as embodiments of the same universal evolution of intellectual thought, i.e., of the same universal enlightenment. Both kinds aimed at promoting education, learning, and a better world for all. In Kireevsky's words, both movements "coincided in the final point of their development in one love, in one striving towards a living, perfect, universal and truly Christian enlightenment."[16]

Like Herder before them, the Slavophiles argued for the intrinsic values and unique development of cultures and for their place on a common scale of progress and perfection. According to their thinking, different cultures corresponded in different epochs to the current state of universal enlightenment. When one culture ceased to be the bearer of enlightenment, this role was simply transferred to another. In every epoch there were nations where learning and culture flourished more fully than in others. These nations represented their epoch, but they did so only as long as their dominant national character coincided with the dominant character of their culture or enlightenment. In other words, they could not have an imitated culture. After reaching perfection in one of the stages of its development, universal enlightenment moved on and consequently changed its character. The nation, which had formerly expressed this character in its national culture, could no longer represent universal history. Other nations, whose originality was in agreement with the coming epoch, would take its place. The new representatives of progress would continue the work of their predecessors, having "harvested all the fruits of their learning and culture and extracted from them the seeds of a new development." European culture, for example, which currently represented universal enlightenment, was in fact a result of the enlightenment of antiquity. In this way, from the beginning of history, there was a continuous link and gradual progress in the life of the human intellect.[17]

This organic view of progress allowed the Slavophiles to argue for a future role for Russia in universal history despite her current backwardness. The Slavophiles argued that Western rationalism had led its enlightenment into a blind alley. Indeed, Khomiakov criticized Western Enlightenment for not having moved humankind forward at all.[18] For

this reason, the European Enlightenment found itself in the same relationship to Russia as the classical enlightenment had been to Europe.[19]
History therefore called upon Russia to take the lead in universal enlightenment because of the "comprehensiveness" and "completeness" of its
national principles. Eventually, Russia would replace Europe as the representative of universal enlightenment. The notion of an original Russian
contribution to humanity and to universal history was a crucial part of
Slavophilism. Hence, in order to understand Slavophile thought, the
striving for both nationality and universality needs to be acknowledged.

ESTABLISHING THE RUSSIAN ENLIGHTENMENT

In order to realize or, perhaps rather, to revive the Russian enlightenment,
the Slavophiles believed that the educated elite had to return to the Russian way of life. As a result of this reunion the Russian enlightenment would
wake up from its slumber and begin to develop. According to Khomiakov,
enlightenment had existed in Russia in the past despite the lack of scientific development. Most importantly, traces of it still remained, although
so far no one had cared about them.[20] This ancient Russian enlightenment
had been something the whole nation participated in; all the members of
the nation played different parts.

Kireevsky described ancient Russia as "a single living organism," held
together not so much by a common language as by the unity of convictions, resulting from a common faith in the guidelines of the Church. He
painted a picture of ancient Russia as covered by a multitude of monasteries, linked together by bonds of spiritual communion. These monasteries
had "radiated a uniform and harmonious light of faith and learning" to all
separate tribes and principalities. The people not only derived their spiritual notions from them, but all their ethical, social, and legal concepts were
subjected to their educational influence; this created a sense of harmony in
them. The clergy, drawn from all layers of society, in turn transmitted to
all social classes the teachings they obtained directly from "the centre of
contemporary learning," which to the Slavophiles meant the religious centers of Constantinople, Syria, and Mount Athos.[21]

Kireevsky argued that because the monasteries were in constant contact with the people, one could assume there was a rich culture or enlightenment among the lower classes in Russia. This enlightenment may not
have been illustrious in a superficial sense, but it was profound; it was not
externally resplendent or materialistic, but inner and spiritual. This old

Russian Christian-Orthodox culture was the foundation of the entire way of life and thinking in Russia.[22] The Slavophiles claimed that traces of an ancient Russian culture were still observable in the customs, manners, and thinking of the common people. In fact, Kireevsky maintained that these traces permeated the soul and the mind of any Russian who had not been transformed by Western education. A century and a half had elapsed since the monasteries were the centers of Russian culture, and the educated elite had largely departed from, or even abandoned, the traditional Russian way of life. But Russia's ancient culture had survived almost intact among the lower classes. This Russian life was still impregnated with the ideas of ancient Russian learning.[23]

Nevertheless, Kireevsky did not argue for a return to these idealized roots. Claiming that Russians could neither expect the restoration of old Russian principles, nor the introduction of Western traditions to the exclusion of the others, he postulated a third alternative. This position was a continuation of Kireevsky's earlier pre-Slavophile standpoint when he argued that an enlightened Russian national culture would be born at the point when European culture coincided with Russian originality. Although in the 1820s and first half of the 1830s Kireevsky believed it necessary to borrow from the West, this was only supposed to be the first stage in the development of a genuine Russian culture since he did not believe Russia had a sufficient basis to develop a national culture from within. What was national was not yet enlightened and progressive. Like Belinsky, the early Kireevsky argued that it was a mistake to search for the national in the uneducated and to develop it at the cost of eschewing European discoveries. The result of such a strategy would be "to chase away enlightenment altogether."[24]

In 1839, in what can be considered as his first Slavophile publication, Kireevsky modified, but did not fundamentally alter, his views to a more positive assessment of Russia's national elements. Yet, he still believed that a third way was possible; it was not a question of whether the Russian or the Western cultural principle was the most valuable, but rather how both principles could be directed to produce beneficial results. Thus, the correct way to pose the question was to ask what direction Russia should take, not which principle she should adopt.[25] However, in a later article, Kireevsky wrote that the solid edifice of Russian enlightenment, built out of mixed and foreign elements, needed to be rebuilt with pure, native stone. Since the essence of Russian civilization lived on in the people and in the Orthodox Church, it was on this foundation that Russia had to erect the edifice of Russian enlightenment.

Although it may seem as if the third way was now closed, this was not the case. The sort of learning to be developed in Russia on the basis of native principles was Western learning.[26] Khomiakov took a similar position, arguing that the future Russian spiritual enlightenment could be united with Western thinking. He saw science, in the broad sense of knowledge, as one of the expressions of the Russian enlightenment.[27] Although the "principles of life," preserved in the doctrine of the Orthodox Church, should be disseminated to every Russian and internalized as an essential part of their beliefs, Western culture was not to be discarded. Rather, these basic principles of the Russian way of life were to give it a "higher meaning" and bring it to "its ultimate development."[28]

This view of the relationship between the Russian and the Western enlightenment demonstrates the universal aspirations of the Slavophiles. They did not want a Russian culture that belonged exclusively to Russians; they wished for a national culture of universal significance that could contribute to the progress of humanity. Clearly, some of the important values of what is usually referred to as Enlightenment thinking, such as universalism, education, and progress, were still upheld by the Slavophiles.

What was needed for the creation of a Russian enlightenment was to appreciate and formulate the principles that formed a basis for the specific Russian way of life. These principles were not as visible in Russian history as were those that formed the basis of Western culture. One had to search for them. Kireevsky suggested that the features of the old culture that remained only hinted at its true meaning. Only some of its primary principles could still be discerned in the impact they had on the minds and lives of Russians. But, fortunately, the Russian way of life had survived among the common people, and it was practised, almost unconsciously, as a matter of tradition even though it was no longer shaped and directed by a guiding thought. It was no longer revived by what Kireevsky called "the concerted influence" of the educated elite, nor was it in harmony with the main current of the country's intellectual life.[29] Yet, although the understanding of the common people had been fragmented, it was nevertheless strong. Kireevsky asserted that "the people's undeveloped understanding of what was not yet articulated," i.e., the founding elements of a Russian culture, constituted the root from which the highest culture of the nation stemmed. It was the moral duty of educated Russians to revive and articulate these elements in order to develop them. In this way, all elements of the enlightenment were connected and constituted an undivided whole.[30] The Russian enlightenment, then, was common property, a force of the entire society and all of the people.[31]

WHO WERE TO BE ENLIGHTENED? THE PEOPLE, THE NATION, AND THE EDUCATED ELITE

The Slavophiles wanted to enlighten all of Russia. However, the object of enlightenment differed between the classes. In the upper classes, both individuals and their culture had to be enlightened; in the lower classes, only the culture needed enlightenment, but it was an enlightenment of a different kind. The inarticulate culture of the people had to be made intelligible and be articulated, while the imported culture of the elite had to be illuminated by the original Russian principles. Therefore, the intellectual and artistic activity of "the thinking part of the nation," i.e., the educated elite, had to return to its national foundation: to the Russian way of life. It was Russia's enlightened, westernized culture, transmitted by and in some sense embodied in its educated elite, that required a genuine, national enlightenment.

The Slavophiles believed that this culture had separated itself from original Russian culture and learning. The foreign enlightenment (or culture) expressed by the educated elite had borne fruit in Western countries, but could not take root in Russia. Here, it proved fruitless. It was based on "alien principles," which could not germinate in a foreign organism. As a consequence, the only existing culture in Russia was separated from "the conditions for historical development" and could not make progress.[32] Torn from its roots, it had neither life, nor spirit. The task of the Russian way of life, which comprised the national idea, was to infuse life into an otherwise barren enlightenment.

The task of Western enlightenment (or learning) was to give common significance to the peculiarity of national life and push it forward on the road to progress. The original Russian culture could not preserve its significance, since the whole of the "external way of life," i.e., the culture of the educated elite, was permeated by different standards based on alien, Western principles. So, for national culture to regain its significance and start developing, Western science had to be transformed into a "Russian meaning," i.e., base itself on national principles. It had to be united with the "true enlightenment" of Russia.

But in order to re-enlighten the imitated culture in Russia, the educated elite had to be enlightened in the first place. As a consequence of this gap between foreign enlightenment and original Russian enlightenment, there was profound ignorance of the ancient "living foundations" of Russia among the majority of the educated.[33] They now had to be able to express the old Russian spiritual enlightenment and be the organs of Russian life, with all of its spiritual and social traditions.

Against this background, one would think the people were in a better position to re-enlighten Russian culture, since they had preserved elements of the old culture. But the Slavophiles, like most of their contemporaries, believed enlightenment could only come about when education, learning, and culture were in progress.[34] In one of his pre-Slavophile articles, Kireevsky wrote that Russian nationality had been uneducated and coarse up until that moment. Now, it had to be elevated, enlightened, and given "the life and strength of progress."[35] The difference between the Slavophiles and the Westernizers on this issue lay in what they saw as the referent of "nationality." While the latter held that nationality entailed some sort of radical, progressive development, whether or not it was found in the educated people, or in the peasants, the former emphasized the Christian element and maintained that it was found only among uneducated people. But even in the Slavophile view, nationality needed to be enlightened in the sense of being joined with learning. The masses were uneducated and could not be the bearers of enlightenment; they could only live Russian life unreflectively—not develop it, or make it progress. The Russian way of life had to be expressed by those who were conscious, who made the spontaneous feelings and actions of the people intelligible by uniting them with rational thinking and scientific knowledge. In short, the educated elite had to contemplate the life of the people in the light of all human knowledge. But the Russian way of life was not to be transformed and made rational in an abstract logical sense; rather, thought and learning were complementary.

In order to fulfil this role, intellectuals had to renounce the degenerated direction of Western enlightenment and re-educate themselves to overcome pride and scepticism. They also had to change their habits.[36] Kireevsky held that Russian enlightenment could only be attained through inner striving towards moral height and perfection. Without this, Russian culture would never flourish.[37] But the national enlightenment could not be recuperated solely through individual moral improvement. Only spiritual union with the people made it possible to clarify their different ideals and express them. Only from a "living community" could an unfruitful, weak individual intellect gain strength and develop. Only then

> would man get out of his egoistic existence and gain the significance of a living organ in the great organism. Only then would every healthy idea and every warm feeling, which emerged in every separate individual, become common property, only then was that enlightenment possible, for which the West was striving without hope.[38]

Each and every life should be in perfect accordance with everyone else's, so that there was no disunity in society or the individual. Individual thinking was only strong and fruitful when it was combined with a strong development of general thinking. General thinking was only possible when the highest level of learning and the individuals who expressed it were connected with the whole social organism through bonds of love.[39] The organic view of the nation meant that its alienated, thinking part had to be re-connected to the people, both as individuals and as a group, so that the original principles of the nation could be regenerated and turned into common principles. These notions would subsequently constitute the basis of a national enlightenment that would direct public life on a new path of development.

The Slavophiles believed that if educated Russians took on the project of articulating the unconscious Russian culture, if they began to learn about their nation, its traditions, customs, and principles and, most importantly, tried to live the Russian life, they would understand it and love it. Then they would be able to connect the remains of this ancient culture with the universal results of science and begin to develop that specific Russian culture, which would correspond to the current demands of universal enlightenment. At that moment it would be possible for philosophy and history to develop in Russia on native principles. The arts could flourish, growing from native roots.[40]

Living the Russian life did not mean the educated elite actually had to live with the peasants in any physical sense. This life could be shared spiritually, so that gentry-intellectuals did not have to leave the security of their country estates. Since the Slavophiles had already defined the meaning of Russian nationality, it was sufficient to study Russian history and the Eastern Church Fathers to "live" the Russian life. The Slavophiles were after the spirit of this life, not its actuality. Yet, this does not mean that they did not know the people at all. The Slavophiles lived on country estates close to their peasant serfs and, like every landowner, had formalized relations with the village commune. However, since most members of the educated elite did not appreciate the unenlightened and, in their view, backward ways of the people, the Slavophiles added a tinge of mystery to their way of life, suggesting there was more to it than Westernized Russians realized. They simply did not comprehend the people. In Khomiakov's words, the "high phenomena" of the people's moral life were almost unknown and therefore little appreciated. He suggested that the inner life of the village commune was full of secret forces and inner harmony and that there were great spiritual principles hiding in Russian life.[41]

Hence, rather than to live the life of the Russian peasants, the educated elite were to be enlightened by this life in order to shape a public, or national, consciousness. As cultural leaders of their country and as representatives of education and progress, Russian intellectuals were responsible for directing public life in a new and original direction.

Kireevsky argued that in forming and basing itself upon a common national consciousness, public life in Russia would proceed in a direction different from that in which Western civilization would lead it. It was the absence of such a common consciousness that concerned both Slavophiles and Westernizers, because without it, there would be no awareness of the nation or of its worth. And without such awareness, the Russian enlightenment could not develop. What was worse, countries, whose people had not formed a common consciousness of its national life, lacked a national character and could not play a part in universal history. Such nations did not live and their existence served no purpose. They were devoid of any significance and useless for the cause of progress.[42] Forming a national consciousness was obviously an extremely important task that entailed a process in two directions. It involved becoming aware of the national way of life and, at the same time, it was a result of bringing this life into public consciousness. This task presented Russian intellectuals with a specific role connected to their nation, thus removing their feelings of inferiority and of embarrassment for Russia's cultural backwardness.

In what sense then was the Slavophile formation of a national consciousness really a question of creating a common consciousness, or a common identity? Clearly the Slavophiles were more interested in the Russian people as a people, or nation, expressing nationality, than as common people. They looked to the people because they were national in the sense of not being influenced by Western education. Through their separation from the state and the educated elite, the people had preserved the remains of the old Russian culture in their way of life. It was manifest in their customs, traditions, and language; in their conceptions, and religious, social, and personal relations.[43] But it was precisely because of their isolation that the people and their way of life was not understood. This was also the reason why the old Russian culture had been halted in its development before it was able to bear any fruit.[44] In the Romantic language of the time, it had been cut off from the thinking part of the organism and thus lost its life. The adoption of Western rationalism produced a gap in Russian society. Therefore, the people's way of life had to be verbalized. It had to be articulated and joined with science. For this reason it may seem as if the Slavophiles really wanted to enlighten the people. It is true that the link between the enlightened elite and the uneducated people had to be restored, but the effort lay solely with the former; the people had only to remain the way they were.

Already in his early writings, Kireevsky focused on the need for an enlightenment of Russian culture, but then it was the genuine Russian culture that needed enlightenment. In his later, Slavophile works, it was the imported culture that had to be enlightened. Nevertheless, in neither case was it a question of educating the common people. It did not involve the making of a socially and politically conscious people. Rather, they were to be made conscious of the spiritual activity and fundamental principles that lay at the basis of their life. Their material well-being, if any, would come as a side effect of enlightenment, rather than constitute its purpose. Ultimately, the Russian enlightenment did not have anything to do with rational education; it was a spiritual enlightenment of the nation and it was the higher learning of those who had attained spiritual wisdom that was to be transmitted to all social groups.

By making Western culture and its Russian exponents national, the people would be incorporated into the intellectual activity of the whole national organism. They would then take part in the higher learning that would be the outcome of the Russian enlightenment.

But then again, this learning would only serve as moral guidance and a revival of their way of life. The common enlightenment would manifest itself to the people as a constant "circular motion of ideas."[45] Since the principles of the Russian enlightenment in a sense already belonged to the people, they needed protection from counterproductive influences more than enlightenment.[46] Here, the writer had an important role. He (or she) was to establish the inner pattern of thought of the people while protecting it at the same time. But, since the writer was not able to do this all by himself, Kireevsky urged all "the thinking people" to cooperate. The role of the educated elite was thus not that of enlightening the people, but of making their thought and life comprehensive; of forming a common, national consciousness in order for the Russian enlightenment to develop.

The enlightenment that would inevitably transcend to the people had to be in accordance with their customs and social relations.[47] The highest stage the enlightenment could reach was when rational thinking was in harmony with the national way of life. Separated from this life, enlightenment would be useless. For example, at the time of the French Enlightenment, Khomiakov argued, books published in the West for the common people were neither bought, nor read because they did not correspond to the needs of the people and therefore lacked what the Slavophiles called

"living fellow-feeling" and "living consciousness," meaning national consciousness.[48] These books were created to teach people what they already
knew. They explained separate scientific questions without any connection
to the central convictions of the people, and without any link to their existence or way of life. These books were not connected to the national
thinking and, consequently, remained useless. Hence, the forming of a national consciousness would benefit the people more than literacy would.

Universal literacy, which the Slavophiles saw as based on Western culture, had many negative consequences, one of which was the separation of
the common people from the Church-Slavonic language, which allegedly
constituted the only source of their inner convictions. Another negative aspect was that the new culture influenced the people differently than it did
the upper classes, where Western learning and culture had been shared by
all. An individual of the lower estates, who adopted Western culture,
would become separated from the whole circle of his earlier relations. He
also had to break away from his inner convictions. No longer supported by
respect for the common views and rules of his circle, and not having inner
strength to resist passions, he declined morally and intellectually. Kireevsky
argued that the spread of foreign culture among the Russian people was
not enforced by "the strength of inner conviction," but by "external temptation and necessity."[49] Consequently, the worst aspects of unbridled individualism and liberalism would influence the people.

Although the Slavophiles obviously expressed rather conservative ideas
concerning the education of common people, one should of course bear in
mind that the French Enlightenment was hardly radical in this respect. But
the fact that the Slavophiles regarded the people as politically passive makes
their nationalism quite different from many types of Western nationalism
where the mobilization of the people is an important element. Certainly in
liberal nationalism, but also in forms of conservative nationalism, the people play an active role in forming the nation. In Slavophile thought, the
nation was explicitly formed by the members of the educated elite.

By looking at the concept of a Russian enlightenment I have shown
the complexity of the cultural nationalism Slavophilism represents. The
Slavophile notion of a Russian enlightenment questions the idea of nationalism as antagonistic to other nations and the formation of a national
identity in opposition to "the Other." It also challenges Liah Greenfeld's
theory of national identity as a "transvaluation of values." Furthermore, it
questions the incompatibility of nationalism and universalism; of Romanticism and Enlightenment; of Russia and Europe; and of conservatism and
progressivism. In the Slavophile view, every people or nation had its own

value and a right to independent development. To establish the Russian nation as a special organism with a distinctive personality therefore constituted an important goal. But in order to counter the feeling of backwardness among Russian intellectuals, the Slavophiles also needed Russia to play a role in the evolution of universal history.[50] This meant that the nation had to contribute to the advancement of humanity.

It was obvious that Russia could not contribute to universal progress by returning to the past. That is why the Slavophiles did not wish to bring medieval Russia back. Although they argued for a return of contemporary culture to its genuine founding principles, they did not want its development to revert, or worse, to stagnate. On the contrary, they wanted Russian culture to progress and not only in relation to national history, but also and especially, in relation to European culture. When the Russian enlightenment reached its perfection, it would constitute a basis for the intellectual life of all individuals and nations. This spiritual foundation would give common meaning and truth to all separate cultural forms and individual truths.[51] Through the notion of a Russian enlightenment, the Slavophiles shaped a specific role for their nation in universal history and furnished Russian intellectuals with a new public role as interpreters of this nation. In this way, it presented a solution to the problem of cultural backwardness. Kireevsky captures the gist of the Slavophile concept of a Russian enlightenment in an appeal to his fellow intellectuals:

> Have conviction, have a religious faith, a patriotic faith, a literary faith. Believe in humankind, in the strength of the genius, in the future, in yourself. Know from where you have come in order to know where you are striving . . . It is not enough to think, you must believe.[52]

In chapter 7 I pursue the investigation of the complex mix of ideas embraced by Slavophilism and characterize their social project in the general framework of Russian intellectual criticism. But before that, I look into the social vision of cultural nationalism in general, thus putting the Slavophile project in a larger context.

Chapter 6

Cultural Nationalism as a Project for Social Change

The study of the Slavophile concept of enlightenment suggests that Slavophilism can be seen as a project for social change. Chapters 6 and 7 are devoted to an analysis of the social vision of cultural nationalism and an attempt is made to characterize this project for change in political terms. This chapter deals with cultural nationalism in general, while chapter 7 concerns the political aspects of Slavophile nationalism specifically.

Cultural nationalism, like Romantic ideas in general, has often been seen as a linguistic, or cultural movement, and not as a social project for change.[1] Both Herder and the German Romantics, who inherited his notion of distinctive organic cultures, have been accused of being apolitical, in the sense of escaping from social and political realities.[2] In the same way Slavophilism has been described as a Romantic nostalgia for a lost ideal, a utopia.[3]

Reinhold Aris writes that the Romantics "revealed the significant fact that men who might have been political leaders took resort to dreams and utopian ideals." He argues that they retreated from an unsatisfactory reality instead of trying to change the existing order. None of them, he claims, played an active part in politics or had any direct influence on the course of political events. This belief has led some scholars to conclude that the Romantics had no political interests or political importance whatsoever.[4] Others, who acknowledge their concern with change, cannot make sense of the Romantics' specific way of realizing their social vision. Frederick Barnard, for example finds it odd that they combine a desire for realism and for solving the problems of their time with an idealistic nostalgia for the past.[5] But, if we try to understand the social project of the Romanticists in its specific context, there is nothing odd about combining the two.

Romantic and cultural nationalistic ideas have been seen as apolitical because of the change of focus from the state to the nation and the community. The fact that the state is regarded with suspicion and the social vision of the Romantics is antagonistic to government and power make them look utopian, politically indifferent, and uninterested in change. The common modern view is that social change has to be realized through the state via political reforms. However, as John Hutchinson shows, the aim of cultural nationalism is not the creation of a representative national state, where nation and state coincide, but the moral regeneration of the historic community and its way of life. This way of life cannot be constructed from above, i. e. from the state, since it is an organic spontaneous social order. It has to be regenerated by artists, writers, historians, and intellectuals in general.[6] By treating Romantic ideas as a utopian escape from reality, they become marginalized; unimportant for the purpose of political and social analysis, which explains why cultural nationalism has been a neglected field of study in the social sciences.

Recently, however, Frederick Beiser has argued that early Romantic ideas, which form the basis of cultural nationalism, were really part of a political project. He points to the common definition of politics, focused on the state, as the reason for overlooking this fact. The fact that the early Romantics did not possess a theory of the state does not mean that they were politically indifferent. Naturally, Herder's anarchism and historicism prevented him from having a theory of the state. But, he did have concrete ideas about the organisation of social life.[7]

PHILOSOPHY, ART, AND RELIGION AS
INSTRUMENTS OF CHANGE

The early Romantics regarded philosophy and art as instruments for change. This was an epoch characterized by elite rule, not mass politics, and the Romantic immersion in aesthetics and poetry was not an escape from political and social problems, but a way to address these problems and offer solutions. Through aestheticism, the Romantics provided a strategy for reform.[8] "Philosophy," they claimed, "should not be disinterested speculation but the guiding force behind all human action." But philosophers did not have to give up abstract theory to discuss political or social issues. Instead ethical, aesthetic, and epistemological theory should be motivated by social concerns and used to justify political ends. According to Beiser, a careful examination of the aims, origins, and context of key Romantic thinkers indicates that their ideas were almost always motivated by social and political objectives, even when they seemed totally concerned with abstract thought. In fact, some major thinkers, such as Johann Gottlieb Fichte, Friedrich Schiller, Johann Gottfried Herder, and Friedrich Schlegel, saw the whole purpose of their authorship as political.[9] Their work was steeped in political consciousness and there is a clear sense of the essential connection between politics, philosophy, literature, and art in their writings. To the Romantics, it was clear that philosophy was a political force and that ideas must serve politics.[10]

They did not confine the discussion of ethical ideas, such as *Humanität* and *Bildung*, to a strictly theoretical sphere. The chief aim of German Romanticism was the rebirth of German culture and public life through the powers of art. It was a struggle for humanity, won only through "the power of spirit and true art."[11] This transformation was not only aesthetic, but involved a social and political regeneration in Germany. Like Herder, Schlegel held that *Humanität* could be attained only under specific political conditions, which is hardly surprising considering that it implied the full realization of all human beings. Political freedom was a prerequisite for the independence of the will and an essential characteristic of the concept of the state.[12] Both political freedom and enlightenment were necessary conditions of *Bildung*. "Experience teaches us," Schlegel wrote, "that a state where education is not as extensive as freedom must degenerate."[13] What is more, art was not only the central organ of *Bildung*, it was also the means to achieve social and political reform. Providing the people with a model of virtue, art alone had the power to bring them together and motivate them to act. In its capacity as the key to change, art should play an essential role in the state. Its main task was to bridge the gap between abstract reason and real life. The highest act of reason was an aesthetic act since to the Romantics, it comprised all ideas. "[T]ruth and goodness are fraternally united only in beauty."

An anonymous Romantic writer asserted:

[b]efore we make ideas aesthetic, i.e. mythological, they will have no interest for the people. Conversely, before mythology is rational, the philosopher must be ashamed of it. Hence . . . mythology must become philosophical to make people rational, and philosophy must become mythological to make philosophers sensuous.

As a result of this unity, the gap between the people and the educated elite would close and the universal freedom and equality of the spirits would rule without repression. "Only then can we expect equal development of all powers, of each individual as well as all individuals."[14] Schiller, who had a great impact on the Romantics, wrote more explicitly about the relationship between aesthetics and politics, contending that "[i]f man is ever to solve the problems of politics in experience, he must take the path through the problem of aesthetics, because it is only through beauty that man attains freedom."[15]

The strong belief in the power of art and philosophy is difficult to understand today, but it is essential to a comprehension of the Romantic movement that art and philosophy were regarded as efficient instruments for social and political transformation. The Romantics' revival of religion should be seen in the same reformist context as their aestheticism, since religion replaced art as a means of realizing humanity. "Liberate religion, and a new humanity will begin," Schlegel wrote. Spiritual rebirth became a prime precondition for social and political freedom. Together with art and philosophy, religion would educate men and thereby liberate them mentally from their submissive attitude. In Schlegel's words, "[n]othing is religious in the strict sense that is not a product of freedom."[16]

The political motivations of the Romantics can also be seen in their general intellectual context. This was a context dominated by the *Aufklärung*, which clearly was a political movement. Most thinkers in late eighteenth-century Germany, including such well-known Romantics as Schlegel, Novalis, and Hölderlin, saw themselves as *Aufklärer*. In fact, one could argue that the early Romantics had a strong connection to Enlightenment thought and preserved some of its ideals such as education, progress, and universality. As a matter of fact, some of the early Romantics were more true to the ideals of the *Aufklärung* than the *Aufklärer* themselves. The Romantics did not believe that literature and philosophy were ends in themselves. They were means to the enlightenment of the public, whose educators they considered themselves to be.[17] Poetry would become "the teacher of humanity." We have already seen that enlightenment was a prerequisite for the highest end of the Romantics. It was a condition for *Bildung*, which alone fostered *Humanität*, the promotion of the common good of humanity.[18] Schlegel maintained that "only through education does a human being become everywhere a human being and penetrated by humanity."[19]

Contrary to the *Aufklärer*, Herder believed that all cultures were unique and of equal value. Consequently, there was no universal culture that could be identified with European culture. "Europe is not the world," he wrote, "it is not mankind."[20] Therefore, European culture could not be "the measure of universal human goodness and human value." Rather, each nation had its peculiar image of *Humanität*, according to the prevailing historical and geographical conditions. In Herder's own words:

> [i]t is fine . . . if the Frenchman and the Englishman depict their humanité and humanity for themselves in English and French; all the less will the foreigner chase after them to his own ruin.

However, the realization of *Humanität* established a link between man as a member of both a nation and humanity at large. Furthering the common good of humanity was a single process, which could be done both on a national and an international level. To Herder, the human species was "a single whole." He borrowed a statement made by Fénelon to express his cosmopolitan outlook: "I love my family more than myself; more than my family my fatherland; more than my fatherland humanity." This universal trait in Herder's thought, which at first glance seems incompatible with the concept of cultural uniqueness, makes perfect sense when seen in the context of his idea of progress and the organic conception of the cosmic order.[21]

The doctrine of organicism also held universal elements in its Romantic version. It contained ideas of harmony and interaction that were not confined to one nation. In Novalis' words:

> [t]his or that people has, like this or that child, a special talent; but the others must not be forgotten in the attempt to develop this one. A talent cultivated in isolation withers early, because it lacks nourishment. This nourishment can come from only other talents. All of the talents make up, as it were, one body.[22]

Taking a standpoint similar to the Slavophiles, German Romantics did not strive for a cultural revival in their country alone. Rather, they believed it was the destiny and cultural mission of the Germans to revive the culture of all mankind.[23] In fact, Romanticism was to radiate outwards from poetry to transform, or poeticize, the whole world. As Schlegel writes, "Romantic poetry is a progressive universal poetry."[24]

UNIVERSAL PROGRESS

To Herder, the progress of humanity constituted the highest objective. Hence, his adherence to the ideals of the *Aufklärung* is unmistakable. But his concept of progress differed from that of the Enlightenment; it was interwoven with his organicism and historicism. If progress was to have enduring effects, it had to be connected to social growth and rooted in a people's historical traditions. Without tradition, progress was "like a plant without roots." For Herder, development was a process of growth in which the latent becomes actual: "Within every grain of seed there lies the plant with all its parts; within every animal seed the creature with all its limbs."[25] But tradition needs progress as much as progress needs tradition.

Herder saw history as a progressive movement, where the old and the new were reconciled at increasingly higher levels.[26] Progress was contained in a variety of cultures, incommensurable with each other. Consequently, one culture was never merely a means to another, even if there was a sense in which mankind as a whole was advancing.[27] According to Herder, certain "fevers and stupidities of humanity" would "cease their ferment with the advance of the centuries and the life-ages [of humanity]."[28] On the one hand, humanity as a whole was moving forward, on the other, each national culture was developing its particular images of humanity. But these were not separate processes. At each stage of the development of a specific culture, the form it had taken and the values it entailed were appropriate to humanity at that stage of its development. The manner and form, which at any given stage the development of a *Volk's* collective consciousness assumes, Herder termed its national culture. Culture was no longer taken to mean civilization and sophistication.

Consequently, in order to assess a culture correctly, one should not, as most Enlightenment thinkers did, apply the standards of a more mature and developed stage of humanity to a primitive, underdeveloped stage. Instead, different standards had to be applied to different cultures. The different "epochs of humanity" should be respected in the same way as the different ages of an individual.[29]

This new conception of culture allowed Herder to argue both for the intrinsic values and unique development of cultures and for their conformity to a single standard. In seeing all cultures on a scale of progress and perfection according to a universal law of nature, he was not advocating a complete incommensurability of cultural standards. Rather, each culture was developing in its own way; and every new epoch was regarded as different from the one that preceded it. Nonetheless, the epochs of the world formed a "moving chain which no individual ring can in the end resist."[30]

Isaiah Berlin argues that this combination of universal progress and uniqueness is impossible. "If all cultures are equal, each in its time and place, the notion of the perfect civilization in which the ideal human being realizes his full potentialities, becomes absurd." In Berlin's view, Herder saw progress as the internal development of a culture towards its own goals. It meant that the historic identity of the nation had to be continuously renovated in terms of the needs of each generation.[31] Against this view, Beiser holds that Herder's aim was to find the middle path between the extremes of ethnocentrism and relativism. This path would show that there is progress in a higher sense. This path was made possible through Herder's organic view of the social order, according to which both nations and individuals were linked to the universal progress of humanity, each in its particular way. The end of human beings was the development and perfection of all their characteristic powers, intellectual, moral, sensitive, and physical. But, in order to realize his humanity, man had to become a single, harmonious whole, because "[t]he existence of each human being is woven together with his whole species." The process of promoting *Humanität* would result in the development of the self not only as an individual, but also as a member of a community. The same could be said to apply to nations, which, through the development of self-consciousness, realized themselves both as unique nations and as members of the community of nations.[32]

Consequently, true progress involved both the development of human beings as integrated wholes, and their development as collective individuals, as cultures and communities, expressing their national consciousness in the arts, sciences, and way of life.[33] Together, then, individuals and nations were part of the progress of humanity. Each image of *Humanität* was unique and yet part of a greater whole, which was moving forward towards understanding, justice, goodness, or "feeling of humanity." Hence, in Herder's thought, universal progress is combined with national uniqueness towards the common goal of *Humanität*. The human species is characterized by "an infinite variety striving for a unity that lies in all, that advances all." Education, social and economic institutions, trade, the arts and the sciences, all provided ways of furthering this aim.[34] Each nation had a distinct role to play in the furthering of *Humanität*. The essential task was for the members of the nations to understand and respect this role and to act on it.[35]

Writing about cultural nationalism in Ireland, Hutchinson points to similar arguments. Only by returning to their unique history and culture could the Irish realize their human potential and contribute to the wider European civilization. While striving to preserve the cultural individuality of a nation, cultural nationalism sought to combine this traditional definition with the modern idea of the community as "an active and equal participator in human progress."[36] This was a vision of the nation as "a high civilisation with a unique place in the development of humanity." Cultural nationalists aimed for a regeneration of their nation at a higher level by integrating both traditional and modern aspects of the community, thus pushing it to the forefront of universal progress.[37]

Andrzej Walicki's distinction between progressive and conservative Romantic nationalism can be seen as an effort to account for the combination of progressive and conservative features in early Romantic thought.[38] In Walicki's notion of conservative Romantic nationalism, each nation represents a unique collective personality. Rather than striving to furnish their national distinctiveness with a universal significance, its proponents encourage nations to cling to their unique traditions and customs. They do not see the realization of their national community as a way of furthering universal progress and the general cause of mankind. According to Walicki, conservative Romantics:

> . . . put the emphasis not on activity but on aesthetic contemplation, not on conscious change but on growth. They saw the national mission not as something which demanded conscious activity, but a function which every nation fulfils without being aware of it, by means of its existence.

This, of course, is really an expression of the mainstream view of cultural, or Romantic, nationalism as apolitical and regressive. Since Walicki regards Polish "Romantic nationalism" as progressive, universal, and active, it does not fit in with the way this nationalism is usually defined. Yet, it is clearly not a version of liberal nationalism. But rather than challenging the common definition of cultural nationalism, Walicki establishes a new category, called "Romantic progressivism." This form of nationalism, he argues, "identified universality with variety, seeing national cultures as unique individualities of mankind." Each nation had a specific role in the history of mankind. It had its own historical mission, serving a universal goal. The realization of the specific national task was the only way of attaining universal progress. Walicki claims that progressive Romantic nationalism was developed in revolutionary France, and in Italy, and Poland, while the conservative Romantic type was characteristic of Germany. According to Walicki, German Romantics saw history as a "slow, organic development and condemned the very spirit of conscious, purposeful activity." This conservative view is contrasted against the main ideas of progressive Romantic nationalism, which are: the idea of universal historical progress; the idea of a national mission; the ethos of activism and moral perfectionism; and a belief in the brotherhood of nations.[39] It is interesting to note that these features, which in Walicki's view are characteristic of progressive Romantic nationalism, are quite similar to the cultural nationalism of the Slavophiles.

Walicki's distinction shows that there are traits in Romantic, or cultural nationalism that seem paradoxical to modern scholars. They do not fit into common categories of political thought. Obviously, this dilemma is not solved by employing present-day ideological distinctions to categorize different elements of Romantic thought, with the purpose of distinguishing more valuable from less valuable nationalist movements.

It is not possible to cleanse original cultural nationalism either from all conservative ideas, or from all radical ones. Rather, it has to be accepted that there might have been conservative ideas in the same movement that later stood for progressive change, and vice versa. It is necessary to acknowledge that Romantic, or cultural nationalism grew out of the context of Enlightenment thought and therefore preserved some of its central ideas while trying to modify others. The philosophical, social, and political problems that the *Aufklärer* tried to confront had not vanished; they still had to be solved. What happened was that intellectuals tried to find another way of solving them. They shifted focus from the state to the nation.

Beiser's main argument, which agrees with my interpretation of Slavophile ideas, is that there is no clear shift between the ideals of the Enlightenment and those of Romanticism. The early Romantics were actually the heirs of the *Aufklärung*.[40] Romantic thought constituted a critique against both the epistemology and ontology of the *Aufklärung*, but was not contrary to its general ideals.[41] Although the early Romantics insisted that there were mystical insights above or beyond the sphere of reason, they never approved of beliefs contrary to reason. Thus, Beiser argues, the Romantic journal, *Athenäum*, which has been seen as a rejection of the *Aufklärung* in devoting itself to radical criticism and education, in fact remained true to two fundamental ideals of the *Aufklärung*.[42]

THE SOCIAL VISION

Having reached the conclusion that the cultural nationalism of Herder and the early Romantics concerned social change and that their project can be seen as a continuation of Enlightenment ideals, the question remains as to what kind of society they envisaged. What was their social vision? We have already seen that *Humanität* and *Bildung* could be realized only under specific political conditions. In fact, Herder maintained that since perfection involved both the individual and his community, any social and political structure, which neglected the development of its members or led it in the wrong direction, would be unacceptable.[43] The state should play a positive role in promoting the self-realization of all its citizens. In Berlin's words, Herder had a liberal conception of culture and an anarchist conception of the state. His social vision was antagonistic to central government, power, and domination and he asserted that human beings were "no slavish people that eternally bends beneath the yoke and turns at chains, but a free happy species." Herder looked upon the state as an artificial product of conquest that tried to coerce both the national and the human personality into mechanical, bureaucratic uniformity. It prevented a free and living spirit to develop. Consequently, there could not be an ideal state. The most noble end of central government was to become dispensable.[44]

Herder believed that as soon as people attained complete enlightenment and autonomy, they would abolish the state. Therefore, the main purpose of philosophy was the education and enlightenment of the public, so they could govern themselves without the oppressive controls of a paternalist state.[45] The Romantics directed their most poignant critique against bourgeois society and its ethic of utility, which they believed acted against the development of humanity. Rather than leading to greater freedom to pursue spiritual goals, modern forms of production enslaved people and turned them into machines. People had to work merely to subsist. If people's lives were regarded as instruments of production, Schlegel warned, religion, literature, and philosophy would simply be treated as a kind of diversion, rather than as the means to freedom and the progress of humanity. Against this utilitarian view Schlegel stressed that human beings were ends in themselves who should never be regarded as commodities. Life should not be treated as if it were a common trade, he wrote, "because the true essence of life consists in the wholeness, completeness, and free activity of all our powers."[46]

Herder recognized a plurality of forms of government. There should be as many forms of government as there were different circumstances. Furthermore, the government should include the broadest range of people, since each estate had an indispensable role to play in the social organism. Herder did not question social hierarchy, or promote the abolition of the estates. Even so, he opposed the division of society into classes, sharply marked off from one another and advocated the cooperation of the different estates.[47] "There exists in the state only a single class," he argued, and that is the people, "to it belongs the king as much as the farmer."[48] Language was regarded as an important bond between social classes. In a plan for the establishment of an Institute of German National Enlightenment,

Herder argued that by developing and disseminating the German language, this institute would reduce the gap between the diverse social classes. "Germany has only one interest: the life and well-being of the whole; not the sectional interests of the princes or the Estates, not the interests of this or that class. All these divisions only give rise to oppressive restrictions." Given his wish to establish a political community without a state apparatus, Herder's concern with class division and rivalry is understandable. In an organic community, social conflict could not be inherent or natural. For this reason, neither was there any need for social contracts. To Herder, as to the Slavophiles, true law was customary law. It was inherent in the traditional mode of life of a natural community. This law did not need external authority or power, because it was an expression of a people's moral consciousness.[49] A society could not be held together only by abstract laws. The purely legal framework of the liberal state was not enough to guarantee a genuine community. A common public spirit was also needed. There had to be genuine affection and love between fellow citizens.

Herder saw the individual as an integral part of a whole, the *Volk*. This did not mean that the individual was lost in the collective. To Herder, "the whole was only meaningful if it was seen as the integration of a great variety of smaller wholes, which were self-regulating units in themselves." True unity could only be realised in diversity. Otherwise it would turn into uniformity.[50] Thus, the early Romantics combined individualism with communalism. They believed in the importance of independence and individuality, but since human beings were social, friendship, love, and communal activities were crucial for the individual. "In thinking, contemplating and learning I need the presence of some beloved person," Schleiermacher insisted, because "there is no individual development without love."[51] The reason for the loss of community in modern life, according to the Romantics, was the growing materialism and egoism of civil society. It was destructive to "bind everyone to the state by self-interest."[52] In an ideal society, where humanity had achieved its ideals of *Bildung*, all laws and distinctions would disappear. "A perfect constitution," Novalis wrote, would make "all written laws superfluous. . . . Laws are the complement of deficient natures and beings, and are therefore synthetic."[53]

Herder advocated a kind of partnership between various social groups within a political framework free from any power center. Barnard describes his notion of the organic state as "a spiritually integrated community engaged in cooperative activity, living under a system devoid of governmental direction and under a law which enshrines the social and moral consciousness of its members."[54] For this community to be viable, it had to be based on a shared culture, or national character, instead of a central-ized state. According to Herder, a political order based on a shared culture expressed the will of the people, since the common beliefs and traditions of a culture were shared by everyone. In such a community, the people freely accepted the law and felt a common purpose. In absolutist states, on the other hand, laws were imposed on each culture so that they could not live according to their own beliefs and traditions. The nation would thus replace the centralized state, rather than justify it.[55]

A RADICAL PROJECT

Against this background, it is possible to argue that Herder was more of a radical than a conservative thinker. One of Beiser's main points is that Herder's historicism was intended to undermine rather than to support claims to authority and that it was originally formulated as a critique of contemporary social, political, and cultural attitudes. Herder presented his ideas as a reaction against the historiographers of the *Aufklärung* who saw the European Enlightenment as the end of history and civilization and found progress only when and where its values were exemplified. In this sense it sanctioned the status quo. Yet, Herder's critique of enlightened despotism and imperialism was only part of a much broader attack upon the *Aufklärung* in general. It was the *Aufklärer* who had supported en-lightened despotism and it was they who had justified oppression, by treat-ing European values as universal, and by recommending that this standard of civilization be extended to "primitive" peoples. In this way the *Aufklärer* justified the extermination of local self-government and the exploitation of native peoples. In Herder's view, nations that the *Aufklärer* called savage or barbaric was in fact much more humane than European nations and "the negro has as much right to consider the white man a degenerate, a born albino freak, as when the white man considers him a beast."[56]

The traditionalism Herder gives expression to was not a source of con-servatism, as it was for Edmund Burke. Herder did not regard tradition as something static, or as sacred prejudice. Rather, tradition was the life of the people, the source of their culture, in the absence of which there would be no progress. Hence, Herder's traditionalism was not a support for the old order, but an instrument for change. There is an egalitarian tendency in Herder's thought, based on the idea that the self-realization of each person should be the moral responsibility of everyone. Everyone had the right to develop his inherent powers. Contrary to his conservative contemporaries, who wanted to restrict education to the social elite, Herder advocated the provision of universal education and social welfare.[57] In addition, the notion of *Humanität* implied that this offer was made under conditions of political freedom, which entailed the abolition of absolutist rule and the absence of political censorship. Herder believed censorship to be inimical to progress because it restrained all that was new and creative. Free investigation and communication was vital for human nature and hence also for society. In an environment of censorship, all efforts towards enlightenment would be futile, and result in economic and cultural stagnation. As a consequence, the social and political foundation of the state would be undermined.[58] The aim of the organic community as formulated by Novalis, Schlegel, and Schleiermacher was not to prevent, but to promote the autonomous self-realization of every individual.[59] The "germs of individual development" should be able to "flourish free from all danger."[60]

A common assumption about cultural nationalism is that it is a regressive response to modernization.[61] Against this accusation Hutchinson argues that, whereas it might be called a defensive response to the impact of modernization, it is a mistake to call it regressive. Cultural nationalists seek not to regress into an idealized past, but to find inspiration for a new path of development. The past is to be used not in order to return to some antique order, but rather "as a means to catapult the nation from present backwardness" to a more advanced stage of social development. In other words, it is not a primitivist, but an "evolutionary vision" of the community.[62] According to Beiser, the early Romantics had a similar view of the past.

Athough these intellectuals admired the handicrafts and guilds of the Middle Ages, they did not explicitly advocate a return to them. Like the Slavophiles, the Romantics were attracted to the medieval state because they saw it as the antithesis of the emerging bourgeois society. Medievalism was in fact a historiographic trend that began with the Enlightenment and was directed against absolutism and centralization. Hence, the fascination with the past could be seen as a progressive vision.[63]

The Romantic philosophy of history did not involve a radical break with the thought of the *Aufklärung*. History was still seen as a progressive evolution. In addition, it was part of "the flow of universal development." Despite its tendencies towards history and transcendence, Romanticism always focused on the present and developed concrete proposals, although in retrospect, these may seem utopian.[64]

Although the Romantics argued against a total transformation of society according to some general plan, again, this should not be interpreted as a pronouncement of conservative political beliefs. Beiser argues that their opposition to radical change was directed as much against the authoritarian policies of absolute princes as against the revolutionary program of French radicals.[65] In *Faith and Love*, for example, Novalis criticizes "the mechanical administration" of Prussia, writing that no state has been run more like a factory than Prussia since the death of Friedrich I.[66] The Romantics also continued to emphasize the importance of an autonomous evolution towards some of the classical ideals of the *Aufklärung*. It is difficult to disregard the element of free evolution in the theory of organism. According to this theory, society, both as a whole and as individual parts, must develop gradually from within by slowly adapting to new conditions. The idea of *Humanität* was the end of this evolution. It signified "the realization of individuality, the development of all intellectual, sensitive, and cognitive powers into a harmonious whole." The realization of *Humanität*, according to Schlegel, was "to know the true, to do the good and to enjoy the beautiful, and then to achieve harmony in knowing, doing, and enjoying."[67] This was quite a radical prospect of freedom, not far from later visions of communism.

Just as Romanticism tried to combine the virtues of both traditionalism and modernism, it sought to reach a middle path between liberalism and conservatism. It tried to avoid the extremes of individual liberalism, which the Romantics believed destroyed all social bonds, and the extremes of communalism, which they felt suppressed individual liberty. The early Romantics held that the people became part of the social organism only insofar as they participated, indirectly or directly, in the government. However, the more the Romantics lost faith in the power of the people to develop a community by themselves, the more they believed in the powers of the state.[68] Still, in the early formative years, there was a strong tendency toward idealism and progressivism in Romantic thought that did not fit into the conservative notion of community.[69] Here, it is easy to draw parallels to the formative phase of Slavophilism.

While the Romantics were committed to the community, the conservatives were loyal to the old paternal state. They defended the status quo against the ideology of the French Revolution. The Romantics, on the other hand, started as "literary revolutionaries, trying to poeticise the world and develop the past as a protest against the present."[70] Beiser's description of the early Romantics, as neither revolutionaries nor reactionaries, but reformers, is very much to the point. As we have seen, the realization of *Bildung* was regarded as the precondition of social and political change. For this reason, the promotion of *Bildung* and *Humanität* was not only a cultural project, in the traditional apolitical sense. It was part of a reformist strategy.[71] Here, the role of the educator merges with the role of the artist, resulting in a vision of an interpreter of the people, or the nation. Cultural nationalism, which bases its ideas on this thinking, is a political movement in the same sense. Hutchinson writes that "it renounces the passive isolationism of the traditionalists and presents the nation as a progressive culture, providing models for communal development." But these models are not universal, since every culture has to follow its own path of development and make its own original contribution to humanity.[72]

This description of cultural nationalism fits well into Walicki's concept of "progressive-Romantic" nationalism, although it ought to be of the "conservative-Romantic" kind if we follow Walicki's own distinctions.[73] The problem is that this distinction does not take the complexity of Romanticism into account. In order to understand cultural nationalism as well as the Romantic thought from which it stems, we have to accept that ideas that today seem incompatible once coexisted harmoniously. For example, as we have seen above, universal progress and organic development do not have to be contradictions. It is now time to return to Slavophilism, to its specific social vision, in order to determine to what extent the arguments presented here can further our understanding of Slavophile thought.

Chapter 7

The Slavophile Project
for Social Change

Chapter 5 established that Slavophilism was a project for social change. This chapter examines what this change was directed at. I focus on the social and political dimension of the Slavophile project by putting it in the context of Russian intellectual criticism. The generation prior to the Slavophiles had been preoccupied with constitutional reforms. The Decembrists wished to give Russia something like a true *Rechtsstaat*, a government of laws and not men. Some were inspired by Jacobin republicanism, but most preferred a constitutional monarchy.[1] The Slavophiles desired limited government as well, but they wanted to transform Russia in a different way. Their focus was not on the state and the law as the basis for society, but on the nation and the community. The importance of the state was played down and instead the vital role played by intellectuals as interpreters of the nation was stressed. The main concern of this chapter is to examine this change of focus. I begin with an investigation of the Slavophile notion of customary, moral law as an alternative to written agreements and formal laws. In the next section I analyse their view of the relationship between the state and society, including their assessment of modern tsarism, the form of rule installed by Peter the Great. Lastly, I deal with the relationship between Slavophilism, nationalism, and conservatism, in an attempt to characterize the Slavophiles' social project as a whole.

CRITICISM AGAINST LEGALISM

The Slavophiles presented their arguments against formal law in the form of opposites, or contrasts, based on their theory of organicism. The major contrast was between written and customary law. As we have seen above, the Slavophiles regarded custom as a crucial pillar of society. The problem was that educated Russians did not appreciate its value, with the result that custom no longer existed for the members of the educated elite. According to Khomiakov, it was their "perpetually changing existence" which made them incapable of turning to custom, consisting, as it did, of "everyday trivialities." However, if educated Russians learned to appreciate the people's way of life, they would realize the value of custom, since custom was the natural expression of the nation.

> Law, written and armed with compulsion, brings the differing private wills into a conditional unity. Custom, unwritten and unarmed, is the expression of the most basic unity of society. It is as closely connected with the personality of a people as the habits of life are connected with the personality of a man. The broader the sphere of custom, the stronger and healthier the society, and the richer and more original the development of its jurisprudence.[2]

The advantages of customary law were illustrated by reference to an idealized version of ancient Russia. There, Kireevsky claimed, customary laws were not formulated in advance by some "learned jurist" and they did not subsequently "fall like an avalanche in the midst of the astounded citizenry," wrecking some existing custom or institution of theirs. A law in ancient Russia was usually not drafted, but merely written down after the idea had been formed in people's minds and gradually, through actual necessity, had become part of their customs and way of life. Ideas of social and personal relationships had slowly evolved into universally held convictions, that became custom, and custom became law. For this reason, customary law "knew nothing of abstract logic," springing as it did from daily life.[3] Although it was seen as a law, at the same time it was distinguished from law by being an internal force that permeated the entire life of the people, i.e., the consciousness and thinking of all its members. Written law, on the other hand, was something external, imposed from the outside, and only accidentally added to life.[4] Because they regarded every nation as a unique organism, it comes as no surprise that the Slavophiles did not accept external law, with its absolute and universal claims. Khomiakov actually denied that law, in its proper meaning, had the right to be called a science, or that it contained any essential basis, or content. Instead, it was tied to history and morals and could not exist separately from them.[5]

The common Slavophile distinction between the artificial and the organic was also applied to the contrast between written and customary law. Accordingly, written law represented dead, empty form, while customary law represented life, full of content. The former was based on the concept of formal legality, the latter on spiritual, or true, legality. The concept of organism was also a basis for the Slavophiles' critique against contractual thinking. Khomiakov argued that a society, based on formal legality, was held together solely by conditional agreements or contracts. These were only artificial bonds, without support from either mores or morals. Such a society lacked faith in people's moral feeling and in human value. A society founded on true legality, on the other hand, was held together by bonds of brotherhood. In such a society, there was a fundamental understanding of justice.[6]

Through communal institutions and courts, people became accustomed to seeking the favourable opinions of their brothers. As a consequence, "the fatal and extremely common indifference among many nations toward public, or common, matters was eliminated." Moreover, Khomiakov held that the introduction of juries, passing verdicts unanimously, together with arbitration courts, free from the confrontational mode of proceedings driven by individual self-interest, would enhance the social and moral element of the courts. All matters concerning courts and justice ought to rest on brotherhood.[7] This idea of a natural, moral brotherhood founded on unity, lay at the core of the Slavophiles' notion of "inner justice." It was contrasted with the idea of conditional agreements and formal Roman law, which in their view, lacked any notion of unity. To the Slavophiles, this law represented "external justice."[8]

The distinction between written and customary law was also characterized as one between egoistic individualism and unselfish communalism. Khomiakov argued that the idea of justice could not reasonably be combined with the idea of a society based on self-interest, only limited by agreements. Self-interest, limited from without, either by the forces of nature, or by other humans, could never form a basis for justice. It had only one meaning and that was power. In order for power to be made into a right, Khomiakov argued, it was necessary for it to be limited by law, but not by external law, which only represented force itself. It had to be limited by inner law, by a moral obligation, recognized by the specific person concerned. This view can be compared to Herder's description of customary law as an expression of moral consciousness. Following this standpoint, Khomiakov insisted that law as a science became rational only in the sense of a science of "the self-acknowledged limits of human strength," i.e., of moral obligations. The understanding of these obligations was dependent on man's common notion of universal moral truth and thus could not constitute a separate subject for a particular science. A reasonable interpretation of rights could only be based on the proclaimed foundations for universal knowledge or belief, which was accepted by every person separately.[9] The universalism of moral truth and belief should not be confused with the universal claims of external law, which the Slavophiles rejected.

The main point of criticism was directed against the idea that individual rights could be granted or gained. The true legality of ancient Russia was presented as a contrast to the contractual thinking of the West. In Russia, Kireevsky argued, even the word "right" was unknown in its Western sense. To Russians, it meant only fairness and justice. Thus, no authority could grant or revoke rights, "since fairness and justice could neither be put up for offer nor taken away." They existed in themselves, independent of formal conventions. What is more, the forces of tradition did not allow despotic legislation, since the relationship between ruler and people had a moral, rather than a formal, basis. Kireevsky asserted that the right to try and to judge people, which the prince possessed in certain cases, could not be put into effect in a way contrary to universal custom, and, for the same reason, this custom could not be interpreted arbitrarily.

This situation is contrasted against the West, but could just as well be compared to the despotism of Nicholas' Russia. Kireevsky described all social relations in the West as based on artificial conventions or agreements. Since these were products of a superficial and formal development, there were no proper relations beyond them, nothing that had grown naturally from inner life.[10] Hence, Western society, just as contemporary Russia, was founded on conditional and artificial bonds, not on natural organic ones. According to the Slavophiles, such a society could not be just. Kireevsky maintained that the law could not be fair unless it was based on customs, traditions, and moral obligations. Consequently, formal Roman law, once a foundation for culture and legal order, was no longer useful, at least not in Russia. The Slavophiles wanted educated Russians to realize that this law was no longer compatible with the demands of the civil order.[11]

The emphasis on an inner, spiritual, and moral law, as opposed to formal, external law, naturally made the Russian Orthodox Church an important factor in the Slavophiles' social vision.[12] In an ideal world, the rules and conceptions of social relations, which formed the foundation of laws, would radiate from the Russian Orthodox Church, and be disseminated by priests, monks, and hermits. It is important to stress here that the intellectuals had an important role to play both in articulating the traditions of the people and in turning their fellowintellectuals towards customary law, inner justice, and true legality. The reason for this new role was that, to the Slavophiles, law no longer belonged to the dominion of the state, but to the dominion of the nation, and the nation was the responsibility of the intellectuals, not to be interfered with by the state. Hence, the purpose of the Slavophiles' nationalism was neither to strengthen the state, nor to participate in the governing of the state. These points will be considered in a discussion of the Slavophiles' notion of the state below.

CRITICISM OF THE STATE

The demand for an organic link between custom and law was not a defence of an unlimited state. On the contrary it can be seen as an attempt to impose restrictions on the autocrat.[13] Although, in Slavophile thought, the government had the power of lawmaking, it did not have the right to decide the content or source of the law. This was determined by the people, or the nation. Because the state held all the negative attributes, such as formalism, compulsion, and corruption, it was vital to keep the nation free from state interference. By separating the nation from the state, it would become possible to build a new foundation for Russia, uncontaminated by the old backward and menacing state. The Slavophiles legitimized this separation by referring to the ancient division between the state and the land. The state was confined to the formal business of government and the land pertained to the whole way of life of the people.

The business of the land, therefore, applied to both communal and spiritual matters, and to economic activities such as agriculture, industry, and trade, whereas the business of the state involved defence, justice, and administration (in a limited sense). Stressing this division, Kireevsky argued that in ancient Russia, the general course of affairs was determined by village communes and local authorities, acting in accordance with old tradition. In effect, the authority of a prince consisted of the command of his troops and in providing armed protection, not in the administration of internal affairs or control of the land. However, in extreme cases when a prince violated his proper relationship with the people and the Church, he was driven out by the people. This interpretation suggests that Kireevsky supported the right to some sort of popular rebellion.[14]

Separation between the state and the land was reflected in a division between the political form and the social and spiritual content of a country, according to which the state gave form to the content filled by the nation.[15] For this reason, the Slavophile project to regenerate the nation had to promote social and spiritual, not political, change. The state and its functions were of no importance to this project, which did not mean that the state could, or should, be abolished. Should this happen, the people would have to assume responsibility for the government and deal with all the corrupt matters of the state. This would prevent the people from spiritual development, and therefore from realizing its moral and communal freedom. The people, as the bearer of the nation would cease to exist, since what defined it was its communal and spiritual freedom separated from the state. The concept of "the people" was of utmost importance to the Slavophiles, not because it was the source of political sovereignty and the driving force behind political reform, but because it was essential to the organic, communal, and spiritual life of the nation.[16]

Thus, the fact that government was autocratic was not a real problem, because it meant the people could free themselves from all participation in governing the state. The important thing was that "society should not be despotic."[17] It had to be independent in spirit, conscience, and thought. Otherwise, the life of the nation could not develop. Therefore, it was essential to the Slavophile project that the people were allowed full freedom in their social and spiritual life. The state had a duty towards the people to safeguard and protect their way of life; to give them material security; and to provide them with all the means and ways necessary for them to prosper, attain their full development, and fulfill their moral destiny. The people's duty to the state was to carry out its demands; to give it the strength it needed to put its plans into execution; and to supply men and money when these were required. Although this relationship can be described as unequal, due to the people's lack of formal power, the government in fact existed for the people, rather than vice versa. The principle of life and of the national spirit was found in the people. Government only provided form for this vital national content.[18]

Hence, in Slavophile thought, the role of the state was clearly delimited. Ideally, its function should be limited to the defence of the people and its aim should be to do all it could to help the nation fulfill its destiny. Quite in line with Herder's anarchist conception of the state, Kireevsky asserted that since the entire virtue of the state consisted in its negative character, the less it existed as a state, the better it accomplished its aim.[19] The wisdom of the government consisted in understanding the spirit of the people, and in allowing this spirit to be its guide. For this reason, it was necessary for people to have both the right of opinion and freedom of speech. Without freedom of thought and speech, the spirit of the people could not be expressed. Hence, these freedoms were an inherent part of moral improvement and human dignity. The repression of them led to total indifference and to the complete destruction of human feeling. It brought about inner discontent and dissension and people lost their trust in the government. Consequently, the government lost confidence in the people and therefore intruded into the life of society.[20]

The Slavophiles maintained that, due to public opinion, the relationship between a powerless people and an omnipotent state could in fact be "free." It did not require a government of force and power. But they made clear that their notion of public opinion did not contain any political element. It had no force other than a moral one. "Public opinion is the living, moral, and in no way political link which can and must exist between state and land," Konstantin Aksakov wrote. By denying that public opinion was a political force, the distinction between the political state and the spiritual nation could be upheld, even when subjects were allowed to speak their mind. The Slavophiles argued that the existence of free public opinion would ensure a sincere union between the sovereign and the people, based on mutual trust. But, if freedom of opinion was essential to the citizens, it was even more vital to the government itself, which without it would "fall into incurable blindness and prepare its own destruction." Being a part of the social organism, the state could not act without knowing the direction of the people, or the nation and its moral activity. It was an obvious role for the intellectuals to reveal the direction of the nation. The Slavophiles saw public opinion as the link between the state and the people, a link that was expressed and communicated by the intellectuals, and which showed the state what the nation needed, how it conceived its purpose, and accordingly, by what principles the state should be guided.[21]

As we have seen, the Slavophiles did not accept the idea that it was the duty of the educated elite to serve the state at all times. But neither did they wish to govern themselves, or believe that a written constitution ought to regulate the actions of the state. The educated elite should belong to the nation, to the social organism, and not to the state. As an organism, the nation was characterized by unity and harmony. Hence, unity had to define its social relations. To the Slavophiles, it was not enough for the different social groups to cooperate, as Herder suggested. They wanted the separation of classes to be abolished and replaced by a form of brotherly, or Christian, equality without "the evil principle, according to which the one was considered a nobleman, the other a commoner."[22] This was indeed a radical position taken by the Slavophiles in the name of the nation. Once again, ancient Russian organic society was contrasted with the formal social organization in the West. According to Kireevsky "ancient Russia knew neither a rigid separation of immobile social estates, nor privileges granted to one estate at the expense of the others." Neither did it know the political and moral struggles that followed from such injustice, or for that matter, class contempt, hatred, or envy. As a result, ancient Russia was spared the inevitable outcome of such a struggle, that is: "artificial formality in public life and a painful process of social development proceeding through the forcible alteration of the laws and the violent overthrow of institutions."[23]

The Slavophiles were modelling their conception of social relations on what Kireevsky described as the Russian ancient social order "without tyranny and slavery, without nobles and commoners." Here, all classes and strata of the population were imbued with "the same spirit, the same convictions and beliefs, and a like desire for the common weal." There might have been differences of opinion on details, but there was hardly ever any discord in essential matters. This society, Kireevsky claimed, was just as free from what he saw as "utopian egalitarianism" as it was from unfair privilege. It could be compared to a ladder with many rungs. These rungs were not meant to be fixed forever, however, for they were set up naturally, as the needs of society required, and not "violently, owing to the contingencies of war, or deliberately, to correspond to logical categories."[24] The nation was based on communal equality, not on political democracy. This social organism had different needs at different times and its constituent parts had their different roles to play according to these needs. But, outside of these roles, every person should be equal to his brother. There should be no high or low except in service to society, which determined the ranks of people according to the diverse virtues or needs of the country. The relationship between various social layers had to be natural, and Khomiakov claimed that if the aristocracy was not part of the common, national spirit, it would divide society and provoke a movement towards political democracy, which to the Slavophiles meant a continuous struggle between differing and separate interests.[25]

According to Khomiakov, the best example of an aristocracy that belonged to the nation was the English. It may seem strange to choose England as a model, since Britain was the most developed, industrialized, urbanized, and democratic country in Europe at the time. Nevertheless, in Khomiakov's view, the English aristocracy was a product of the soil and history of its nation, rather than a formal institution or a separate force in society. This organic relationship was preserved by means of unchanged customs and traditions combined with "the special character of domestic life" in England. It was also strengthened through public education. Khomiakov maintained that English aristocrats did not represent ideas of privileges, power, or administrative forms. Instead, they had given strength to the people and their way of life. Most importantly, the English aristocracy counteracted the fragmentation of village life following the decay of the village. As a consequence, village communities had now been revived.[26] This was obviously an ideal towards which the Russian aristocracy should strive: to be part of the nation. It was the task of the intellectuals to take them there.

As part of their belief in Christian equality, the Slavophiles desired a simple life. Khomiakov asserted that the luxury of the individual always meant "theft and the detriment of society." Instead the rich person should use his surplus wealth to aid the poor, or promote common welfare and enlightenment.[27] Kireevsky stressed that the formation of wealth was a secondary factor in a country's life and should therefore be entirely subordinate to other, more elevated, pursuits.[28] In this context the Slavophiles emphasized the importance of restraining the violence of the strong and of protecting the weak and defenceless. This should not be done by means of contracts and laws, but by means of moral obligations. Duty was the only source of rights. Khomiakov argued that knowledge of one's rights merely strengthened one's will. This led to inequality, since the very weakness of a powerless person made his rights negligible. On the other hand, knowledge of duty imposed limitations on a strong person's will, while for the weak it created and clarified his rights. In Khomiakov's words, "egotism spoke of rights and brotherly love spoke of duty."[29]

The aim of Slavophile nationalism was neither to strengthen the state, nor to tie the nation to it. It was the people, not the state, who were to fulfil the nation's destiny, and it was the intellectuals, not the central government, who were responsible for accomplishing the vital social and moral task necessary for the nation's fulfillment. Consequently, the Slavophiles did not have to concern themselves with the state when they presented their case for social change. It was through the nation that important changes would be made. And in the centre of the nation was the Orthodox Church, not the tsar.[30] This church, the only true Christian one according to the Slavophiles, was closer to the people and thus to the nation than any other Church. It was not as authoritarian as the Catholic Church and not as individualistic as the Protestant Church. While the former represented unity without freedom, and the latter freedom without unity, the Orthodox Church was unity in freedom. It was a free union made through love. Khomiakov claimed that since love could only be found where there was inner freedom, and strength only where there was love, the spiritual forces belonged to the people and its Church and not to the government.[31] Thus, in Slavophile thinking, the Church was connected to the people and the nation, not to the state. Both the Orthodox Church and the Russian people played a vital role in the moral regeneration of the nation.

In order for social relations to be organic and natural, they had to be based on social unity and convictions, rather than artificial contracts.[32] In Russia, social unity had been based on common spiritual principles. According to the Slavophiles, this vital unity had now been shattered. It was not that formal structures had withered, but that faith, by which societies and their members lived, was in decay. This deadening of the human spirit manifested itself in the convulsions of social institutions, for, in Khomiakov's words, "man cannot live without faith."[33] If society had lost its spiritual foundations, neither individuals nor society could develop. The result was moral apathy, lack of conviction, and widespread egoism.[34] What Russia needed was a spiritual and moral revival. The unity, that according to the Slavophiles was lacking in society, was found in the Orthodox Church. Through faith, as an act of spiritual freedom, a Russian society would emerge "full of living and organic forces" and based on the local existence of the community, expressing moral and Christian ideas. Freedom in this sense, found only in the Orthodox faith, meant freedom from formality, legality, and any type of compulsion.[35]

According to this organic concept of freedom, social unity could not be enforced on the nation. It had to be organically developed from within. Hence, the moral revival of society could not be imposed from above, i.e., from the state. Instead, the intellectuals were given the task of restoring the living principles of "Holy Russia" and guiding Russia's culture in a new direction. They were to create a free social unity, that is, to shape a harmonious relationship between all the parts of the nation. Such a unity would constitute a basis for healing the wound inflicted on Russian enlightenment through the gulf between the people and the educated elite. "What was needed was communion, fellowship, consisting of a living change, not of certain concepts, but of feelings . . . and of the sharing, not only of sorrow, but also of the joy of living." Only a fellowship like this might bring Russian intellectuals back to the foundation of real life from the condition of "non-national abstraction" and "dead arbitrary reason." It might bring them to a comprehensive participation in the traditions and ideas of the people.[36] It might bring them back to the nation.

The Slavophiles desired to make the "living principles," preserved in the doctrine of the Orthodox Church part and parcel of the beliefs of all estates and strata of Russian society. Their spiritual force should permeate all relations between people in society and thus create social unity.[37] However, the spiritual and moral values, expressed by these principles, had to be in concert with the customary values of the people. The reason for this was that the principles for a moral revival were not only found in the Orthodox Church and its holy monasteries, but also in the customs of the people, institutionalized in the village commune and the town assemblies.[38] In short, the social principles and norms found both in the Church and the people, the institutions based upon them, and the system they had generated, were to be revived and developed so that they could produce an original Russian culture. In this way, Russian national elements could contribute to all branches of human knowledge and activity. But, as the old institutions, as well as their basic principles, were organic, they could not be revived in some dead old form without "living content." Ideally, they should grow out of the Russians themselves, embodying their inner life.

In a society where life rested on a basic unanimity of views, any impairment of the sanctity of tradition, or the continuity of customary relationships, was bound to destroy the very fabric of social life. In such a society, every change introduced by force as a result of logical reasoning would harm the social organism.[39] According to the Slavophiles this was precisely what happened in Russia as a result of the reforms of Peter the Great. Much of the Slavophile critique of the state was actually presented as criticism against Peter the Great and the modern tsarism he had established.

CRITICISM AGAINST MODERN TSARISM

The Slavophiles maintained, that Peter the Great had adopted a style of autocracy alien to Russian traditions. In trying to reform Russia, through foisting Western civilization on the Russian people, he had broken the organic union between the state and the people. This ancient union was replaced with the domination of the state over the people, or the land. The state had infringed on the freedom of life of the community. The freedom of conscience, thought and opinion had been restricted, turning the people into slaves. Consequently, the trust between the government and the people was destroyed and the monarch became a despot. With the destruction of organic spiritual unity, it became necessary to create a physical, formal unity, resulting in a hierarchical system expressed by serfdom and the *oprichnina*.

As a consequence of this alien system, foreign ideas filtered into Russia and the upper classes lost touch with their native Russian soil. The practice of imitating everything Western had begun and with this the creation of the gulf in Russian society between the educated elite and the people. Previously, the Slavophiles argued, the upper classes identified with the people by sharing their ideas, way of life, customs, and manner of dress. They now suffered more than anyone from Peter the Great's encroachments upon the moral principles which governed their daily life.[40] They became alienated from the life of the people and thereby from spiritual freedom. Hence, modern tsarism could be blamed for the backwardness of the Russian nation. This system of rule was seen as a Western phenomenon with its bureaucratic rationalism, centralization, and expansionist policies. Moreover, the important distinction the Slavophiles made between internal and external truth and between moral and formal law stood in sharp contrast to the realities of the Petersburg regime. The artificial and compulsory nature of government organs, basing themselves on formal, external law, was far from the notion of a natural, voluntary association of people, united through mutual love.

The Slavophile attack against Peter the Great and modern tsarism was seen by Nicholas I as an assault against the regime and on himself as the heir of Peter's legacy. According to official ideology, Peter the Great had elevated the power and glory of Russia to its present splendour. In addition, although trying to legitimate his rule by referring to nationality and orthodoxy, Nicholas wanted to be a European emperor rather than a Russian tsar in the ancient tradition. The Slavophiles' idealized picture of pre-Petrine Russia implied criticism of the bureaucratic autocracy established by Peter the Great. Furthermore, the concept of nationality, propounded by the regime, was quite different from that of the Slavophiles, who found it in the Orthodox faith and in the traditions and custom of the people. To the tsar, nationality had to do with patriotism and traditional loyalty to crown and country. The Russian Church was to serve the tsar, not the reverse. Nicholas did not see his power as bequeathed to him by the people and for this reason he had no intention of changing his method of government to suit traditional custom or religious values.[41] In addition, the tsar must have looked with suspicion on any division between the state and the nation which threatened his control over the whole country. He could not have been satisfied with the limited sphere of government the Slavophiles offered him. Nicholas certainly had good reasons for his misgivings about this group of nationalists.

A RADICAL PROJECT?

It is obvious that changing the focus from the state and the law to the nation and the community implied a radical standpoint at the time. Both the Slavophiles' explicit position against an unlimited state and in favor of a society free from the interference of the state, as well as their notion of brotherly equality, indicate this. As does the importance attached to the role of intellectuals in relation to the nation. In this way, Slavophilism did not just entail a change of focus from the state to the nation, but a change of initiative from the state to the intellectuals. In spite of this, the Slavophiles' social vision has been described by various scholars as conservative, regressive, and as striving to realize a reactionary utopia, in the same way that cultural nationalism in general has been portrayed. The Slavophiles have been accused of being reactionaries, and of rejecting the major social and intellectual developments of their time, i.e., rationalism, secularism and the industrial revolution. Furthermore, Slavophilism has been regarded as an antimodern ideology, "a Russian expression of the counter-revolutionary impulses in Europe, pronounced by spokesmen for an older social order increasingly threatened by new social forces and institutions."[42]

Walicki argues that their social ideal was reactionary and conservative because it was located in the past. But he acknowledges that, in this instance, conservatism cannot be equated with the acceptance of status quo in Russia or opposition to any kind of change. "It was less defence of the present than romantic nostalgia for a lost ideal."[43] Nevertheless, Walicki still regards Slavophilism as conservative, precisely because of its reactionary character. His major reason for this is that the Slavophiles belonged to the aristocracy. His Slavophilism is seen as the ideology of the hereditary nobility, who, "reluctant to stand up for their own selfish interest, attempted to sublimate and universalise traditional values and to create an ideological platform that would unite all classes and social strata representing ancient Russia."[44] Although Walicki suggests that Slavophilism set out to represent the precapitalist social structure as a whole and not the specific interest of the gentry, he nevertheless defines it by the class of its propagators. The problem with this definition is that it makes the Slavophiles look more conservative than they actually were.

Michael Hughes has offered a slightly different interpretation, arguing that the Slavophiles were well-attuned to the opportunities offered to them and their class by the development of an agricultural market in Russia. He finds it problematic to argue that their social and political thought was inspired by fear of economic and social change, when several members of the

Slavophile circle managed their estates in a way that relied on the existence of an agricultural market and the adoption of modern farming methods.[45] Even if selfish class interest had been the sole motive behind their ideas (a position which seems hard to prove), it is clear that their ideas did not represent an antiprogressive defence of status quo. I have shown that their interest in ancient Russia and its traditional values must be seen in a wider intellectual context to be fully understood. Moreover, since both Westernizers and Slavophiles came from the same social stratum but held divergent ideas, reference to class does not exhaust the meaning of their ideas.

How did the Slavophiles themselves describe their social project? First, they portrayed it as a progressive project for social change. Taking part in the progress-oriented European discourse of Romanticism and idealism, they realized that going backwards was not an option. It is true that the Slavophiles wanted to restore the essential principles of, and the basis for, ancient Russia, but this does not mean that they wanted to reestablish medieval Russia. "We certainly did not want to resurrect ancient Russia," Aleksandr Koshelev, a member of the Slavophile circle, wrote in his memoirs. "We were far from rejecting the great discoveries and improvements accomplished in the West."[46] Kireevsky explicitly declared that the Russia of the past could not be restored or brought back. He argued that the distinctive feature of Russian life lay in its living source of pure Christianity, and that this way of life had declined as the spirit weakened. Therefore, this extinct way of life could be of no value today. Kireevsky also asserted that it would be ridiculous, if not actually harmful, to try to resurrect it by force. On one occasion, he wrote that if he ever dreamt that some external feature of Russia's former life had suddenly been revived and, in its former shape, become part of his present existence, it would cause him grief.

> For such an intrusion of the past into the new, the dead into the living, would be tantamount to transferring a wheel from one machine into another, of a different type and size: in such a case, either the wheel or the machine must break.

It is important to realize that it was not the ancient Russian society the Slavophiles wanted to restore, but its "living principles." These principles were seen as the starting point of something new and it was the role of the intellectuals to develop them and to steer them in a new direction. Educated Russians had to study their country's former life in order to comprehend how an original culture could be developed and what principles it entailed. This would result in the evolution of public life in Russia in a completely new direction.[47] Thus, Khomiakov believed in the peasant commune not because it was an old remnant of ancient Russia, but because he believed that an entirely new social order might evolve from its development.[48] This change inevitably involved critique of contemporary Russian society.

We have already seen that the Slavophiles were against imitation, a position that may seem antithetical to the idea of progress. However, according to the Slavophiles, everything that was morally harmful should be rejected, but not that which would entail spiritual or material improvement, "be it art, the steam engine or the railroad." Such improvements should not be repudiated on the pretext that they were dangerous to the unity of life. Khomiakov regarded it as the duty of educated Russians to adopt everything that could enrich the land, expand trade, and improve public welfare. Everything based on wholesome and honest ideas should be adopted. The results of abstract and applied sciences were presented as examples of useful adoption. In this field, Khomiakov argued, the civilized world constituted a whole and every people used the discoveries and inventions of other people without downgrading their own value or losing their ability for independent development.

The main argument was that there was a difference between ideas of universal human value, which the Russians imported from the West, and the local, temporary forms they were dressed in there. It was the latter that could not be adopted in Russia.[49] The Slavophiles' notion of social change was in fact closely related to their concept of the nation and its role. The view of the nation as a provider of national form to universal human values made it possible for Russia to contribute something original to humanity while preserving its unique character. The fact that the Slavophiles used the West as their point of reference meant that they neither wished to, nor could, isolate themselves from developments in the West. Their nationalism was linked to a belief in progress.

The Slavophiles themselves presented their social project as a national mission, rather than as a conservative, or indeed any other political enterprise. Their focus was on the nation and its moral regeneration, not on the state and its politics. To them, this was an important distinction. But, it was equally essential to demonstrate that progress could be found in the nation. Khomiakov expressed this view of the relationship between nationalism, conservatism, and progress in his "Letter on England." There, he challenged those who labelled Tories "conservatives" and called Whigs "friends of progress", because he found that when it came to improvements in laws, institutions, and social structure, they came as often from

Tories as from Whigs. According to Khomiakov's interpretation, Whigs, or the "friends of freedom," tried hard to eliminate the freedom of instruction, which the Tories tried to protect. What is more, the Whigs, who were not only friends of freedom, but also democrats, imported aristocratic power and supported it for a long time, while Tories fought against it. Centralization, which Khomiakov believed to be harmful for the free development of life, was always defended by Whigs and denigrated by Tories. Whigs disliked the multitude of communities, which had developed organically. Therefore, they tried to detach people from these communities and attach them to the political centre and its formal law. As a result, natural social bonds were destroyed and replaced by conditional bonds. These bonds, Khomiakov argued, seemed less severe, but were actually less free, precisely because they were conditional, and not based on love.[50]

The reason why Toryism often appeared as stagnant conservatism, even when, in Khomiakov's words, it tried to "develop the germs already lying in society," was that it was constituted by an organic, living, historical force, which was already weakened by the decay of the village community and its way of life and also by the scepticism of Protestantism.

Whigism, on the other hand, was based on an individual and analytic force, which had no connections to its past. It had been established by the same decay of village life and was made stronger by the demoralizing force of Protestantism. For this reason Whigism often appeared to be a liberating force, even when it actually hampered life. In fact, Khomiakov claimed, noble voices in the service of humanity and truth against violence and conquest were more often heard from the ranks of the Tory party than from the Whigs. "One-sided development of the individual mind, rejecting the history and traditions of society, that was the meaning of Whigism in England, or in any country."[51]

Khomiakov's assertion that the terms Whig and Tory did not have a political, but a social meaning, constitutes a good example of the limited role the Slavophiles assigned to the state and the government. These terms had a social meaning because they defined the way of life of the English people. Khomiakov argued that Toryism was to be found just as much among ordinary people as among the highest ranks of society. It had nothing to do with how people voted. Khomiakov was well aware that merchants and artisans gave their vote to the Whigs. He believed this was only natural, since they acted according to their conviction of the commonweal or social benefit, but, he argued, in their heart they loved the Tories. This was so because Toryism epitomized Englishness. "Whigism—that is the daily bread; Toryism—that is every joy of life." Hence, because he was

English, a Whig was really a Tory in his soul.[52] The reason for this, in Khomiakov's opinion, was that Whigism in England retained its bonds with the people and with the spiritual essence of the country even when it broke with its traditions and its historical past. In Russia, on the other hand, "Whigism" (or essentially liberalism) had not been generated by the inner law of the people's spiritual life. As a consequence, it turned into a protest against the very essence of this life. It renounced the entire Russian foundation and broke away from it.[53]

It is clear that the Slavophiles, or at least Khomiakov, favoured conservatism, but not as a regressive or preservationist ideology. Khomiakov did believe in a conservative utopia, but only as a means to something new. One could say that he believed in conservatism as a progressive force that was also a national force. Slavophilism was a national project, not a political one, in the sense of dealing with power and government. Since progress was found in the nation, and conservatism was concerned with the development of the nation, it had to be a progressive force. To take but one example: Khomiakov wrote in a comment on Iurii Samarin's, project, that his (Samarin's) work was truly progressive because it was truly conservative. "I find great comfort in the fight which is now taking place by the fact that among many mistaken conservatives I see the beginning of a real progress, which I do not often meet among imaginary progressives."[54]

Conclusion

To Russian intellectuals of the 1830s and 1840s, the imitated character of Russian culture constituted a central problem. It was emphasized by representatives of all kinds of ideological currents. Previously, imitation had been regarded as a way to modernize Russia. In the eighteenth century, the role of the Russian intellectuals had been to absorb, express, and disseminate European culture. In this role, they saw themselves as European intellectuals, identifying with European culture and learning. The Decembrists were the last representatives of this view.

With the new Romantic agenda this practice became unacceptable. Now, demands for a unique, national culture were raised. In order to be part of Europe, Russia had to offer a genuine contribution to European culture; but she had nothing to offer. Her imitated culture was no longer of value. To the contrary, Russia's lack of cultural originality became a sign of backwardness. It questioned Russia's role as a nation, and as a consequence, it questioned the role of Russian intellectuals as cultural leaders.

Regarding themselves as representatives of education, civilization, and progress in their country, the intellectuals had to assume responsibility for the absence of a genuine Russian culture. They could not act as cultural leaders if there was no culture to lead. Since the role of both the nation and the intellectuals were questioned simultaneously, both suffered from a crisis of identity.

Hence, Slavophilism was not just a reactionary response to modernization, or a conservative utopia as it has sometimes been described. Nor should it be seen merely as an argument in defence of Russia against the criticism of Chaadaev, de Custine, and Belinsky. Slavophilism was formulated as a conscious attempt to counter the sense of backwardness among members of Russia's educated elite and find a way out of a dual crisis of identity. Since these two problems were intertwined, the solution had to accommodate both the need for a national identity and an identity for the intellectuals.

According to the new intellectual agenda, every person was connected to a specific context, which constituted an essential basis for his or her development. In other words, while in the eighteenth century educated Russians had to be European in order to be part of Europe, in the nineteenth century, they now had to be Russian. Romanticism was responsible for both identifying imitation as a problem in the first place, and for the solution to this problem. Romanticism purported that there was a national spirit inherent in every people or nation, which in turn gave a specific character to its culture and way of life. However, if the culture of a nation was not "national," i.e. did not express its national spirit, it was possible to resuscitate the dormant national spirit through a moral regeneration of the national community.

This was precisely what the Slavophiles suggested through their notion of a specific Russian enlightenment. It was an attempt to develop a latent Russian culture so it could make a Russian contribution to universal enlightenment, that is, to the universal development of culture and learning. In contrast to the material, empirical enlightenment of the West, the Russian enlightenment was presented as a spiritual enlightenment. Traces of an ancient Russian culture were preserved in the traditional life of the people, but it had to be articulated and interpreted in order to develop. In fact, a Russian enlightenment would not start to develop until the Russian way of life was joined with the progress of science. The customs of the people had to be articulated and developed in a process that involved a union between Western science and the principles of the Russian way of life. It was not a question of making these spiritual principles rational in a logical sense, but of adding thought and learning to them. On the one hand, Western learning was to give common significance to the peculiarity of the Russian way of life and push it forward, although without transforming it. On the other hand, the principles of the Russian way of life were to give Western science higher meaning; and to develop it to its ultimate perfection so it could be joined with the "true" enlightenment of Russia on a higher level. By giving intellectuals and artists the responsibility to carry out this task, the Slavophiles solved their crisis of identity.

The notion of a Russian enlightenment created a new role for educated Russians as exponents of their culture's fundamental principles. They were to express this original culture and present it to the world. As a consequence, Russia's role in universal history could be realized. Thus, as regards the realization of the Russian enlightenment, the Slavophiles placed the initiative clearly with the intellectuals. In contrast, both the people and the state were to remain passive in the process of regenerating the national community.

The nationalism of the Slavophiles was not a state-oriented nationalism aimed at political power. Rather, it was oriented towards national culture, and focused on the nation and the intellectuals in a symbiotic relationship. The nation, in the sense of the Russian way of life, needed the intellectuals as its interpreters and articulators. The intellectuals, on their part, needed the nation as their source for moral development.

Despite its orientation towards culture, Slavophilism can be seen as a conscious project for social change. The fact that the Slavophiles chose to turn away from the state did not imply that they rejected the idea of social improvements, but it did imply that the transformation of society should not be carried out through the state. Instead, social change should be achieved through moral regeneration of the nation. No longer were the state, and the constitution, seen as the means for reform, as they had to the previous generation of Russian intellectuals, and would be to Russian liberals in the second half of the nineteenth century.

The change of focus, from the state and the law as the basis of society to the nation and the community, involved similar intellectual criticism against the unlimited state and the central government. But, while the Decembrists had seen the creation of a constitutional monarchy as the solution to Russia's predicament, the Slavophiles saw the solution in the rebirth of the nation. In order for the nation to develop its moral and spiritual principles, it had to be safeguarded from the harmful influence of the state. The moral regeneration had to be developed organically from within the life of the people, not formally enforced from above. Dead form could not revive living content. For this reason, it was the duty of the educated Russians to rejoin the nation, from which they had alienated themselves; and to restore its dormant principles and direct them on a new path.

In Slavophilism, Enlightenment ideals of progress, enlightenment, and universalism were still upheld. One of the Slavophiles' main objectives was to make it possible for Russia to present a cultural contribution to humanity. In its wish to contribute to a common European culture and to incorporate the learning of the West into the Russian enlightenment, this version of Russian nationalism was not antagonistic to the West. The study therefore questions the notion that Russian nationalism is defined in opposition to Europe. A case in point is the use of Slavophile ideas as an inspiration for the formulation of Russian socialism. Alexander Herzen used the Slavophile notion of a specific Russian communal structure in order to argue that conditions for the realization of socialism were especially favourable there. He also made use of the Slavophile critique of Western industrialism, capitalism, and individualism, while praising Russian peasants and the village commune. Like the Slavophiles, Herzen tried to fuse native Russian principles with European achievements. In his view, the traditional Russian way of life, free of bourgeois tendencies, could be used to make a national contribution to world socialism. To Herzen, it was in fact the only remaining hope for socialism after the failure of the European Revolutions in 1848.[1]

Interpreting Slavophilism as a conscious project for social change, this book also questions the notion of cultural nationalism as a movement without any political significance. It argues that the dichotomy between cultural/conservative and political/liberal nationalism needs to be reformulated in order to point to differences in aims and strategies, rather than in ideological basis. The conclusion to be drawn from this reformulation is that all nationalism is about social change and thus of political significance. Nevertheless, the Slavophiles' project was a failure, in the sense that it did not lead to any movement of consequence before intellectual life was taken over by more extreme ideas. The liberalization of society after the death of the repressive tsar Nicholas I, brought with it a feeling of urgency among Russian intellectuals; a wish to make up for lost time. When social changes were suddenly feasible, they wished for rapid, far-reaching changes. Romantic ideas about a moral regeneration of the nation seemed irrelevant to those who believed radical social change could only be achieved through political means.

The radicalization of the socialists made the position of the conservatives equally uncompromising. On the one hand were those who wanted an immediate and radical transformation of Russian society; on the other hand were those who wished to preserve the autocracy against what they saw as the dangerous effects of a revolution. Hence, to the conservatives, Slavophile ideas were just as inappropriate. The polarization in Russian intellectual life after the death of Nicholas I, between extreme conservatives and extreme revolutionaries, can perhaps account for the failure of the comparably moderate Slavophiles. Their ideas were adopted by representatives of various ideological currents and transformed in different directions. Both socialists, conservatives, and pan-Slavists made use of their ideas.

Miroslav Hroch has developed a model for the process by which national movements shape modern nations. He distinguishes three structural phases between the starting point of any given national movement and its successful conclusion. During the initial period, Phase A, activists are devoted to scholarly enquiry into the linguistic, cultural, social, and historical attributes of their ethnic group. They engage in disseminating an awareness of these attributes, but do not press specifically national de-mands. In Phase B, a new range of activists try to persuade all members of their ethnic group to join in the project of creating a future nation, by im-planting or awakening a national consciousness among them. Once the major part of the population has come to value their national identity, a mass movement is formed, which Hroch has termed Phase C. During this phase, when a full organizational structure has come into being, the move-ment differentiates into conservative, liberal, and democratic wings.[2]

The relationship between the transition from one of these phases to another and the transition to a constitutional society, has led Hroch to dis-tinguish between four types of national movements. In the first two types, national agitation began under the old regime of absolutism. In the first type, such as the Norwegian and the Czech movements, the transition to a mass movement occurred at a time of revolutionary changes in the polit-ical system, when an organized labour movement was beginning to assert itself. In the second type, the transition was delayed until a constitutional revolution had been completed, as in Lithuania, Slovenia, and the Ukraine. In the third type, which was confined to the European posses-sions of the Ottoman Empire, the national movement acquired a mass character already under absolutism, leading to armed insurrection. In the fourth type, national agitation first began under constitutional conditions, as in the Basque lands and Catalonia.[3]

Obviously, Slavophile nationalism does not correspond to any of these types. It never entered Phase C in Hroch's model, the final period when a mass movement was being formed. Indeed, it never even reached Phase B since the new range of activists, who were to turn the scholarly project into a popular social movement, never came to be part of the original Slavophile movement. Very likely, an important reason for this was that the Russians were not oppressed by another dominant ethnic or cultural group. Instead, they themselves constituted the dominant group of the empire. Whereas the nation and the nation-state were not congruent; the state was domi-nated by Russians. To nationalists, this was a nation oppressed by her own government and by the westernized elite, but most of all by cultural imita-tion. However, when social mobility allowed the middle-classes to be edu-cated, they did not take on the scholarly project of the nationalists. Instead they chose to devote themselves to a more radical movement with a pro-gramme of greater political relevance to them. Since they did not belong to a suppressed ethnic group, but to an inferior social group, class analysis of society was far more appropriate than ethnic analysis for solving their predicament. Therefore, in the long run, Russian nationalism as a political force lost its impetus. It was superseded by another more radical, but similarly elitist, modernizing movement whose members, unlike the Slavophiles, were conscious of the power of the masses and the necessity to control the state in order to reform society.

According to John Hutchinson, cultural nationalism is seldom able to extend beyond the educated strata. He argues that, in terms of its communitarian goals, cultural nationalism is bound to fail. It is forced to adopt state-oriented strategies to institutionalize its ideals in the social order. The goals of cultural nationalism have to be translated into concrete social, economic, or political programs by political nationalists.[4] In Russia, this political driving force of cultural nationalism was lacking. Hence, the transition from Hroch's Phase A to Phase B was never accomplished. In this respect, Slavophilism was a double failure. It did not succeed in realizing any full-scale social transformation, nor did it achieve its communitarian goals by shifting into state politics, and eliciting political nationalism.

Yet, the claim that Slavophilism was a failure is true only if its aim was to achieve mass mobilization or enforced social transformation. According to the Slavophiles' own goals and strategies, their project was in many ways a success. They did not have any intention of forming a mass movement. Their main ambition was to create an impetus for cultural and moral transformation in their homeland by altering the way in which people thought about Russia. The Slavophiles strove for a moral regeneration of the nation in order for a genuine Russian culture to evolve and they certainly succeeded in that endeavour.

In the decades following the formulation of Slavophilism, the most remarkable phase of cultural production appeared in Russia, which left no one in doubt as to Russia's contribution to European culture.[5] What is more, the Slavophiles formed a notion of a Russian nationality, a new identity for the Russian nation based on spiritual and communal values. This identity has continued to be articulated and reformulated by Russian artists and intellectuals. It is a recurrent idea that has appeared in different forms at times of ideological transformation and social unrest before, during, and after the Soviet period.[6] Hutchinson may be right that by rejecting the state, cultural nationalists cannot transform social institutions according to their communitarian ideals, but that does not mean that they are incapable of making cultural changes that have a bearing on a people's values and self-perceptions and, ultimately, on society.

The first clear post-Slavophile manifestation of the Russian idea appeared in the compilation of essays called *Vekhi* (Landmarks), published as a reaction to the experience of the Revolution of 1905.[7] Common to all contributors was their rejection of Marxism in favour of spiritual values. A fundamental tendency in the essays was a call for a religious, metaphysical worldview in contrast to the dominating positivistic and materialistic view.[8] Many of the writers claimed that material socialism was an outcome of Western individualistic rationalism, since both socialism and individualism idealized freedom and lacked norms and morality. The adherence to utilitarian ethics among members of the radical intelligentsia prevented them from understanding real, i.e. divine truth. The *Vekhi*-writers were afraid that the nihilism of the radicals would lead people away from Christian values to a world where everything would be allowed as long as it was done in the name of the common good. The recommendation of the writers was to turn to Russia's own tradition instead of importing Western doctrines. The "Russian idea" would save the country from the destruction to which nihilism would inevitably lead it.

The main criticism against the radical intelligentsia was that in their efforts to overthrow the existing regime, they had subordinated all considerations of truth, morality, and intellectual integrity. Just like the Slavophiles, the *Vekhi*-writers stressed the inner, spiritual life over the external forms of society. Hence, moral self-perfection was far more important than social and political reforms. In their view, the real task was for each individual to change himself, rather than to transform society. In this way, society would be transformed through a transformation of its members.[9] The mechanistic worldview, promulgated by radical intellectuals, gave birth to the idea that man was God and everything that was wrong could be corrected by man via external reforms. This led to an absence of principles and norms in society. Another argument taken from the Slavophiles was that Russia did not need a written constitution. Inner law was more important than formal law. The relationship between ruler and the ruled should be based on solidarity, mutual confidence, and ethical motives rather than on laws and guarantees.

After the October Revolution, it seemed as if Slavophile thought had played out its role once and for all, but after Stalin's death, the Slavophile notion of the Russian way of life reappeared. The disclosure of Stalin's crimes, made in the name of Marxism-Leninism, paved the way for public criticism of society. Intellectuals searched for alternative ideas and voices were raised for Russia to choose a "third path" between the East and the West, i.e. for a specific Russian way. In this more open intellectual climate, the "Russian idea" had a renaissance. In the works of the so-called village writers, Marxism-Leninism was depicted as a Western doctrine and its negative effects were criticized. This group was antiprogressive and antimodern in a way the Slavophiles had not been. Not only did the village writers disapprove of industrialization and urbanization, but of progressive thinking on the whole. Modernization was seen as a completely un-Russian phenomenon, which caused moral degeneration. The main criticism of these writers was directed against the decay of the Russian village, which, in their view, had led to the spread of egoism and "cold rationalism" in Soviet life. They idealized the Russian village community and stressed that it needed protection against the growth of individualism because it destroyed the feeling of solidarity between people. The village writers believed that the Russian way of life was preserved in the Russian village, and that it was expressed in the moral values and popular traditions of the countryside. In line with the Slavophiles, they exhorted the Russian intelligentsia to stop adopting Western ideas and change their negative attitude towards the "Russian idea."[10]

In 1975, a compilation, considered a follower of the *Vekhi* collection, called *From Under the Rubble*, was published.[11] It was the most pronounced position in favour of the "Russian idea" during the Soviet epoch. Certain traits common with Slavophilism can be recognized, such as the critique against adopting Western ideas and the call for a moral regeneration of the nation. Marxism was accused of striving to extinguish Russian tradition and history. A society without history, traditions, religion, and morals would lead humanity to its destruction.[12]

Capitalism was just as bad as communism, however, basing itself on the same idea of constant growth. Both systems led to rootlessness and degeneration. The main thesis of the contributors was that there was a third way for Russia, a road away from modernization, growth, centralization, and atheism led by spiritual experience rather than by logic.[13] The social structure should be founded on spiritual and moral principles and develop organically. Hence, internal rather than external development should be promoted. An example to be avoided was the Western practice of replacing unconditional equality before God with conditional equality before the law. In such a society, man was turned into a juridical abstraction. What Russia needed was a development towards moral aims and inner perfection.[14] But in order to restore vital spiritual values to society, a moral regeneration of Russia was needed. The contributors to *From Under the Rubble* felt that Russian national feeling had been repressed far too long.[15]

Since the fall of the Soviet Union, there has been a resurgent interest in the Russian idea. Once again the question of the identity of the Russian nation and its relation to Europe was at the centre stage of intellectual discussions. Questions like "Who are we?" and "What makes us special?" were posed. The nation's originality and objective value had to be determined. Russia was regarded as neither a higher nor an inferior civilization compared to other countries, only a different one. Once again, intellectuals assumed the task of formulating concrete conceptions about the genuine basis from which Russia should develop.[16] Many intellectuals stressed the importance of turning to national traditions and of getting to know Russia's history, religion, philosophy, and literature. The national character had to be revitalized and the moral principles associated with it had to be regenerated. A rebirth of the nation and its distinctive traditions and culture, still preserved in the people, was considered essential for the future of Russia.[17]

Many nationalists expressed discontent with the imitation of Western ideas. In their view, both socialism and capitalism were antinational ideologies, which deprived man of his communal native roots. Communism was transferred to Russia from the West without any regard for national history and traditions. Because these foreign ideas were badly adjusted to the conditions of social life in Russia, they caused great harm to the nation. In the name of Western rationalism, morality, and social bonds were destroyed. According to several nationalists, people's life should be based on moral and spiritual principles rather than on logic or mathematical calculations.[18]

The right way for Russia is, therefore, inner development and perfection. It is a road of humility and love, founded on spiritual values. The new Russia should be built on community and its social structure must grow organically from the culture and history of the nation.[19] In making this claim, nationalists distinguish the organic community from an individualistic society based on law. Just like the Slavophiles, they argue that contracts and laws are needed only if there is no faith, no confidence in other people.[20]

Even the Communist leader, Gennadii Ziuganov, uses the "Russian idea" to mobilize people. He talks about the need for a spiritual regeneration and the protection of national traditions, culture, spiritual values, and moral ideals. The purpose of the state, he holds, should be "to organise life in accordance with truth, conscience, and justice."[21] Some contemporary intellectuals present an answer to the query as to Russia's future identity in a way that reminds us of the Slavophiles' effort to combine ostensibly conflicting values. They portray a picture of Russia as a union between universal and national values, and as a perfect blend of national traditions, faith, and foreign experience.[22]

The notion of a specific "Russian idea" has constituted an important part of the self-perception of Russian intellectuals ever since it was first formulated in the second quarter of the nineteenth century. Whether it is a useful basis for the contemporary Russian nation is an open question, and it has not been the purpose of this study to answer it. Clearly, however, there is a similarity between the national problems expressed by the Slavophiles and those articulated by contemporary Russian intellectuals. The perception of backwardness, and of not being admitted as an equal partner in Europe which motivated the Slavophile project, is presented as Russia's greatest predicament today. Yet, as far as the original national idea formulated by the Slavophiles is concerned, the answer to this predicament lies neither in isolationism nor in an antagonistic posture towards the West, but in working towards a Russian contribution to a common European culture.

Notes

INTRODUCTION

1. Although the Slavophiles have exerted great influence on Russia's intellectual life and on present-day nationalists, they have not attracted the interest of Western scholars in the same way. The main works on the Slavophiles published in the West are F. Rouleau, *Ivan Kireievski et la naissance du Slavophilisme* (Namur: Culture et verité, 1990); A. Walicki, *The Slavophile Controversy* (Oxford: Clarendon, 1975); A. Gleason, *European and Muscovite: Ivan Kireevsky and the Origins of Slavophilism* (Cambridge, MA: Harvard University Press, 1972); P. K. Christoff, *An Introduction to Nineteenth Century Slavophilism*, vol. I, *A. S. Xomjakov* (The Hague: Mouton, 1961); vol. II, *I. V. Kireevsky* (The Hague: Mouton, 1972); vol. III, *K. S. Aksakov* (Princeton, NJ: Mouton, 1982); vol. IV, *Iu. Samarin* (Boulder: Mouton, 1991); N. V. Riasanovsky, *Russia and the West in the Teaching of the Slavophiles* (Cambridge, MA: Harvard University Press, 1952). Notable recent works in Russian are E. A. Dudzinskaia, *Slavianofily v poreformennoi Rossii* (Moscow, 1994); B. F. Yegorov, V. A. Kotelnikov, and Iu. V. Stennik, eds., *Slavianofilstvo i sovremennost* (St. Petersburg, Russia, 1994); N. I. Tsimbaev, *Slavianofilstvo: iz istorii russkoi obshchestvenno-politicheskoi mysli XIX veka* (Moscow: Izdatelstvo Moskovskogo universiteta, 1986); E. A. Dudzinskaia, *Slavianofily v obshchestvennoi borbe* (Moscow, 1983); Iu. Z. Iankovskii, *Patriarkhalno-dvorianskaia utopiia* (Moscow: Khudozhestvennaia literatura, 1981).

2. Walicki, *The Slavophile Controversy*, pp. 6, 450–54.

3. See Walicki, *The Slavophile Controversy*; A. Walicki, *A History of Russian Thought from the Enlightenment to Marxism* (Stanford: Stanford University Press, 1979); M. Raeff, *Russian Intellectual History. An Anthology* (New York: Harcout, 1966); A. Gleason, *European and Muscovite*; Iankovskii, *Patriarkhalno-dvorianskaia utopiia*; S. Carter, *Russian Nationalism. Yesterday, Today, Tomorrow* (London: Pinter, 1990); L. Greenfeld, *Nationalism. Five Roads to Modernity* (Cambridge, MA: Harvard University Press, 1993). For a different view, see Dudzinskaia *Slavianofily v obshchestvennoi borbe*; E. A. Dudzinskaia, *Slavianofily v poreformennoi Rossii* (Moscow, 1994); Tsimbaev, *Slavianofilstvo: iz istorii russkoi obshchestvennoi-politicheskoi mysli XIX veka*; D. Saunders, *Russia in the Age of Reaction and Reform 1801–1881* (New York: Longman, 1992).

4. F. Meinecke, *Cosmopolitanism and the National State* (Princeton: Princeton University Press, 1970), pp. 10, 12.

5. H. Kohn, *The Idea of Nationalism* (New York, 1945), pp. 3–4, 329–31. See J. Plamenatz, "Two Types of Nationalism" in *Nationalism*, ed. E. Kamenka (Canberra: Australian National University Press, 1973) for a similar distinction between Eastern and Western nationalism.

6. M. Hughes, *Nationalism and Society. Germany 1800–1945* (London: Arnold, 1988), pp. 22–23. See R. Brubaker for a similar view, *Citizenship and Nationhood in France and Germany* (Cambridge, MA: Harvard University Press, 1992). Liah Greenfeld upholds this distinction between a culturally based "ethnic nationalism" and a political "civic nationalism" in her *Nationalism*. See also M. Ignatieff, *Blood and Belonging: Journeys into the New Nationalism* (New York: Farrar, Straus and Giroux, 1993); P. Sugar, ed., *Eastern European Nationalism in the Twentieth Century* (Washington, DC: American University Press, 1995). Andrzej Walicki talks about two different types of Romantic nationalism; the progressive and the conservative, see *Philosophy and Romantic Nationalism: The Case of Poland* (Oxford: Clarendon, 1982), p. 77.

7. W. Kymlicka, "Misunderstanding Nationalism"; K. Nielsen, "Cultural Nationalism, Neither Ethnic nor Civic"; B. Yack, "The Myth of the Civic Nation" in R. Beiner, ed., *Theorizing Nationalism* (Albany: State University of New York Press, 1999).

8. See E. Kedourie, *Nationalism* (London: Hutchinson, 1966), p. 58; E. Gellner, *Nations and Nationalism* (Oxford: Blackwell, 1983), pp. 57–61; A. D. Smith, *Theories of Nationalism* (London: Duckworth, 1983), pp. 171–211; J. Breuilly, *Nationalism and the State* (Manchester, England: Manchester University Press,1993), pp. 1–2; Greenfeld, *Nationalism*; Kohn, *Idea of Nationalism*; Hughes, *Nationalism and Society*.

9. F. C. Beiser, *Enlightenment, Revolution, and Romanticism: The Genesis of Modern German Political Thought 1790–1800* (Cambridge, MA: Harvard University Press, 1992); J. Hutchinson, *The Dynamics of Cultural Nationalism: The Gaelic Revival and the Creation of the Irish Nation State* (London: Allen & Unwin, 1987).

10. Beiser, *Enlightenment, Revolution, and Romanticism*, pp. 8, 206–208.

11. Hutchinson, *Dynamics of Cultural Nationalism*. See also K. Yoshino, *Cultural Nationalism in Contemporary Japan* (London: Routledge, 1992); A-chin Hsiau, *Contemporary Taiwanese Cultural Nationalism* (London: Routledge, 2000); G. Jusdanis, *The Necessary Nation* (Princeton, NJ: Princeton University Press, 2001).

12. Hutchinson, *Dynamics of Cultural Nationalism*, pp. 2–3.

13. Ibid., pp. 9, 14–16; I. Berlin, *Vico and Herder: Two Studies in the History of Ideas* (London: Hogarth Press, 1976), p. 26.

14. S. Huntington, *The Clash of Civilizations and the Remaking of World Order* (New York: Simon & Schuster, 1996).

15. R. Pipes, *The Russian Revolution* (New York: Knopf, 1990); Pipes, *Russia under the Bolshevik Regime* (New York: Knopf, 1994); Pipes, *Russia under the Old Regime*; Pipes, *Property and Freedom* (New York: Knopf, 1999).

16. See for example, T. Szamuely, ed., *The Russian Tradition* (London: Secher & Warburg, 1974); A. Yanov, *The Origins of Autocracy: Ivan the Terrible in Russian History* (Berkeley: University of California Press, 1981); J. Steele, *Eternal Russia: Yeltsin, Gorbachev,*

and the Mirage of Democracy (London: Faber & Faber, 1994); Pipes, *Russia under the Old Regime*. For a more favourable view of Russia's distinctiveness, although with different emphasis, see N. O. Lossky, *History of Russian Philosophy* (New York: International University Press, 1951); J. M. Edie, J. P. Scanlan, and M. Zeldin, eds., *Russian Philosophy*, vol. 1 (Chicago: Quadrangle books, 1965); N. Berdiaev, *The Russian Idea* (London, 1947) and *The Origin of Russian Communism* (London: The Centenary Press, 1937); J. Billington, *The Icon and the Axe: An Interpretive History of Russian Culture* (New York: Knopf, 1966); Christoff, *An Introduction to Nineteenth Century Slavophilism* I;. M. Lotman and B. A. Uspenskii, "Binary Models in the Dynamics of Russian Culture" in *The Semiotics of Russian Cultural History*, ed. A. D. Nakhimovsky and A. S. Nakhimovsky (Ithaca, NY: Cornell University Press, 1985); Tim McDaniel takes a more neutral position arguing for the uniqueness of the cultural pattern of social change in Russia in *The Agony of the Russian Idea* (Princeton: Princeton University Press, 1996).

17. Kohn, *Idea of Nationalism*; Yanov, *The Russian New Right: Right-Wing Ideologies in the Contemporary USSR* (Berkeley: University of California Press, 1978); Yanov, *The Russian Challenge and the Year 2000* (Oxford: Blackwell, 1987); Pipes, *The Russian Revolution*; S. Carter, *Russian Nationalism*, pp. 147–49; Greenfeld, *Nationalism*; T. Parland, *The Rejection in Russia of Totalitarian Socialism and Liberal Democracy. A Study of the Russian New Right* (Helsinki: Finnish Society of Sciences and Letters, 1993), pp. 11–13, 23, 48; I. Neumann, *Russia and the Idea of Europe* (London: Routledge, 1996).

18. Kohn, *Idea of Nationalism*, p. 330.

19. Yanov, *The Russian Challenge*, p. xii; D. G. Rowley, "Russian Nationalism and the Cold War," *American Historical Review* 99 (February 1994): 169–70; Greenfeld, *Nationalism*, chap. 1.

20. Kohn, *Idea of Nationalism*, p. 330.

21. Neumann, *Russia and the Idea of Europe*, pp. 1–2; I. Prizel, *National Identity and Foreign Policy. Nationalism and Leadership in Poland, Russia and Ukraine* (Cambridge: Cambridge University Press, 1998), pp. 16–18, 23–29, 166–67.

22. Greenfeld, *Nationalism*, pp. 15–17. See also G. A. Hosking, *Russia: People and Empire, 1552–1917* (Cambridge, MA: Harvard University Press, 1997), p. 275–76

23. Liah Greenfeld perceives the conflict between socialists and liberals as one between Russia and the West (Greenfeld, *Nationalism*, pp. 263–70).

24. Gleason, *European and Muscovite*; Walicki, *Slavophile Controversy*; Neumann, *Russia and the Idea of Europe*, pp. 28–39; D. Offord, *Portraits of Early Russian Liberals. A Study of the Thought of T. N. Granovsky, V. P. Botkin, P. V. Annenkov, A. V. Druzhinin, and K. D. Kavelin* (Cambridge: Cambridge University Press, 1985), pp. 9–10. It should be noted that both David Saunders and Nikolai Tsimbaev treat the Slavophiles as liberals. See D. Saunders, *Russia in the Age of Reaction and Reform*; Tsimbaev, *Slavianofilstvo*.

25. Christoff makes this point although he does not pursue it. P. Christoff, *The Third Heart: Some Intellectual-Ideological Currents and Cross Currents in Russia 1800–1830* (The Hague: Mouton, 1970). See also L. Schapiro and J. Billington for a similar view, although Billington emphasizes the Slavophilism of the Westernizers more. L. Schapiro, *Rationalism and Nationalism in Russian Nineteenth-Century Political Thought* (New Haven: Yale

University Press, 1967), p. 64; Billington, *Icon and the Axe*, pp. 320, 324. Alexander Herzen arrives at a similar conclusion in his memoirs *My Past and Thoughts: The Memoirs of Alexander Herzen*, 4 vols. (London: Chatto & Windus, 1968).

26. M. Malia, *Russia under Western Eyes. From the Bronze Horseman to the Lenin Mausoleum* (Cambridge, MA: Harvard University Press, 1999), pp. 12–14.

27. Unless stated otherwise, all translations from Russian are mine.

28. There were other liberal Westernizers, such as Konstantin Kavelin and Aleksandr Druzhinin. But they are not discussed here, since I am only concerned with the radical Westernizers. For a detailed account of the liberal Westernizers see Offord, *Portraits of Early Russian Liberals*. See also P. R. Roosevelt, *Apostle of Russian Liberalism: Timofei Granovsky* (Newtonville: Oriental research partners, 1986); G. M. Hamburg, *Boris Chicherin and Early Russian Liberalism, 1828–1866* (Stanford: Stanford University Press, 1992); A. Walicki, *Legal Philosophies of Russian Liberalism* (Oxford: Clarendon, 1987).

29. A. Walicki, *A History of Russian Thought*, p. 147.

30. See P. Boobbyer, "Russian Liberal Conservatism," in *Russian Nationalism Past and Present*, ed. G. Hosking and R. Service (Basingstoke: Macmillan Press, 1998); Greenfeld, *Nationalism*.

31. Romanticism is used here in a very broad sense, including both the political thought of J. G. Herder and the idealistic philosophy of F. W. Hegel.

32. Riasanovsky, *Russia and the West in the Teaching of the Slavophiles*, p. 11; Saunders, *Russia in the Age of Reaction and Reform*, pp. 117, 162.

33. M. Malia, "What Is the Intelligentsia?" *Daedalus* (Summer 1960): 451; Riasanovsky, *Russia and the West in the Teaching of the Slavophiles*, p. 11; Saunders, *Russia in the Age of Reaction and Reform*, pp. 162, 166; Schapiro, *Rationalism and Nationalism*, pp. 62–63, 67.

34. F. C. Copleston, *Philosophy in Russia. From Herzen to Lenin and Berdyaev* (Notre Dame: University of Notre Dame Press, 1986), p. 47.

35. Riasanovsky, *Russia and the West in the Teaching of the Slavophiles*, p. 154; Saunders, *Russia in the Age of Reaction and Reform*, pp. 154–55.

36. The Third Department was a police agency founded by Nicholas I in 1826, which was known for its malevolence (Saunders, *Russia in the Age of Reaction and Reform*, p. 117).

37. Saunders, *Russia in the Age of Reaction and Reform*, pp. 154–57; Pipes, *Russia under the Old Regime*, pp. 292–93.

38. See Gleason, *European and Muscovite*; Walicki, *Slavophile Controversy*; Offord, *Portraits of Early Russian Liberals*; M. Hughes, "'Independent Gentlemen': The Social Position of the Moscow Slavophiles and Its Impact on Their Political Thought," *The Slavonic and East European Review* 71, no. 1 (1993); Lotman and Uspenskii, "Binary Models in the Dynamics of Russian Culture"; N. Berdiaev, *The Russian Idea*.

39. See F. Steppun, "Nemetskii romantizm i russkoe slavianofilstvo," *Russkaia Mysl* (March 1910); Lossky, *History of Russian Philosophy*; Riasanovsky, *Russia and the West in the Teaching of the Slavophiles*; I. Berlin, "Russian Thought and the Slavophile Controversy,"

The Slavonic and East European Review 59, no. 4 (1981); Christoff, *An Introduction to Nine-teenth Century Slavophilism* I, II, III.

40. Q. Skinner, "Motives, Intentions and the Interpretation of Texts," in *Meaning and Context. Quentin Skinner and His Critics*, ed. J. Tully, pp. 70, 73–78 (Cambridge: Polity Press, 1988).

41. See for example the recent study by Rouleau, *Ivan Kireievski et la naissance du Slavophilisme*.

CHAPTER ONE

1. A. D. Smith, *Theories of Nationalism*, 2nd ed. (London, 1983); *The Ethnic Revival* (Cambridge: Cambridge University Press, 1981); E. Gellner, *Nations and Nationalism* (Oxford: Blackwell, 1983); E. J. Hobsbawm, *Nations and Nationalism since 1780* (Cambridge: Cambridge University Press, 1992); L. Greenfeld, *Nationalism. Five Roads to Modernity* (Cambridge, MA: Harvard University Press, 1993); B. Anderson, *Imagined Communities: Reflections on the Origin and Spread of Nationalism* (London: Verso, 1991).

2. Gellner, *Nations and Nationalism*, pp. 1, 24, 47–49, 95.

3. Anderson, *Imagined Communities*, p. 46.

4. W. L. Blackwell, *The Industrialization of Russia: A Historical Perspective*, 3rd ed. (Arlington Heights: Harlan Davidson, Inc., 1994), pp. 1–22.

5. E. J. Hobsbawm, "The Invented Nation" in *The Invention of Tradition*, ed. Hobsbawm and Ranger, p. 303 (Cambridge: Cambridge University Press, 1983). See also *Intellectuals and the Articulation of the Nation*, ed. R. G. Suny and M. P. Kennedy (Ann Arbor: University of Michigan Press, 1999). Here writers look specifically at the role of intellectuals in the making of nations.

6. Greenfeld, *Nationalism*, pp. 14–17.

7. Ibid., pp. 15–17.

8. Smith, *Theories of Nationalism*, pp. 231–48.

9. For Marxist-Leninist theories on the Slavophiles see S. S. Dmitriev, "*Slavianofily i slavianofilstvo*," *Istorik-Marksist*, no. 1 (1941) and "*Podkhod dolzhen byt konkretno-istoricheskii*," *Voprosy Literatury*, no. 12 (1969); S. A. Pokrovskii, "*Literaturnaia kritika rannikh slavianofily*," *Voprosy Literatury*, nos. 5, 7, 10, 12 (1969).

10. A. Walicki, *A History of Russian Thought from the Enlightenment to Marxism* (Stanford: Stanford University Press, 1979), pp. 106–7; A. Gleason, *European and Muscovite: Ivan Kireevsky and the Origins of Slavophilism* (Cambridge, MA: Harvard University Press, 1972), pp. 151, 169.

11. D. Lieven, *The Aristocracy in Europe, 1815–1914* (Basingstoke: Macmillan, 1992), pp. 9–10. See also D. Offord, *Portraits of Early Russian Liberals: A Study of the Thought of T. N. Granovsky, V. P. Botkin, P. V. Annenkov, A. V. Druzhinin, and K. D. Kavelin* (Cambridge: Cambridge University Press, 1985).

12. Gleason, *European and Muscovite*, pp. 178–79. M. Hughes writes about this rural trend, but he locates it in the nineteenth century in "'Independent Gentlemen': The Social Position of the Moscow Slavophiles and Its Impact on Their Political Thought," *The Slavonic and East European Review* 71, no. 1 (1993).

13. P. K. Christoff, I, p. 245, *An Introduction to Nineteenth-Century Slavophilism* vol. II: *I. V. Kireevsky* (Princeton: Mouton, 1972), p. 326.

14. I. V. Kireevsky cited in Gleason, *European and Muscovite*, p. 204.

15. Gleason, *European and Muscovite*, pp. 280, 169.

16. I. V. Kireevsky, *Polnoe sobranie sochinenii*, ed. Gershenzon, 2 vols. (Moscow, 1911), I, p. 208.

17. Christoff, *Introduction to Nineteenth-Century Slavophilism* II, p. 306.

18. Ibid., p. 295; Gleason, *European and Muscovite*, p. 291.

19. P. K. Christoff, *An Introduction to Nineteenth-Century Slavophilism*, vol. I: *A. S. Xomjakov* (The Hague: Mouton, 1961), pp. 45–46, 232–33.

20. N. O. Lossky, *History of Russian Philosophy* (New York: International University Press, 1951), p. 47; Zernov, *Three Russian Prophets* (London: S.C.M. Press, 1944), pp. 72–73. Von Haxthausen discussed the Russian commune already in 1843 in *Studies on the Interior of Russia* (Chicago: University of Chicago Press, 1972).

21. A. S. Khomiakov, *Polnoe sobranie sochinenii* (Moscow, 1900–1914), III, pp. 465–66.

22. J. M. Edie, J. P. Scanlan, and M. Zeldin, eds., *Russian Philosophy*, vol. I (Chicago: Quadrangle books, 1965), p. 163; A. S. Khomiakov, "To the Serbians," in Christoff, *Introduction to Nineteenth-Century Slavophilism* I, p. 266; N. Zernov, *Three Russian Prophets*, p. 72.

23. Khomiakov, *Polnoe sobranie sochinenii*, I, pp. 137–38.

24. Khomiakov, "To the Serbians," p. 266.

25. E. Wirtschafter, *Social Identity in Imperial Russia* (Dekalb: Northern Illinois University Press, 1997), pp. 22, 47; Lieven, *Aristocracy in Europe*, pp. 214–15.

26. Wirtschafter, *Social Identity in Imperial Russia*, pp. 97–98, 87.

27. N. V. Riasanovsky, "Notes on the Emergence and Nature of the Russian Intelligentsia," in *Art and Culture in Nineteenth Century Russia*, ed. T. G. Stavrou, p. 6 (Bloomington: Indiana University Press, 1983).

28. Marquis de Custine, *Letters from Russia* (London: Penguin Books, 1991), p. 44.

29. Wirtschafter, *Social Identity in Imperial Russia*, pp. 30, 17.

30. Ibid., p. 32. It is interesting to note that some of these eighteenth-century concepts remained central to the Slavophiles.

31. M. Malia, "What Is the Intelligentsia?" *Daedalus* (Summer 1960): 453. Compared to other European countries, as Prussia and, especially, England, the Russian schools and universities were much more democratic in their intake (Lieven, *Aristocracy in Europe*, p. 176).

32. R. Pipes, "The Historical Evolution of the Russian Intelligentsia," *Daedalus* (Summer 1960): 488; Lieven, *Aristocracy in Europe*, p. 180; Riasanovsky, "Emergence and Nature of the Russian Intelligentsia," p. 5.

33. M. Raeff, "The People, the Intelligentsia and Russian Political Culture," *Political Studies* 41 (1993): 96–97; Pipes, "Historical Evolution of the Russian Intelligentsia," p. 488; Lieven, *Aristocracy in Europe*, pp. 19, 179–80.

34. Raeff, "The People, the Intelligentsia," pp. 97–98.

35. D. Pospielovsky, "A Comparative Enquiry into Neo-Slavophilism and Its Antecedents in the Russian History of Ideas," *Soviet Studies*, no. 3 (1979): 319; Christoff, *Introduction to Nineteenth-Century Slavophilism* II, p. 261; M. Raeff, *Political Ideas and Institutions in Imperial Russia* (Boulder: Westview Press, 1994), pp. 70–71.

36. Malia, "What Is the Intelligentsia?" p. 449; M. Raeff, *Origins of the Russian Intelligentsia: The Eighteenth-Century Nobility* (New York: Harcourt, Brace & World, 1966), p. 170; D. Saunders, *Russia in the Age of Reaction and Reform 1801–1881* (New York: Longman, 1992), p. 148.

37. Malia, "What Is the Intelligentsia?" p. 450.

38. Wirtschafter, *Social Identity in Imperial Russia*, pp. 167–68; Riasanovsky, "Emergence and Nature of the Russian Intelligentsia," pp. 22–23.

39. Lieven, *Aristocracy in Europe*, p. 245.

40. Ibid.

41. Raeff, "The People, the Intelligentsia," p. 98. The nobility were emancipated from compulsory service in 1762.

42. Lieven, *Aristocracy in Europe*, p. 245.

43. Malia, "What Is the Intelligentsia?" pp. 449–50, 453, 455, 443.

44. See Smith for the view of nationalism as a solution to the clash between traditional identities and a modern state, *Theories of Nationalism*.

45. Edie et al., eds., *Russian Philosophy*, pp. 4–6; Lossky, *History of Russian Philosophy*, pp. 10, 13.

46. Christoff, *Introduction to Nineteenth-Century Slavophilism* II, pp. 338–39.

47. I. M. Lotman and B. A. Uspenskii, "Binary Models in the Dynamics of Russian Culture," in *The Semiotics of Russian Cultural History*, ed. A. D. Nakhimovsky and A. S. Nakhimovsky, pp. 30–66 (Ithaca, NY: Cornell University Press, 1985).

48. Ibid., pp. 31–32. Although Lotman and Uspenskii do not apply their argument to the Slavophiles, others do. See for example P–A. Bodin, *Ryssland och Europa. En kulturhistorisk studie* (Stockholm, 1993).

49. It is clear that at least Kireevsky read Novikov. In the "Review of Russian Literature for 1829" Kireevsky praised him and said that he had done much to further the development of Russian culture. See *Izbrannye stati* (Moscow: Sovremennik, 1984), p. 42.

50. H. Rogger, *National Consciousness in Eighteenth-Century Russia* (Cambridge, MA: Harvard University Press, 1960), pp. 1–2, 265, 75, 84, 77.

51. Ibid., pp. 266–67, 84, 77, 3–4. See also E. C. Thaden, "The Beginnings of Romantic Nationalism in Russia," *The American Slavic and East European Review* 13, no. 4 (1954) for a similar view.

52. Iu. V. Stennik, "*Ob istokakh slavianofilstva v russkoi literature XVIII veka*" in *Slavianofilstvo i Sovremennost*, ed. B. F. Yegorov, V. A. Kotelnikov, and Iu. V. Stennik, p. 5 (St. Petersburg: Nauka, 1994).

53. A. Martin, *Romantics, Reformers, Reactionaries. Russian Conservative Thought and Politics in the Reign of Alexander I* (Dekalb: Northern Illinois University Press, 1997), pp. 15, 17, 33–34; N. V. Riasanovsky, *Russia and the West in the Teaching of the Slavophiles* (Cambridge, MA: Harvard University Press, 1952), p. 5.

54. Martin, *Romantics, Reformers, Reactionaries*, pp. 26, 31–34, 36, 25.

55. Zernov, *Three Russian Prophets*, 1944, p. 54.

56. Gleason, *European and Muscovite*, pp. 112, 114–15. See A. Koyré, *La Philosophie et la problème national en Russie au début du XIX siècle* (Paris: Champion, 1929) on the subject of Chaadev's influence on Kireevsky and E. Müller, *Russischer Intellekt in Europäischer Krise: Ivan V. Kireevskij (1806–1856)* (Köln: Böhlau, 1966), for a critique of this argument.

57. Chaadaev cited in Lossky, *History of Russian Philosophy*, 1951, p. 51.

58. Edie et al., eds., *Russian Philosophy*, p. 157–60, 168, 217; Zernov, *Three Russian Prophets*, 1944, pp. 52–53; Gleason, *European and Muscovite*, pp. 3–4; Christoff, *Introduction to Nineteenth-Century Slavophilism* I, p. 44; Walicki, *History of Russian Thought*, p. 106.

59. Riasanovsky, *Russia and the West*, pp. 166, 171, 210, 174.

60. Steppun, "Nemetsky romantizm i russkoe slavianofilstvo," *Russkaia mysl* (March 1910): 73–75.

61. Christoff, *Introduction to Nineteenth-Century Slavophilism II*, pp. 253, 158, 146.

62. Christoff, *Introduction to Nineteenth-Century Slavophilism I*, pp. 126, 39, 197.

63. H. Lanz, "The Philosophy of Ivan Kireevsky," *The Slavonic Review* IV (1925): 604; Lossky, *History of Russian Philosophy*, pp. 23, 13–14.

64. Gleason, *European and Muscovite*, pp. 32, 282–83.

CHAPTER TWO

1. I. V. Kireevsky, *Izbrannye stati* (Moscow: Sovremennik, 1984), p. 60.

2. P. Chaadaev, *Philosophical Letters & Apology of a Madman* (Knoxville: University of Tennessee Press, 1969), pp. 36–37, 39, 41.

3. V. G. Belinsky, *Selected Philosophical Works* (Moscow: Foreign Languages Pub. House, 1956), p. 5–8, 44.

4. Belinsky, *Selected Philosophical Works*, p. 383.

5. V. F. Odoevsky, "Russkie nochi," in *Sochineniia kniazia V. F. Odoevskago* (St. Petersburg: Ivanov, 1844), p. 10.

6. D. Venevitinov, *Polnoe sobranie sochinenii* (Moscow, 1934), pp. 216–17.

7. Kireevsky, *Izbrannye stati*, p. 60.

8. This concept was used to describe the philosophical basis of a culture in a specific way, which I will discuss in chapter 4.

9. Kireevsky, *Izbrannye stati*, p. 146.

10. Ibid., p. 84.

11. Ibid., pp. 150–51.

12. A. S. Khomiakov, *Polnoe sobranie sochinenii*, 8 vols. (Moscow, 1900–1914), III, pp. 115–16.

13. Kireevsky, *Izbrannye stati*, p. 276.

14. Khomiakov, *Polnoe sobranie sochinenii* III, p. 111.

15. Belinsky, *Selected Philosophical Works*, p. 372.

16. Belinsky, *Selected Philosophical Works*, p. 29.

17. A. Herzen, *Selected Philosophical Works* (Moscow: Foreign Languages Pub. House, 1956), p. 18.

18. A. Herzen, "Dilettantism in Science," in *A Documentary History of Russian Thought*, ed. W. J. Leatherbarrow and D. C. Offord, pp. 140, 144 (Ann Arbor: Ardis, 1987).

19. Khomiakov, *Polnoe sobranie sochinenii* I, pp. 22, 33.

20. Ibid., p. 60. This refers to the Romantic contrast between mind and spirit, which will be discussed below.

21. Kireevsky, *Izbrannye stati*, p. 95; Khomiakov, *Polnoe sobranie sochinenii* I, p. 97.

22. Khomiakov, *Polnoe sobranie sochinenii* I, pp. 61, 64, 66.

23. Ibid., p. 61.

24. There is a discussion of this idea by McNally in his introduction to *Philosophical Works of Peter Chaadaev*, pp. 15–16.

25. Chaadaev, *Philosophical Letters*, p. 39.

26. Ibid., p. 12.

27. Kireevsky, *Izbrannye stati*, pp. 147, 276.

28. Khomiakov, *Polnoe sobranie sochinenii* I, p. 74.

29. Ibid. III, pp. 117–18

30. Kireevsky, *Izbrannye stati*, p. 51.

31. Ibid., pp. 156–57.

32. Khomiakov, *Polnoe sobranie sochinenii* I, p. 47.

33. Kireevsky, *Izbrannye stati*, pp. 192–93.

34. Ibid., p. 76.

35. Ibid., p. 151.

36. Khomiakov, *Polnoe sobranie sochinenii* I, p. 83.

37. Ibid., p. 77.

38. Ibid., p. 160.

39. Ibid., p. 165, 11, 28; Vol. V, pp. 24, 47.

40. Ibid., pp. 20, 22–23.

41. L. Greenfeld, *Nationalism. Five Roads to Modernity* (Cambridge, MA: Harvard University Press, 1993).

42. Khomiakov, *Polnoe sobranie sochinenii* I, p. 150.

43. Ibid., p. 132.

44. Kireevsky, *Izbrannye stati*, p. 280.

45. Ibid., p. 67.

46. Ibid., pp. 67–68.

47. Ibid., 144–145.

48. Khomiakov, *Polnoe sobranie sochinenii* III, p. 20.

49. Ibid., I, 1900, p. 66.

50. Ibid., p.13.

51. Kireevsky, *Izbrannye stati*, p. 120.

52. Kireevsky, *Izbrannye stati*, p. 61.

53. Khomiakov, *Polnoe sobranie sochinenii* I, pp. 93, 43; Kireevsky, *Izbrannye stati*, p. 276.

54. Chaadaev, *Philosophical Letters*, p. 40.

55. Lieven, *The Aristocracy in Europe, 1815–1914* (Basingstoke: Macmillan, 1992), pp. 179–80.

56. Belinsky, *Selected Philosophical Works*, p. 365.

57. Khomiakov, *Polnoe sobranie sochinenii* I, p. 171.

58. Belinsky, *Selected Philosophical Works*, p. 365.

59. A. S. Khomiakov, *Izbrannye sochineniia* (New York: Izdatelstvo imeni Chekhova, 1955), p. 331.

60. Chaadaev, *Philosophical Letters*, pp. 34, 41.

61. Kireevsky, *Izbrannye stati*, p. 155.

62. Ibid., pp. 151–52, 147.

63. See Chaadaev, *Philosophical Letters*.

64. Khomiakov, *Polnoe sobranie sochinenii* III, p. 111; ibid. I, p. 41; Kireevsky, *Izbrannye stati*, p. 276.

65. Khomiakov, *Polnoe sobranie sochinenii* I, pp. 33–34, 24, 64, 80.

66. Kireevsky, *Izbrannye stati*, pp. 277–78.

67. Khomiakov, *Polnoe sobranie sochinenii* I, p. 28.

68. Kireevsky, *Izbrannye stati*, pp. 60, 160, 330, 151.

69. Khomiakov, *Polnoe sobranie sochinenii* V, p. 358.

70. Ibid. I, 1900, p. 37.

71. Ibid., pp. 174, 152, 156–57, 96; Kireevsky, *Izbrannye stati*, pp. 60, 160, 330, 151.

72. Kireevsky, *Izbrannye stati*, p. 160.

73. Ibid., pp. 323, 330.

74. Khomiakov, *Polnoe sobranie sochinenii* III, pp. 166–67.

75. Belinsky, *Selected Philosophical Works*, pp. 382–83.

76. Khomiakov, *Polnoe sobranie sochinenii*, I, pp. 19, 9, 43.

77. Ibid., p. 93.

78. Ibid., pp. 156, 6, 52, 8–9.

79. Herzen, *My Past and Thoughts: The Memoirs of Alexander Herzen*, 4 vols. (London: Chatto & Windus, 1968), I, p. 313; ibid. II, pp. 424, 527; V. G. Belinsky, *Polnoe sobranie sochinenii*, 13 vols. (Moscow: Izdatelstvo Akademii nauk SSSR, 1953–1959), V, p. 124; ibid. XI, p. 526.

80. Belinsky, *Selected Philosophical Works*, pp. 355, 362.

81. Ibid., pp. 190–91.

82. Khomiakov, *Polnoe sobranie sochinenii* I, pp. 44, 92, 96, 24.

83. Ibid. III, p. 167.

84. Kireevsky, *Izbrannye stati*, p. 165.

85. Khomiakov, *Polnoe sobranie sochinenii* I, pp. 24, 66, 9, 42, 17, 44–45; vol. III, p. 167.

86. Belinsky, *Selected Philosophical Works*, p. 325.

87. Chaadaev, *Philosophical Letters*, p. 39.

88. Khomiakov, *Polnoe sobranie sochinenii* I, pp. 6–9.

89. Chaadaev, *Philosophical Works*, p. 121.

90. At this time *narodnost* was used instead of *natsionalnost* to express "nationality."

91. Khomiakov, *Polnoe sobranie sochinenii* I, p. 18.

92. Ibid., pp. 22, 33, 46, 65, 73.

93. Herzen, *Selected Philosophical Works*, pp. 51, 65, 54–55, 59, 80, 84.

94. Khomiakov, *Polnoe sobranie sochinenii* I, p. 77.

95. Ibid., p. 16.

96. Kireevsky, *Izbrannye stati*, pp. 288–89.

97. Khomiakov, *Polnoe sobranie sochinenii* I, p. 98; Kireevsky, *Izbrannye stati*, p. 323.

98. Khomiakov, *Polnoe sobranie sochinenii* I, pp. 163–64. This is a story about men, although female writers are sometimes acknowledged.

99. Ibid., pp. 75, 96.

100. Kireevsky, *Izbrannye stati*, p. 174.

101. Khomiakov, *Polnoe sobranie sochinenii* I, pp. 169, 152, 22, 88, 86.

102. Kireevsky, *Izbrannye stati*, pp. 288, 277.

103. Khomiakov, *Polnoe sobranie sochinenii* I, p. 6; Kireevsky, *Izbrannye stati*, p. 95.

104. Khomiakov, *Polnoe sobranie sochinenii* I, pp. 169, 152.

105. Ibid., pp. 86, 156.

Chapter Three

1. L. Greenfeld, *Nationalism. Five Roads to Modernity* (Cambridge, MA: Harvard University Press, 1993), p. 9.

2. See note 4 in the Introduction.

3. Quoted in E. J. Hobsbawm, *Nations and Nationalism since 1780* (Cambridge: Cambridge University Press, 1992), p. 19.

4. "Political" is used in the traditional limited sense of pertaining to the state and government.

5. B. Anderson, *Imagined Communities: Reflections on the Origin and Spread of Nationalism* (London: Verso, 1991), p. 6.

6. Greenfeld, *Nationalism*, p. 3.

7. E. J. Sieyès, *What Is the Third Estate?* (London: Pall Mall Press, 1963), p. 58; Hobsbawm, *Nations and Nationalism*, p. 20.

8. J. S. Mill, *Utilitarianism, Liberty and Representative Government* (London: Dent, 1910), pp. 359–66.

9. Greenfeld, *Nationalism*, pp. 10, 6–7.

10. E. Renan, *Qu'est-ce qu'une nation?* (Paris, 1882), p. 27. John Breuilly rejects the concept of the subjective, voluntarist view of the nation, because it makes it impossible to identify any specific nation, based on a collective identity. He argues that Renan's position, to be meaningful, has to rest upon shared views of what being French means, which together with their political organization constitute a form of nationalism. For his purposes, there has to be a collective idea of a distinctive nation, in the name of which nationalist movements can justify its politics. See J. Breuilly, *Nationalism and the State* (Manchester: Manchester University Press, 1993), pp. 6, 2.

11. Sieyès, *What Is the Third Estate?*

12. E. Gellner, *Nations and Nationalism* (Oxford: Blackwell, 1983), p. 1

13. Hobsbawm, *Nations and Nationalism*, p. 37.

14. See E. Kedourie, *Nationalism* (London: Hutchinson, 1966, 3d. erd); A. D. Smith, *Theories of Nationalism* (London: Duckworth, 1983).

15. J. Hutchinson, *The Dynamics of Cultural Nationalism: The Gaelic Revival and the Creation of the Irish Nation State* (London: Allen & Unwin, 1987), pp. 12–13.

16. See for example M. Hroch, "From National Movement to Fully-Fledged Nation," *New Left Review*, nr. 198 (1993); Hobsbawm, *Nations and Nationalism*; Anderson, *Imagined Communities*; Gellner, *Nations and Nationalism*; Smith, *Theories of Nationalism*; C. Tilly, ed., *The Formation of National States in Western Europe* (Princeton: Princeton University Press, 1975).

17. T. Nipperdey, p. 8, cited in M. Guibernau, *Nationalisms. The Nation-State and Nationalism in the Twentieth Century* (Cambridge: Polity Press, 1996), p. 56.

18. Guibernau, *Nationalisms*, pp. 55–56. See also T. Nipperdey, "In Search of Identity," in *Romantic Nationalism in Europe*, ed. J. C. Eade, p. 6 (Canberra: Australian National University Press, 1983).

19. Hutchinson, *Dynamics of Cultural Nationalism*, p. 9. There are interesting parallels between cultural nationalists' view of the nation as a moral community and Renan's portrayal of the nation as a moral conscience created by an aggregation of men (Renan, *Qu'est-ce qu'une nation*, p. 29).

20. For literature that discuss the importance of cultural nationalism, see Hutchinson, *Dynamics of Cultural Nationalism*; Yoshino, *Cultural Nationalism in Contemporary Japan*; Hsiau, *Contemporary Taiwanese Cultural Nationalism*; G. Jusdanis, *The Necessary Nation* (Princeton, NJ: Princeton University Press, 2001).

21. Kedourie, *Nationalism*, p. 58; Gellner, *Nations and Nationalism*, pp. 57–61.

22. Smith, *Theories of Nationalism*, pp. 171, 178–80, 186, 192–93, 197–98, 210, 211.

23. Breuilly, *Nationalism and the State*, pp. 1–2, 420–21. Another interesting consequence of Breuilly's approach is that he excludes from consideration political movements which demand independence on the basis of universal principles. Such ideas only become nationalist when combined with other ideas about a distinctive cultural identity (p. 5). The consequences of this view is that the formation of the American nation, for example, cannot be defined as a nationalism.

24. B. Yack, "The Myth of the Civic Nation," in *Theorizing Nationalism*, ed. R. Beiner (Albany: State University of New York Press, 1999); Hutchinson, *Dynamics of Cultural Nationalism*.

25. Liah Greenfeld refers to the culturally based nationalism as an ethnic nationalism, opposed to the civic form and characterised by its collectivistic-authoritarian character, *Nationalism*, p. 11.

26. I. Berlin, *Vico and Herder: Two Studies in the History of Ideas* (London: Hogarth Press, 1976), pp. 158, 163; Hutchinson, *Dynamics of Cultural Nationalism*, pp. 13, 2–3.

27. Berlin, *Vico and Herder*, p. 26.

28. Hutchinson, *Dynamics of Cultural Nationalism*, 1987, pp. 14–15; Berlin, *Vico and Herder*, pp. 203–4.

29. F. Barnard, *Herder's Social and Political Thought* (Oxford: Clarendon Press, 1965), pp. 37, 31.

30. See D. von Engelhardt, "Romanticism in Germany," in *Romanticism in National Context*, ed. R. Porter and M. Teich, p. 113 (Cambridge: Cambridge University Press, 1988), p. 113; F. C. Beiser, *Enlightenment, Revolution, and Romanticism: The Genesis of Modern German Political Thought 1790–1800* (Cambridge, MA: Harvard University Press, 1992), pp. 236, 238.

31. Berlin, *Vico and Herder*, p. 177; Barnard, *Herder's Social and Political Thought*, p. 70.

32. Berlin, *Vico and Herder*, pp. 168–77.

33. Barnard, *Herder's Social and Political Thought*, pp. 54–55.

34. F. C. Beiser, ed., *The Early Political Writings of the German Romantics* (Cambridge: Cambridge University Press, 1996), p. xxvii–xxviii; Beiser, *Enlightenment, Revolution, and Romanticism*, pp. 237–38.

35. Barnard, *Herder's Social and Political Thought*, pp. 57, 141–42, 84.

36. Berlin, *Vico and Herder*, pp. 194–97.

37. Ibid., pp. 180, 188–89. How the principle of incommensurability may be combined with the notion of universal progress will be discussed in chapter 6.

38. J. G. Herder cited in Barnard, *Herder's Social and Political Thought*, p. 61.

39. Barnard, *Herder's Social and Political Thought*, p. 149; Berlin, *Vico and Herder*, pp. 186–87.

40. Beiser, *Enlightenment, Revolution, and Romanticism*, p. 206.

41. Berlin, *Vico and Herder*, p. 197; Barnard, *Herder's Social and Political Thought*, p. 102.

42. J. G. Herder cited in Berlin, *Vico and Herder*, p. 182.

43. Berlin, *Vico and Herder*, p. 180.

44. Beiser, *Enlightenment, Revolution, and Romanticism*, p. 206.

45. Berlin, *Vico and Herder*, pp. 195, 214–15.

46. Barnard, *Herder's Social and Political Thought*, pp. 117–18.

47. Berlin, *Vico and Herder*, pp. 198, 201, 203–4.

48. Barnard, *Herder's Social and Political Thought*, pp. 118, 131, 143.

49. J. G. Herder cited in Barnard, *Herder's Social and Political Thought*, p. 93, 105.

50. Barnard, *Herder's Social and Political Thought*, pp. 93, 78, 134.

51. Beiser, *Enlightenment, Revolution, and Romanticism*, p. 197; Berlin, *Vico and Herder*, p. 204.

52. Barnard, *Herder's Social and Political Thought*, pp. 73–74.

53. J. G. Herder cited in Barnard, *Herder's Social and Political Thought*, pp. 76–77.

54. Barnard, *Herder's Social and Political Thought*, pp. 76, 82.

55. Beiser, *Enlightenment, Revolution, and Romanticism*, pp. 266, 233, 229, 255.

56. Ibid., pp. 259–60, 227, 231.

57. Ibid., 1992, p. 228. See also F. G. Nauen, *Revolution, Idealism and Human Freedom: Schelling, Hölderlin and Hegel and the Crisis of Early German Idealism* (The Hague: Nijhoff, 1971), pp. 20, 22.

58. Novalis cited in Beiser, *Enlightenment, Revolution, and Romanticism*, p. 276.

59. Beiser, *Enlightenment, Revolution, and Romanticism*, pp. 229, 240–41.

60. Nauen, *Revolution, Idealism and Human Freedom*, pp. 3, 13.

61. Beiser, *Enlightenment, Revolution, and Romanticism*, p. 99.

62. Some scholars characterize Slavophilism as a Romantic movement. There are at least two reasons for why cultural nationalism is a better term for the purpose of this study. First, it is the idea of the nation that is most crucial to the Slavophiles at the time. Romanticism is such a wide concept and the idea of the organic nation is just one aspect of it. Secondly, calling it a Romantic movement might lead people to think that it did not contain any strivings for social change.

63. See Barnard, *Herder's Social and Political Thought*, p. 62.

CHAPTER FOUR

1. V. G. Belinsky, *Selected Philosophical Works* (Moscow: Foreign Languages Pub. House, 1956), pp. 87–88, 14.

2. Belinsky, *Selected Philosophical Works*, p. 8.

3. Ibid., pp. 21, 39, 89, 91, 365, 40, 373.

4. A. Herzen, *Selected Philosophical Works* (Moscow: Foreign Languages Pub. House, 1956), pp. 51, 54–55, 61, 80, 84.

5. Belinsky held this view in common with the liberal Westernizers, Granovsky, and Annenkov.

6. Herzen, *Selected Philosophical Works*, pp. 484–85, 489, 346.

7. Belinsky, *Selected Philosophical Works*, pp. 219, 224–25, 220.

8. Ibid., pp. 89, 215, 376, 380, 220.

9. Ibid., p. 205.

10. Herzen, *Selected Philosophical Works*, pp. 61, 69, 83–84, 313, 64, 173, 65.

11. Ibid., p. 64; M. A. Bakunin, "The Confession to Tsar Nicholas I" [1851] and "Statism and Anarchy" [1873], both in *Selected Writings* (London: Jonathan Cape, 1973), pp. 70, 350.

12. Belinsky, *Selected Philosophical Works*, pp. 206, 101, 228, 358, 361, 102, 362.

13. Ibid., pp. 101, 321. It was only East of the Rhine that idealism was combined with nationalism, Romanticism, and historicism. See M. Malia, *Alexander Herzen and the Birth of Russian Socialism 1812–1855* (Cambridge, MA: Harvard University Press, 1961), p. 73.

14. A. Herzen, "Dilettantism in Science," in *A Documentary History of Russian Thought. From the Enlightenment to Marxism*, ed. W. J. Leatherbarrow and D. C. Offord, pp. 144–46 (Ann Arbor: Ardis, 1987).

15. Belinsky, *Selected Philosophical Works*, pp. 380, 47.

16. Ibid., pp. 12, 20.

17. Ibid., pp. 325–26.

18. Herzen, *Selected Philosophical Works*, p. 94.

19. Belinsky, *Selected Philosophical Works*, p. 322, 328, 338. The idea underlying universal history, according to Belinsky, should be that of humanity as a unitary, individual, and personal subject and the aim was to sketch the picture of humanity's progress from the savage state to what it was today, pp. 325, 328.

20. Herzen, *Selected Philosophical Works*, pp. 323, 480.

21. Ibid., p. 321.

22. Belinsky, *Selected Philosophical Works*, pp. 365–68.

23. Herzen, *Selected Philosophical Works*, p. 242.

24. Belinsky, *Selected Philosophical Works*, pp. 384, 400.

25. Herzen, *Selected Philosophical Works*, pp. 212, 214–16.

26. P. Chaadaev, *Philosophical Works of Peter Chaadaev*, ed. R. T. McNally and R. Tempest (Dordrecht, 1991), pp. 158, 161.

27. Herzen, *Selected Philosophical Works*, pp. 237, 213.

28. V. G. Belinsky, "Letter to N. V. Gogol," in *Russian Intellectual History: An Anthology*, ed. M. Raeff, p. 254 (New York: Harcourt, 1966).

29. Belinsky, *Selected Philosophical Works*, pp. 362, 357.

30. V. G. Belinsky, "Letter to Gogol," p. 254.

31. Herzen, *Selected Philosophical Works*, pp. 499, 342.

CHAPTER FIVE

1. K. S. Aksakov, "On the Internal State of Russia," in *Russian Intellectual History: An Anthology*, ed. M. Raeff, p. 241. (New York: Harcourt, 1966).

2. A. Walicki, *The Slavophile Controversy* (Oxford: Clarendon, 1975); N. V. Riasanovsky, *Russia and the West in the Teaching of the Slavophiles* (Cambridge, MA: Harvard University Press, 1952); A. Gleason, *European and Muscovite: Ivan Kireevsky and the Origins of Slavophilism* (Cambridge, MA: Harvard University Press, 1972); I. Berlin, "Russian thought and the Slavophile controversy," *Slavonic and East European Review* 59, no. 4 (1981).

3. V. F. Odoevsky, "Russkie nochi," in *Sochineniia kniazia V. F. Odoevskago* (St. Petersburg: Ivanov, 1844), pp. 313–14.

4. I. V. Kireevsky, *Izbrannye stati* (Moscow: Sovremennik, 1984), p. 61.

5. See Belinsky's notion of public life in chapter 4. For an example of the translation of culture as prosveshchenie, see V. Snow's translation of Kiereevsky in *Russian Intellectual History*, ed. M. Raeff, pp. 175–207 (New York: Harcout, 1966).

6. Kireevsky, *Izbrannye stati*, pp. 71, 277.

7. A. S. Khomiakov, *Polnoe sobranie sochinenii*, 8 vols. (Moscow, 1900–1914) I, p. 26.

8. I. V. Kireevsky, "On the Nature of European Culture and Its Relation to the Culture of Russia," in *Russian Intellectual History: An Anthology*, ed. M. Raeff, p. 192 (New York: Harcourt, 1966).

9. Khomiakov, *Polnoe sobranie sochinenii*, I, p. 80.

10. Kireevsky, "On the Nature of European Culture," pp. 192–94.

11. Khomiakov, *Polnoe sobranie sochinenii*, I, pp. 26–27, 80.

12. Kireevsky, *Izbrannye stati*, p. 277.

13. Khomiakov, *Polnoe sobranie sochinenii*, I, p. 23.

14. Kireevsky, *Izbrannye stati*, pp. 77–78.

15. Khomiakov, *Polnoe sobranie sochinenii*, I, pp. 26–27.

16. Kireevsky, *Izbrannye stati*, p. 160.

17. Kireevsky, *Izbrannye stati*, p. 77–78.

18. Khomiakov, *Polnoe sobranie sochinenii*, I, pp. 174, 34.

19. See Herzen's description of this relationship in chapter four.

20. Khomiakov, *Polnoe sobranie sochinenii*, I, pp. 26, 170–72.

21. Kireevsky, "On the Nature of European Culture," p. 194.

22. Kireevsky, *Izbrannye stati*, pp. 125, 276.

23. Kireevsky, "On the Nature of European Culture," pp. 175, 195.

24. Kireevsky, *Izbrannye stati*, pp. 118, 78, 97.

25. Ibid., p. 118.

26. Kireevsky, "On the Nature of European Culture," pp. 206–7.

27. Khomiakov, *Polnoe sobranie sochinenii*, I, pp. 26–27.

28. Kireevsky, "On the Nature of European Culture," p. 207.

29. Ibid., pp. 180, 195.

30. Kireevsky, *Izbrannye stati*, pp. 191, 147.

31. Khomiakov, *Polnoe sobranie sochinenii*, I, p. 27.

32. Ibid., p. 22; Kireevsky, *Izbrannye stati*, p. 278.

33. Khomiakov, *Polnoe sobranie sochinenii*, I, pp. 100–101, 28, 66; Kireevsky, *Izbrannye stati*, pp. 276–78.

34. See for example V. G. Belinsky, *Selected Philosophical Works* (Moscow: Foreign Languages Pub. House, 1956), pp. 205–6, 215, 381.

35. Kireevsky, *Izbrannye stati*, p. 97.

36. Khomiakov, *Polnoe sobranie sochinenii*, I, p. 66.

37. Kireevsky, *Izbrannye stati*, p. 277.

38. Khomiakov, *Polnoe sobranie sochinenii*, I, pp. 99–101.

39. Ibid., pp. 173–74, 22, 97–98, 6.

40. Ibid., pp. 27–28, Kireevsky, *Izbrannye stati*, pp. 193, 276–77.

41. Khomiakov, *Polnoe sobranie sochinenii*, I, pp. 59, 44; III, p. 99.

42. Ibid., vol. 1, pp. 27–28, Kireevsky, "On the Nature of European Culture," p. 207. See note 5.

43. To complicate things, Khomiakov sometimes described the people's way of life not only as the Russian national life, but as a common, universal way of life (Khomiakov, *Polnoe sobranie sochinenii*, I, p. 92). It seems likely that by this he meant that the people's way of life was spiritual and in this sense common to all, although at this particular moment it was the Russian people who lived this life, or the remains of it.

44. Kireevsky, *Izbrannye stati*, pp. 153, 276, 278.

45. Kireevsky, "On the Nature of European Culture," pp. 194, 200; Khomiakov, *Polnoe sobranie sochinenii*, I, pp. 80, 22.

46. Kireevsky, *Izbrannye stati*, p. 191.

47. Ibid., pp. 191–93.

48. Khomiakov, *Polnoe sobranie sochinenii*, I, pp. 21–22.

49. Kireevsky, *Izbrannye stati*, pp. 191–92, 278.

50. Khomiakov, *Polnoe sobranie sochinenii*, III, p. 115.

51. Kireevsky, *Izbrannye stati*, p. 156.

52. Kireevsky, ibid., p. 197.

Chapter Six

1. See J. Hutchinson, *The Dynamics of Cultural Nationalism: The Gaelic Revival and the Creation of the Irish Nation State* (London: Allen & Unwin, 1987), p. 8; E. Gellner, *Nations and Nationalism* (Oxford: Blackwell, 1983), pp. 60–61; M. Hughes, *Nationalism and Society. Germany 1800–1945* (London: Arnold, 1988), p. 22.

2. R. Aris, *History of Political Thought in Germany from 1789–1815* (London: Allen & Unwin, 1936), p. 212; F. C. Beiser, *Enlightenment, Revolution, and Romanticism: The Genesis of Modern German Political Thought 1790–1800* (Cambridge, MA: Harvard University Press, 1992), p. 7.

3. M. Raeff, *Russian Intellectual History: An Anthology* (New York: Harcourt, 1966), p 230; A. Walicki, *The Slavophile Controversy* (Oxford: Clarendon, 1975).

4. Aris, *History of Political Thought in Germany*, pp. 208, 218.

5. F. M. Barnard, *Herder's Social and Political Thought: From Enlightenment to Nationalism* (Oxford: Clarendon, 1965), pp. 155–56.

6. J. Hutchinson, *Dynamics of Cultural Nationalism*, p. 16.

7. Beiser, *Enlightenment, Revolution, and Romanticism*, p. 190.

8. Ibid., pp. 229, 259, 100, 190.

9. Ibid., pp. 1, 8, 225.

10. D. Simpson, *German Aesthetic and Literary Criticism. Kant, Fichte, Schelling, Schopenhauer, Hegel* (Cambridge: Cambridge University Press, 1984), p. 3; F. G. Nauen, *Revolution, Idealism and Human Freedom: Schelling, Hölderlin and Hegel and the Crisis of Early German Idealism* (The Hague: Nijhoff, 1971), p. ix.

11. F. D. Schleiermacher, *Monologues II and III*, in *The Early Political Writings of the German Romantics*, ed. F. C. Beiser, p. 196 (Cambridge: Cambridge University Press, 1996).

12. F. Schlegel, *Ideas* in *Early Political Writings*, ed. Beiser, p. 127; Schlegel, *Essay on the Concept of Republicanism Occasioned by the Kantian Tract 'Perpetual Peace,'* in ibid., p. 100.

13. F. Schlegel, "Über die Diotima," in *Kritische Ausgabe*, ed. E. Behler, p. 88 (Paderborn: Schöningh, 1979), vol. 1.

14. Anonymous author, *The Oldest Systematic Programme of German Idealism*, in *Early Political Writings*, ed. Beiser, pp. 4–5; Beiser, *Enlightenment, Revolution, and Romanticism*, pp. 227, 247, 212, 229, 259, 100.

15. F. Schiller, "Über die ästhetische Erziehung des Menschen in einer Reihe von Briefen," in *Schillers Werke: Nationalausgabe*, ed. L. Blumenthal and B. von Wiese, p. 315 (Weimar: Böhlau, 1943–1967), XX.

16. Beiser, *Enlightenment, Revolution, and Romanticism*, p. 241; Nauen, *Revolution, Idealism and Human Freedom*, p. 4; F. Schlegel, *Ideas*, in *Early Political Writings*, ed. Beiser, pp. 125–26; Schlegel, *Athenæum Fragments*, in ibid., p. 119.

17. Beiser, "Introduction," in *Early Political Writings*, ed. Beiser, pp. xi–xxix; Beiser, *Enlightenment, Revolution, and Romanticism*, pp. 9–10.

18. Barnard, *Herder's Social and Political Thought*, p. 88.

19. Schlegel, *Ideas*, in *Early Political Writings*, ed. Beiser, p. 131.

20. J. G. Herder, "Ideen zur Philosophie der Geschichte der Menschkeit," in *Herders Sämmtliche Werke*, ed. von B. Suphan, p. 455 (Berlin: Weidmann, 1877–1913), XIII.

21. Herder, "Letters for the Advancement of Humanity (1793–1797)—tenth collection," in *Philosophical Writings*, ed. M. N. Forster, pp. 419, 389, 396 (Cambridge: Cambridge University Press, 2002); Barnard, *Herder's Social and Political Thought*, pp. 97, 94, 87.

22. Novalis, *Fragments from the Notebooks*, in *Early Political Writings*, ed. Beiser, pp. 87–88.

23. F. Meinecke, *Weltbürgertum und Nationalstaat: Studien Zur Genesis des deutschen Nationalstaats* (Munich, 1908), pp. 67–88, 74–76; Beiser, *Enlightenment, Revolution, and Romanticism*, p. 238.

24. L. R. Furst, *Romanticism* (London: Methuen, 1969), p. 40; Schlegel, *Athenæum Fragments*, in *Early Political Writings*, ed. Beiser, p. 116.

25. Herder, "Ideen zur Philosophie," in *Sämmtliche Werke*, XIII, p. 347; II, p. 62.

26. Barnard, *Herder's Social and Political Thought*, p. 130.

27. I. Berlin, *Vico and Herder: Two Studies in the History of Ideas* (London: Hogarth Press, 1976), pp. 191, 189.

28. Herder, "Letters—tenth collection," in *Philosophical Writings*, ed. Forster, p. 418.

29. Beiser, *Enlightenment, Revolution, and Romanticism*, pp. 208–9; Barnard, *Herder's Social and Political Thought*, p. 118; Herder, "Letters—tenth collection," in *Philosophical Writings*, ed. Forster, p. 416.

30. Herder, "Letters for the Advancement of Humanity (1793–1797) [excerpt on patriotism]," in *Philosophical Writings*, ed. M. N. Forster, p. 377; Beiser, *Enlightenment, Revolution, and Romanticism*, pp. 209; Barnard, *Herder's Social and Political Thought*, p. 118; Berlin, *Vico and Herder*, p. 191.

31. Berlin, *Vico and Herder*, pp. 212, 192.

32. Beiser, *Enlightenment, Revolution, and Romanticism*, pp. 208-209, 214; Herder, "Letters—tenth collection," in *Philosophical Writings*, ed. Forster, p. 422; Barnard, *Herder's Social and Political Thought*, p. 80.

33. Berlin, *Vico and Herder*, p. 191.

34. Herder, "Letters—tenth collection," in *Philosophical Writings*, ed. Forster, pp. 424, 422–23; Beiser, *Enlightenment, Revolution, and Romanticism*, p. 212; Barnard, *Herder's Social and Political Thought*, p. 105.

35. See Berlin, *Vico and Herder*, p. 180. Herder had a universal notion of Christianity, which he saw as a religion that embraces all human beings and all people, that transcends all local and temporary loyalties in the worship of what is universal and eternal. This thesis was characteristic of the Christian humanism of the German *Aufklärung*, which was pantheist (Berlin, *Vico and Herder*, p. 157; Beiser, *Enlightenment, Revolution, and Romanticism*, p. 205).

36. The idea of a unique identity can of course only be called traditional if it is not taken to mean a national identity.

37. Hutchinson, *Dynamics of Cultural Nationalism*, pp. 1–2, 32–33.

38. A. Walicki, *Philosophy and Romantic Nationalism: The Case of Poland* (Oxford: Clarendon, 1982), pp. 74–77. Walicki's distinction is almost equivalent to the one made by Georg Lukács between "liberal romanticism," which stands for the ideology of moderate progress and "romantic reaction," the apologetic glorification of the Middle Ages. See G. Lukács, *The Historical Novel* (London: Merlin, 1962), pp. 63, 68, 33.

39. Walicki, *Philosophy and Romantic Nationalism*, pp. 74–76.

40. Beiser, *Enlightenment, Revolution, and Romanticism*, pp. 225, 227.

41. D. von Engelhardt, "Romanticism in Germany," in *Romanticism in National Context*, ed. R. Porter and M. Teich, p. 113 (Cambridge: Cambridge University Press, 1988).

42. Beiser, *Enlightenment, Revolution, and Romanticism*, pp. 230, 255.

43. Barnard, *Herder's Social and Political Thought*, p. 133.

44. Herder, "Letters—tenth collection," in *Philosophical Writings*, ed. Forster, p. 421; Berlin, *Vico and Herder*, p. 181; Beiser, *Enlightenment, Revolution, and Romanticism*, p. 212. See also Herder, "Ideen zur Philosophie," in *Sämmtliche Werke*, XIII.

45. Beiser, *Enlightenment, Revolution, and Romanticism*, pp. 190, 212.

46. F. Schlegel, cited in Beiser, *Enlightenment, Revolution, and Romanticism*, pp. 260, 234.

47. Beiser, *Enlightenment, Revolution, and Romanticism*, pp. 200–1.

48. Herder, "Letters Concerning the Progress of Humanity (1792)," in *Philosophical Writings*, ed. M. N. Forster, p. 364.

49. Herder, "Kleine Schriften. 1791–1796," in *Herders Sämmtliche Werke*, ed. von B. Suphan, XVIII, p. 384; Barnard, *Herder's Social and Political Thought*, pp. 58, 68.

50. Barnard, *Herder's Social and Political Thought*, pp. 67–68.

51. Schleiermacher, *Monologues II and III*, in *Early Political Writings*, ed. Beiser, 182, 183, 178–79. See Furst, *Romanticism*, pp. 39–40; Beiser, *Enlightenment, Revolution, and Romanticism*, p. 270; von Engelhardt, "Romanticism in Germany," p. 120.

52. Novalis, *Faith and Love*, in *Early Political Writings*, ed. Beiser, p. 45.

53. Beiser, *Enlightenment, Revolution, and Romanticism*, pp. 270, 252, 235, 231–32, 267; Novalis, *Fragments from the Notebooks*, in *Early Political Writings*, ed. Beiser, pp. 87, 84.

54. Barnard, *Herder's Social and Political Thought*, pp. 67, 86, 63; Beiser, *Enlightenment, Revolution, and Romanticism*, pp. 213–14.

55. Barnard, *Herder's Social and Political Thought*, p. 139; Beiser, *Enlightenment, Revolution, and Romanticism*, pp. 211–12.

56. Herder, "This Too a Philosophy of History for the Formation of Humanity," in *Philosophical Writings*, ed. Forster, pp. 268–358; Beiser, *Enlightenment, Revolution, and Romanticism*, pp. 206–7, 203; Herder, "Letters—tenth collection," in *Philosophical Writings*, ed. Forster, pp. 386, 394–95.

57. Beiser, pp. 211, 214–15; Barnard, *Herder's Social and Political Thought*, p. 77.

58. Herder, "Letters for the Advancement of Humanity (1793–1797)," in *Philosophical Writings*, ed. Forster, pp. 370–73; Barnard, *Herder's Social and Political Thought*, p. 77; Beiser, *Enlightenment, Revolution, and Romanticism*, p. 210.

59. Beiser, *Enlightenment, Revolution, and Romanticism*, p. 227. The organic concept was later developed by Adam Müller into a theory which served conservative ends. See Beiser, *Enlightenment, Revolution, and Romanticism*, p. 238.

60. Schleiermacher, *Monologues II and III*, in *Early Political Writings*, ed. Beiser, p. 185.

61. See Hans Kohn, *The Idea of Nationalism* (New York, 1945) and Gellner, *Nations and Nationalism.*

62. Hutchinson, *Dynamics of Cultural Nationalism*, pp. 9–10, 30–33.

63. Beiser, *Enlightenment, Revolution, and Romanticism*, pp. 236, 252, 275; Beiser, ed., *Early Political Writings*, p. xxix.

64. See Herder, "This Too a Philosophy of History," in *Philosophical Writings*, ed. Forster, pp. 268–358; von Engelhardt, "Romanticism in Germany," in *Romanticism in National Context*, ed. Porter and Teich, pp. 114–15, 126; Novalis, "Christianity or Europe: A Fragment," in *Early Political Writings*, ed. Beiser, p. 64.

65. Beiser, *Enlightenment, Revolution, and Romanticism*, pp. 239, 276, 238.

66. Novalis, "Faith and Love," in *Early Political Writings*, ed. Beiser, p. 45.

67. F. Schlegel, cited in Beiser, *Enlightenment, Revolution, and Romanticism*, pp. 246–47.

68. Hutchinson, *Dynamics of Cultural Nationalism*, p. 33; Beiser, *Enlightenment, Revolution, and Romanticism*, pp. 223, 287.

69. Beiser, ed., *Early Political Writings*, p. xxix.

70. Beiser, *Enlightenment, Revolution, and Romanticism*, p. 281–82; Aris, *History of Political Thought in Germany*, p. 219.

71. Ibid., p. 229.

72. Hutchinson, *Dynamics of Cultural Nationalism*, pp. 35–36, 46.

73. Walicki, *Philosophy and Romantic Nationalism*, p. 77.

CHAPTER SEVEN

1. M. Raeff, *Understanding Imperial Russia. State and Society in the Old Regime* (New York, 1984), pp. 141–42; H. Seton-Watson, *The Russian Empire 1801–1917* (Oxford: Clarendon, 1988), p. 186. See also A. G. Mazour, *The First Russian Revolution, 1825. The Decembrist Movement. Its Origins, Development, and Significance* (Stanford: Stanford University Press, 1961), pp. 64–117; A. Yarmolinsky, *Road to Revolution. A Century of Russian Radicalism* (Princeton: Princeton University Press, 1986), pp. 15–57.

2. A. S. Khomiakov, *Polnoe sobranie sochinenii*, 8 vols. (Moscow, 1900–1914), III, p. 75.

3. I. V. Kireevsky, *Izbrannye stati* (Moscow: Sovremennik, 1984), p. 122; I. V. Kireevsky, "On the Nature of European Culture and Its Relation to the Culture of Russia," in *Russian Intellectual History: An Anthology*, ed. M. Raeff, p. 198 (New York: Harcourt, 1966).

4. Khomiakov, *Polnoe sobranie sochinenii*, I, p. 164.

5. Ibid., p. 14.

6. Ibid., pp. 15, 54.

7. A. S. Khomiakov, "To the Serbians. A Message from Moscow," in *An Introduction to Nineteenth-Century Slavophilism*, P. Christoff, vol. I: *A. S. Xomjakov* (The Hague: Mouton, 1961), pp. 266, 254; Khomiakov, *Polnoe sobranie sochinenii*, III, pp. 333–34.

8. Khomiakov, *Polnoe sobranie sochinenii*, I, pp. 98–99.

9. Ibid., pp. 14–15.

10. Kireevsky, *Izbrannye stati*, pp. 122–23.

11. Ibid., p. 80.

12. Khomiakov, "To the Serbians," p. 254.

13. This point is also made by Andrzej Walicki in *A History of Russian Thought from the Enlightenment to Marxism* (Stanford: Stanford University Press, 1979), p. 110.

14. Kireevsky, *Izbrannye stati*, p. 123.

15. K. S. Aksakov, "On the Internal State of Russia," in *Russian Intellectual History: An Anthology*, ed. M. Raeff (New York: Harcout, 1966), pp. 251, 241.

16. Khomiakov, *Polnoe sobranie sochinenii*, VIII, pp. 200–201; K. S. Aksakov, *Polnoe sobranie sochinenii*, 3 vols. (Moscow, 1861–1880), I, p. 292.

17. Khomiakov, "Letter to Countess A. D. Bludova," 1848, *Polnoe sobranie sochinenii*, VIII.

18. Aksakov, "On the Internal State of Russia," pp. 236–37 234, 239.

19. Ibid., p. 233; I. V. Kireevsky, *Polnoe sobranie sochinenii*, 2 vols. (Moscow, 1911), II, p. 272.

20. Aksakov, "On the Internal State of Russia," pp. 233, 248, 250; Khomiakov, "To the Serbians," p. 267.

21. Aksakov, ibid., pp. 248, 239–40, 250; Khomiakov, ibid.

22. Khomiakov, "To the Serbians," p. 254.

23. Kireevsky, "On the Nature of European Culture," p. 197.

24. Kireevsky, *Izbrannye stati*, p. 125.

25. Khomiakov, "To the Serbians," pp. 254–55; Khomiakov, *Polnoe sobranie sochinenii*, I, p. 131.

26. Ibid., pp. 130–32.

27. Khomiakov, "To the Serbians," pp. 263–64.

28. Kireevsky, "On the Nature of European Culture," p. 203.

29. Khomiakov, "To the Serbians," pp. 251, 267.

30. Kireevsky, *Izbrannye stati*, pp. 122–23.

31. Khomiakov, *Polnoe sobranie sochinenii*, II, pp. 3–6, 312–13; ibid. III, pp. 27–28.

32. Ibid., I, pp. 14, 38.

33. A. S. Khomiakov, "On Humboldt," in *Russian Intellectual History*, ed. M. Raeff, p. 212.

34. Kireevsky, *Izbrannye stati*, p. 120.

35. Khomiakov, *Polnoe sobranie sochinenii*, III, p. 29; Khomiakov, "To the Serbians," p. 253.

36. Khomiakov, ibid., I, pp. 130, 85, 98.

37. Khomiakov, "To the Serbians," p. 253; Kireevsky, "On the Nature of European Culture," p. 207.

38. Khomiakov, "On Humboldt," p. 226; Kireevsky, *Izbrannye stati*, pp. 125–26.

39. Kireevsky, *Izbrannye stati*, p. 198.

40. Kireevsky, ibid, p. 126; Aksakov, "On the Internal State of Russia," pp. 233, 242–45.

41. Walicki, *History of Russian Thought*, p. 110; F. C. Copleston, *Philosophy in Russia. From Herzen to Lenin and Berdyaev* (Notre Dame: University of Notre Dame Press, 1986), pp. 46–47.

42. A. Gleason, *European and Muscovite: Ivan Kireevsky and the Origins of Slavophilism* (Cambridge, MA: Harvard University Press, 1972), pp. 4, 151, 169. See also Iu. Z. Iankovsky, *Patriarkhalno-dvorianskaia utopiia* (Moscow: Khuclozhestvennoia literatura, 1994), and S. Carter, *Russian Nationalism. Yesterday, Today, Tomorrow* (London: Pinter, 1990).

43. Walicki, *History of Russian Thought*, pp. 111, 107.

44. A. Walicki, *The Slavophile Controversy* (Oxford: Clarendon, 1975), pp. 177–78.

45. M. Hughes, "'Independent Gentlemen': The Social Position of the Moscow Slavophiles and Its Impact on their Political Thought," *The Slavonic and East European Review* 71, no. 1 (1993): 67, 73, 75, 84. See also E. A. Dudzinskaia, *Slavianofily v obshchestvennoi borbe* (Moscow, 1983).

46. A. Koshelev, *Zapiski* (Berlin: B. Behr's Verlag, 1884), pp. 76–77. David Saunders takes this as evidence for that the Slavophiles were not as conservative as Walicki describes them. See Saunders, *Russia in the Age of Reaction and Reform 1801–1881* (New York: Longman, 1992), p. 163. In 1952 Hugh Seton-Watson contended that they were no less discontented than the Westernizers with the regime of Nicholas I. They were well aware of the backwardness and ignorance of the Russian people, the wrongs of the serfs and the absence of civil liberties. The Slavophiles wanted to remedy these things. They wished to reform Russia and, above all, to emancipate the serfs. See *The Russian Empire*, pp. 22, 24.

47. Kireevsky, *Izbrannye stati*, pp. 126, 118; Kireevsky, "On the Nature of European Culture," p. 207.

48. Khomiakov, *Polnoe sobranie sochinenii*, III, p. 462.

49. Ibid., pp. 115–16.

50. Khomiakov, *Polnoe sobranie sochinenii*, I, pp. 123, 129.

51. Ibid., pp. 128, 123; Khomiakov cited in Christoff, *Introduction to Nineteenth-Century Slavophilism*, I, p. 218.

52. Khomiakov, *Polnoe sobranie sochinenii*, I, pp. 128–30.

53. Khomiakov, "On Humboldt," pp. 217–18.

54. Khomiakov, "On Recent Developments in Philosophy," in *Russian Philosophy*, ed. Edie et al. (Chicago: Quadrangle books, 1965), vol. I, p. 245.

CONCLUSION

1. A. Walicki, *A History of Russian Thought from the Enlightenment to Marxism* (Stanford: Stanford University Press, 1979), pp. 162–70.

2. M. Hroch, "From National Movement to Fully-Fledged Nation," *New Left Review*, no. 198 (1993): 6–7.

3. Ibid., pp. 7–8.

4. J. Hutchinson, *The Dynamics of Cultural Nationalism: The Gaelic Revival and the Creation of the Irish Nation State* (London: Allen & Unwin, 1987), pp. 17, 38. See also A. D. Smith, *Theories of Nationalism*, 2nd ed. (London: Duckworth, 1983); A. D. Smith, *The Ethnic Revival* (Cambridge: Cambridge University Press, 1981).

5. H. Muchnic, *Rysk litteratur före 1900* (Stockholm: Aldus/Bonnier, 1968), pp. 56–77.

6. See R. Aizlewood, "The Return of the 'Russian Idea' in Publications, 1988–91," *Slavonic and East European Review* 71, no. 3 (1993) and S. B. Dzhimbinov, "The Return of Russian Philosophy," in *Russian Thought after Communism: The Recovery of a Philosophical Heritage*, ed. J. Scanlan (Armonk, NY: Sharpe, 1994) for a review of the recent revival. See S. Hudspith, *Dostoevsky and the Idea of Russianess* (London: Routledge Curzon, 2004) for the influence of Slavophile thought on Dostoevsky's writing.

7. *Landmarks: A Collection of Essays on the Russian Intelligentsia 1909 [Vekhi]*, ed. B. Shragin and A. Todd (New York: Howard, 1977, [1909]).

8. C. Read, *Religion, Revolution and the Russian Intelligentsia 1900–1912* (London: Macmillan, 1979), p. 120.

9. S. Tompkins, "Vekhi and the Russian Intelligentsia," *Canadian Slavonic Papers*, II (1957), pp. 22–23, 19; E. Lampert, "Vekhi and the Vekhovtsy: A Critical Re-examination," *New Zealand Slavonic Journal*, no. 2 (1978): 43–44.

10. D. Brown, *Soviet Russian Literature since Stalin* (Cambridge: Cambridge University Press, 1978), pp. 219–21; J. Dunlop, *The Faces of Contemporary Russian Nationalism* (Princeton: Princeton University Press, 1983), pp. 111, 130, 94–105, 40; S. Carter, *Russian Nationalism. Yesterday, Today, Tomorrow* (London: Pinter, 1990), pp. 93, 100, 84.

11. A. Solzhenitsyn, ed., *From under the Rubble* (London: Collins & Harvill, 1975).

12. A. Solzhenitsyn, "Repentance and Self-Limitation in the Life of Nations," in *From under the Rubble*, pp. 122, 126–27; V. Borisov, "Personality and National Awareness," in ibid., pp. 219–22.

13. A. Solzhenitsyn, "Repentance," in *From under the Rubble*, pp. 139–40; A. B., "The Direction of Change," in ibid., pp. 145–48; F. Korsakov, "Russian Destinies,"

in ibid., p. 153; E. Barabanov, "The Schism between the Church and the World," in ibid., p. 191; V. Borisov, "Personality and National Awareness," in ibid., p. 200; I. Shafarevich, "Does Russia Have a Future?" in ibid., p. 294; M. Agurskii, "Contemporary Socioeconomic Systems and Their Future Prospects," in ibid., pp. 67–73.

14. Korsakov, "Russian Destinies," in *From under the Rubble*, p. 157; Borisov, "Personality and National Awareness," in ibid., pp. 200, 213; A. Solzhenitsyn, "As Breathing and Consciousness Return," in ibid., pp. 19–25.

15. A. Solzhenitsyn, "The Smatterers," in *From under the Rubble*, p. 263; Solzhenitsyn, "Repentance," p. 116.

16. V. Shchukin, "Kulturnyi mir russkogo zapadnika," *Voprosy filosofii*, no. 5 (1992): 74; V. Rubanov, "Bezopasnost i budushchee Rossii," *Svobodnaia mysl*, no. 10 (1995): 4, 7–8.

17. V. Diakov, "Slavianskaia ideia v istorii i sovremennosti," *Svobodnaia mysl*, no. 4 (1992): 82; "Rossiia i Zapad," *Voprosy Filosofii*, no. 6 (1992): 23; N. Ivanova, "Russkii vopros," *Znamia*, no. 1 (1992): 156; Iu. Borodai, "Tretii put," *Nash Sovremennik*, no. 9 (1991): 147; A. Solzhenitsyn, *"The Russian Question" at the End of the Twentieth Century* (New York: Farrar, Straus & Giroux, 1995), pp. 106–107; V. L. Manilov, "Natsionalnaia bezopasnost: tsennosti, interesy i tseli," *Voiennaia Mysl*, no. 6 (1995): 35, 37.

18. Diakov, "Slavianskaia ideia," p. 82; "Rossiia i Zapad," p. 23; Rubanov, "Bezopasnost i budushchee Rossii," pp. 5, 7; I. Troitskii, *Shto Takoe Russkaia Sobornost?* (Moscow: AKIRN, 1993), p. 5; Borodai, "Tretii put," pp. 131–35, 140–43; A. Andreev, "Zemlia i derzhava," *Nezavisimaia Gazeta* (96-03-19), p. 2.

19. P. Tulaev, "Rossiia i Evropa," *Nash Sovremennik*, no. 11 (1991): 161–62; Rubanov, "Bezopasnost i budushchee Rossii," pp. 9, 11; A. Solzhenitsyn, *"The Russian Question,"* p. 89; D. Ilin, "Russkaia ideia na poligone demokratii," *Nash Sovremennik*, no. 3 (1991): 23–24; Borodai, "Tretii put," pp. 143–45; Troitskii, *Shto Takoe Russkaia Sobornost?* pp. 6–7.

20. "Rossiia i Zapad," p. 22; Ilin, "Russkaia ideia na poligone demokratii," pp. 6, 26.

21. G. Ziuganov, "Rossiia i sovremennyi mir," *Transition*, no. 11 (1996): 16–17; Sovietskaia Rossiia, 19/3 (1996): 2.

22. Manilov, "Natsionalnaia bezopasnost: tsennosti, interesy i tseli," pp. 32–33; Troitskii, *Shto Takoe Russkaia Sobornost?* p. 19.

Bibliography

A. B. "The Direction of Change." In *From Under the Rubble*, edited by A. Solzhenitsyn, pp. 144–50. London: Collins & Harvill Press, 1975.

Agurskii, M. "Contemporary Socioeconomic Systems and their Future Prospects." In *From Under the Rubble*, edited by A. Solzhenitsyn, pp. 67–87. London: Collins & Harvill Press, 1975.

Aizlewood, R. "The Return of the 'Russian Idea' in Publications, 1988–91." *Slavonic and East European Review* 71, no. 3 (1993): 490–99.

Aksakov, K. S. *Polnoe sobranie sochinenii.* 3 vols. Moscow, 1861–1880.

———. "On the Internal State of Russia." In *Russian Intellectual History: An Anthology*, edited by M. Raeff, pp. 231–51. New York: Harcourt, 1966.

Andreev, A. "Zemlia i derzhava." *Nezavisimaia Gazeta*, 96-03-19.

Anderson, B. *Imagined Communities: Reflections on the Origin and Spread of Nationalism.* London: Verso, 1991.

Anonymous. *The Oldest Systematic Programme of German Idealism.* In *The Early Political Writings of the German Romantics*, edited by F. C. Beiser, pp. 1–5. Cambridge: Cambridge University Press, 1996.

Aris, R. *History of Political Thought in Germany from 1789–1815.* London: Allen & Unwin, 1936.

Bakunin, M. A. "The Confession to Tsar Nicholas I." In *Selected Writings.* London: Jonathan Cape, 1973.

———. "Statism and Anarchy." In *Selected Writings.* London: Jonathan Cape, 1973.

Barabanov, E. "The Schism between the Church and the World." In *From Under the Rubble*, edited by A. Solzhenitsyn, pp. 172–93. London: Collins & Havill Press, 1975.

Barnard, F. M. *Herder's Social and Political Thought: From Enlightenment to Nationalism.* Oxford: Clarendon Press, 1965.

Bauman, Z. *Legislators and Interpreters.* Cambridge: Polity Press, 1987.

Beiser, F. C. *Enlightenment, Revolution, and Romanticism: The Genesis of Modern German Political Thought 1790–1800.* Cambridge, MA: Harvard University Press, 1992.

————, ed. *The Early Political Writings of the German Romantics*. Cambridge: Cambridge University Press, 1996.

Belinsky, V. G. *Selected Philosophical Works*. Moscow: Foreign Languages Pub. House, 1956.

————. "Letter to N. V. Gogol." In *Russian Intellectual History. An Anthology*, edited by M. Raeff, pp. 253–61. New York: Harcourt, 1966.

————. *Polnoe sobranie sochinenii*. 13 vols. Moscow: Izdatelstvo Akademii nauk SSSR, 1953–1959.

Berdiaev, N. *The Origin of Russian Communism*. London: The Centenary Press, 1937.

————. *The Russian Idea*. London, 1947.

Berlin, I. *Vico and Herder: Two Studies in the History of Ideas*. London: Hogarth Press, 1976.

————. *Russian Thinkers*. Edited by H. Hardy, and A. Kelly. London: Hogarth Press, 1978.

————. "Russian Thought and the Slavophile Controversy." *The Slavonic and East European Review* 59, no. 4 (1981): 572–86.

Billington, J. *The Icon and the Axe: An Interpretive History of Russian Culture*. New York: Knopf, 1966.

Blackwell, W. L. *The Industrialization of Russia: A Historical Perspective*. 3rd ed. Arlington Heights: Harlan Davidson, Inc., 1994.

Bodin, P. A. *Ryssland och Europa. En kulturhistorisk studie*. Stockholm, 1993.

Boobyer, P. "Russian Liberal Conservatism." In *Russian Nationalism Past and Present*, edited by G. Hoskin and R. Service, pp. 35–54. Basingstoke: Macmillan Press, 1998.

Borisov, V. "Personality and National Awareness." In *From Under the Rubble*, edited by A. Solzhenitsyn, pp. 194–228. London: Collins & Harvill Press, 1975.

Borodai, I. "Tretii puti." *Nash sovremennik*, no. 9 (1991): 130–47.

Brown, D. B. *Soviet Russian Literature since Stalin*. Cambridge: Cambridge University Press, 1978.

Breuilly, J. *Nationalism and the State*. Manchester, England: Manchester University Press, 1993.

Brubaker, R. *Citizenship and Nationhood in France and Germany*. Cambridge, MA: Harvard University Press, 1992.

Carter, S. *Russian Nationalism. Yesterday, Today, Tomorrow*. London: Pinter, 1990.

Chaadaev, P. *Philosophical Letters and Apology of a Madman*. Knoxville: University of Tennessee, 1969.

————. *Philosophical Works of Peter Chaadaev*. Edited by R. T. McNally and R. Tempest. Dordrecht: Kluwer Academic Publishers, 1991.

Christoff, P. K. *An Introduction to Nineteenth-Century Slavophilism*. Vol. I: *A. S. Xomjakov*, The Hague: Mouton, 1961; Vol. II: *I. V. Kireevsky*, The Hague: Mouton, 1972; Vol. III: *K. S. Aksakov*, Princeton, NJ: Princeton University Press, 1982; Vol. IV: *Iu. F. Samarin*, Boulder: Mouton, 1991.

————. *The Third Heart: Some Intellectual-Ideological Currents and Cross Currents in Russia 1800–1830*. The Hague: Mouton, 1970.

Copleston, F. C. *Philosophy in Russia. From Herzen to Lenin and Berdyaev*. Notre Dame: University of Notre Dame Press, 1986.

Custine, Marquis de. *Letters from Russia*. London: Penguin Books, 1991.

Diakov, V. "Slavianskaia ideia v istorii i sovremennosti." *Svobodnaia mysl*, no. 4 (1992): 73–83.

Dmitriev, S. "Slavianofily i slavianofilstvo." *Istorik-Marksist*, no. 1 (1941).

Dmitriev, S. S. "Podkhod dolzhen byt konkretno-istoricheskii." *Voprosy literatury*, no. 12 (1969): 73–84.

Dudzinskaia, E. A. *Slavianofily v obshchestvennoi borbe*. Moscow, 1983.

————. *Slavianofily v poreformennoi Rossii*. Moscow, 1994.

Dunlop, J. *The Faces of Contemporary Russian Nationalism*. Princeton: Princeton University Press, 1983.

Dzhimbinov, S. B. "The Return of Russian Philosophy." In *Russian Thought after Communism: The Recovery of a Philosophical Heritage*, edited by J. Scanlan, pp. 11–22. Armonk, NY: Sharpe, 1994.

Edie, J. M. J. P. Scanlan,and M. Zeldin, eds. *Russian Philosophy*. Vol. 1. Chicago: Quadrangle books, 1965.

Furst, L. R. *Romanticism*. London: Methuen, 1969.

Gellner, E. *Nations and Nationalism*. Oxford: Blackwell, 1983.

Gleason, A. *European and Muscovite: Ivan Kireevsky and the Origins of Slavophilism*. Cambridge, MA: Harvard University Press, 1972.

Greenfeld, L. *Nationalism. Five Roads to Modernity*. Cambridge, MA: Harvard University Press, 1993.

Guibernau, M. *Nationalisms. The Nation-State and Nationalism in the Twentieth Century*. Cambridge: Polity Press, 1996.

Hamburg, G. M. *Boris Chicherin and Early Russian Liberalism, 1828–1866*. Stanford: Stanford University Press, 1992.

Herder, J. G. *Herders Sämmtliche Werke*. Edited by B. von Suphan. Berlin: Weidmann, 1877–1913.

————. *Philosophical Writings*. Edited by M. N. Forster. Cambridge: Cambridge University Press, 2002.

Herzen, A. *My Past and Thoughts: The Memoirs of Alexander Herzen*. 4 vols. London: Chatto & Windus, 1968.

————. *Selected Philosophical Works*. Moscow: Foreign Languages Pub. House, 1956.

————. "Dilettantism in Science." In *A Documentary History of Russian Thought*, edited by W. J. Leatherbarrow and D. C. Offord, pp. 136–46. Ann Arbor: Ardis, 1987.

Hobsbawm, E. J. *Nations and Nationalism since 1780: Programme, Myth, Reality.* Cambridge: Cambridge University Press, 1992.

Hobsbawm, E. J., and T. Ranger, eds. *The Invention of Tradition.* Cambridge: Cambridge University Press, 1983.

Hosking, G. A. *Russia: People and Empire, 1552–1917.* Cambridge, MA: Harvard University Press, 1997.

Hroch, M. "From National Movement to Fully-Fledged Nation." *New Left Review,* no. 198 (March/April 1993).

Hsiau, A. *Contemporary Taiwanese Cultural Nationalism.* London: Routledge, 2000.

Hudspith, S. *Dostoevsky and the Idea of Russianess: A New Perspective on Unity and Brotherhood.* London: Routledge Curzon, 2004.

Hughes, M. *Nationalism and Society. Germany 1800–1945.* London: Arnold, 1988.

Hughes, M. "'Independent Gentlemen': The Social Position of the Moscow Slavophiles and Its Impact on Their Political Thought." *The Slavonic and East European Review* 71, no. 1 (1993): 66–88.

Huntington, S. P. *The Clash of Civilizations and the Remaking of World Order.* New York: Simon & Schuster, 1996.

Hutchinson, J. *The Dynamics of Cultural Nationalism: The Gaelic Revival and the Creation of the Irish Nation State.* London: Allen & Unwin, 1987.

Iu. Z. Iankovskii. *Patriarkhalno-dvorianskaia utopiia.* Moscow: Khudozhestvennaia literatura, 1981.

Ignatieff, M. *Blood and Belonging: Journeys into the New Nationalism.* New York: Farrar, Straus and Giroux, 1994.

Ilin, D. "Russkaia ideia na poligone demokratii." *Nash sovremennik,* no. 3 (1991): 5–27.

Intellectuals and the Articulation of the Nation. Edited by R. G. Suny and M. P. Kennedy. Ann Arbor: University of Michigan Press, 1999.

Ivanova, N. "Russkii vopros." *Znamia,* no. 1 (1992): 191–204.

Jusdanis, G. *The Necessary Nation.* Princeton, NJ: Princeton University Press, 2001.

Kedourie, E. *Nationalism.* 3rd ed. London: Hutchinson, 1966.

Khomiakov, A. S. *Polnoe sobranie sochinenii* [Complete collected works]. 8 vols. Moscow, 1900–1914.

———. *Izbrannye sochineniia* [Selected works]. New York: Izdatelstvo imeni chekhova, 1955.

———. "To the Serbians. A Message from Moscow." In *An Introduction to Nineteenth Century Slavophilism.* Vol. 1: *A. S. Xomjakov,* edited by P. Christoff, pp. 247–68. The Hague: Mouton, 1961.

———. "On Recent Developments in Philosophy." In *Russian Philosophy,* edited by J. M. Edie, J. P. Scanlan, and M. Zeldin, pp. 221–69. 2 vols. Chicago: Quadrangle books, 1965.

———. "On Humboldt." In *Russian Intellectual History: An Anthology*, edited by M. Raeff, pp. 209–29. New York: Harcourt, 1966.

Kireevsky, I. V. *Polnoe sobranie sochinenii*. Edited by M. O. Gershenzon. 2 vols. Moscow, 1911.

———. *Izbrannye stati* [Selected articles]. Moscow: Sovremennik, 1984.

———. "On the Nature of European Culture and Its Relation to the Culture of Russia." In *Russian Intellectual History: An Anthology*, edited by M. Raeff, pp. 175–207. New York: Harcourt, 1966.

Kohn, H. *The Idea of Nationalism*. New York, 1945.

Korsakov, F. "Russian Destinies." In *From Under the Rubble*, edited by A. Solzhenitsyn, pp. 151–71. London: Collins & Harvill, 1975.

Koshelev, A. *Zapiski*. Berlin: B. Behr's Verlag, 1884.

Koyré, A. *La Philosophie et la problème national en Russie au début du XIX siècle*. Paris: Champion, 1929.

Kymlicka, W. "Misunderstanding Nationalism." In *Theorizing Nationalism*, edited by R. Beiner, pp. 131–40. Albany: State University of New York Press,1999.

Lampert, E. "Vekhi and the Vekhovtsy: A Critical Re-examination." *New Zealand Slavonic Journal*, no. 2 (1978): 41–58.

Lanz, H. "The Philosophy of Ivan Kireevsky." *The Slavonic Review* IV (1925): 594–604.

Leatherbarrow, W. J., and D. C. Offord, eds. *A Documentary History of Russian Thought. From the Enlightenment to Marxism*. Ann Arbor: Ardis, 1987.

Leighton, L. G. *Russian Romanticism: Two Essays*. The Hague: Mouton, 1975.

Lieven, D. *The Aristocracy in Europe, 1815–1914*. Basingstoke: Macmillan, 1992.

"Literaturnaia kritika rannikh slavianofilov." *Voprosy literatury*, nos. 5, 7, 10, 12 (1969): 90–135; 116–52; 103–44; 73–140.

Lossky, N. O. *History of Russian Philosophy*. New York: International University Press, 1951.

Lotman, I. M., and B. A. Uspenskii. "Binary Models in the Dynamics of Russian Culture." In *The Semiotics of Russian Cultural History*, edited by A. D. Nakhimovsky and A. S. Nakhimovsky, pp. 30–66. Ithaca, NY: Cornell University Press. 1985.

Lukács, G. *The Historical Novel*. London: Merlin, 1962.

Malia, M. "What Is the Intelligentsia?" *Daedalus* 89, no. 3 (Summer 1960): 441–58.

———. *Alexander Herzen and the Birth of Russian Socialism 1812–1855*. Cambridge, MA: Harvard University Press, 1961.

———. *Russia Under Western Eyes. From the Bronze Horseman to the Lenin Mausoleum*. Cambridge, MA: Harvard University Press, 1999.

Manilov, V. L. "Natsionalnaia bezopasnost: tsennosti, interesy i tseli." *Voennaia mysl*, no. 6 (1995).

Martin, A. *Romantics, Reformers, Reactionaries. Russian Conservative Thought and Politics in the Reign of Alexander I.* Dekalb: Northern Illinois University Press, 1997.

Mazour, A. G. *The First Russian Revolution, 1825. The Decembrist Movement. Its Origins, Development, and Significance.* Stanford: Stanford University Press, 1961.

McDaniel, T. *The Agony of the Russian Idea.* Princeton: Princeton University Press, 1996.

McNally, R., and R. Tempest, eds. *Philosophical Works of Peter Chaadaev.* Dordrecht: Kluwer Academic Publishers, 1991.

Meinecke, F. *Weltbürgertum und Nationalstaat: Studien Zur Genesis des deutschen Nationalstaats.* Munich, 1908. English translation of 1963 ed. by F. Meinecke, *Cosmopolitanism and the National State.* Princeton: Princeton University Press, 1970.

———. *Cosmopolitanism and the National State.* Princeton: Princeton University Press, 1970.

Mill, J. S. *Utilitarianism, Liberty and Representative Government.* London: Dent, 1910.

Muchnic, H. *Rysk litteratur före 1900.* Stockholm: Aldus/Bonnier, 1968.

Müller, M. *Russischer Intellekt in Europäischer Krise: Ivan V. Kireevskij (1806–1856).* Köln: Böhlau, 1966.

Nauen, F. G. *Revolution, Idealism and Human Freedom: Schelling, Hölderlin and Hegel and the Crisis of Early German Idealism.* The Hague: Nijhoff, 1971.

Neumann, I. *Russia and the Idea of Europe.* London: Routledge, 1996.

Nielsen, K. "Cultural Nationalism, Neither Ethnic nor Civic." In *Theorizing Nationalism,* edited by R. Beiner, pp. 119–30. Albany: State University of New York Press, 1999.

Nipperdey, T. "In Search of Identity." In *Romantic Nationalism in Europe,* edited by J. C. Eade, pp. 1–16. Canberra: Australian National University Press, 1983.

Novalis. "Christianity or Europe: A Fragment." In *The Early Political Writings of the German Romantics,* edited by F. C. Beiser, pp. 59–79. Cambridge: Cambridge University Press, 1996.

———. "Faith and Love." In *The Early Political Writings of the German Romantics,* pp. 33–49. Cambridge: Cambridge University Press, 1996.

———. "Fragments from the Notebooks." In *The Early Political Writings of the German Romantics,* pp. 81–92. Cambridge: Cambridge University Press, 1996.

Odoevsky, V. F. "Russkie nochi." In *Sochineniia kniazia V.F. Odoevskago.* St. Petersburg: Ivanov, 1844.

Offord, D. *Portraits of Early Russian Liberals. A Study of the Thought of T. N. Granovsky, V. P. Botkin, P. V. Annenkov, A. V. Druzhinin, and K. D. Kavelin.* Cambridge: Cambridge University Press, 1985.

Parland, T. *The Rejection in Russia of Totalitarian Socialism and Liberal Democracy. A Study of the Russian New Right.* Helsinki: Finnish Society of Sciences and Letters, 1993.

Pipes, R. "The Historical Evolution of the Russian Intelligentsia." *Daedalus* (Summer 1960): 487–502.

———. *Russia under the Old Regime*. 2nd ed. London: Penguin, 1995.

———. *The Russian Revolution*. New York: Knopf, 1990.

———. *Russia under the Bolshevik Regime*. New York: Knopf, 1993.

———. *Property and Freedom*. New York: Knopf, 1999.

Plamenatz, J. "Two Types of Nationalism." In *Nationalism*, edited by E. Kamenka, pp. 22–36. Canberra: Australian National University Press, 1973.

Pospielovsky, D. "A Comparative Enquiry into Neo-Slavophilism and Its Antecedents in the Russian History of Ideas." *Soviet Studies* 31, no. 3 (1979): 319–42.

Prizel, I. *National Identity and Foreign Policy. Nationalism and Leadership in Poland, Russia and Ukraine*. Cambridge: Cambridge University Press, 1998.

Raeff, M. *Origins of the Russian Intelligentsia: The Eighteenth-Century Nobility*. New York: Harcourt, Brace & World, 1966.

———. *Russian Intellectual History: An Anthology*. New York: Harcourt, 1966.

———. *Understanding Imperial Russia: State and Society in the Old Regime*. New York: Columbia University Press, 1984.

———. *Political Ideas and Institutions in Imperial Russia*. Boulder: Westview Press, 1994.

———. "The People, the Intelligentsia and Russian Political Culture." Special Issue, *Political Studies* 41 (1993).

Read, C. *Religion, Revolution and the Russian Intelligentsia 1900–1912*. London: Macmillan, 1979.

Renan, E. *Qu'est-ce qu'une nation?* Paris, 1882.

Riasanovsky, N. V. *Russia and the West in the Teaching of the Slavophiles*. Cambridge, MA: Harvard University Press, 1952.

———. "Notes on the Emergence and Nature of the Russian Intelligentsia." In *Art and Culture in Nineteenth Century Russia*, edited by T. G. Stavrou, pp. 3–25. Bloomington: Indiana University Press, 1983.

Rogger, H. *National Consciousness in Eighteenth-Century Russia*. Cambridge, MA: Harvard University Press, 1960.

Roosevelt, P. R. *Apostle of Russian Liberalism: Timofei Granovsky*. Newtonville: Oriental research partners, 1986.

"Rossiia i Zapad." *Voprosy filosofii*, no. 6 (1992): 3–49.

Rouleau, F. *Ivan Kireievski et la naissance du Slavophilisme*. Namur: Culture et verité, 1990.

Rowley, D. G. "Russian Nationalism and the Cold War." *American Historical Review* 99, no. 1 (February 1994): 155–71.

Rubanov, V. "Bezopasnost i budushchee Rossii." *Svobodnaia mysl*, no. 10 (1995): 3–11.

Saunders, D. *Russia in the Age of Reaction and Reform 1801–1881*. New York: Lognman, 1992.

Schapiro, L. *Rationalism and Nationalism in Russian Nineteenth-Century Political Thought*. New Haven: Yale University Press, 1967.

Schiller, F. "Über die ästhetische Erziehung des Menschen in einer Reihe von Briefen." In *Schillers Werke: Nationalausgabe*, edited by L. Blumenthal and B. von Wiese, pp. 309–412. Weimar: Böhlau, 1943–1967, XX.

Schlegel, F. "Athenæum Fragments." In *The Early Political Writings of the German Romantics*, edited by F. C. Beiser, pp. 113–22. Cambridge: Cambridge University Press, 1996.

———. "Essay on the Concept of Republicanism Occasioned by the Kantian Tract 'Perpetual Peace.'" In *The Early Political Writings of the German Romantics*, pp. 93–112. Cambridge: Cambridge University Press, 1996.

———. "Ideas." In *The Early Political Writings of the German Romantics*, pp. 123–40. Cambridge: Cambridge University Press, 1996.

———. "Über die Diotima." In *Kritische Ausgabe*, edited by E. Behler, pp. 70–115. Paderborn: Schöningh, 1979.

Schleiermacher, F. D. "Monologues II and III." In *The Early Political Writings of the German Romantics*, edited by F. C. Beiser, pp. 169–97. Cambridge: Cambridge University Press, 1996.

Seton-Watson, H. *The Decline of Imperial Russia 1855–1914*. London: Praeger, 1952.

———. *The Russian Empire 1801–1917*. Oxford: Clarendon, 1988, (1967).

Shafarevitch, I. "Does Russia Have a Future?" In *From Under the Rubble*, edited by A. Solzhenitsyn, pp. 279–94. London: Collins & Harvill Press, 1975.

Shchukin, V. "Kulturnyi mir russkogo zapadnika." *Voprosy filosofii*, no. 5 (1992): 74–86.

Shragrin, B., and A. Todd, eds. *Landmarks: A Collection of Essays on the Russian Intelligentsia 1909 [Vekhi]*. New York: Howard, 1977, [1909].

Sieyès, E. J. *What Is the Third Estate?* London: Pall Mall Press, 1963.

Simpson, D. *German Aesthetic and Literary Criticism. Kant, Fichte, Schelling, Schopenhauer, Hegel*. Cambridge: Cambridge University Press, 1984.

Skinner, Q. "Motives, Intentions and the Interpretation of Texts." In *Meaning and Context, Quentin Skinner and His Critics*, edited by J. Tully. Cambridge: Polity Press, 1988.

Smith, A. D. *Theories of Nationalism*. 2nd ed. London: Duckworth, 1983.

———. *The Ethnic Revival*. Cambridge: Cambridge University Press, 1981.

Solzhenitsyn, A. "Repentance and Self-Limitation in the Life of Nations." In *From under the Rubble*, pp. 105–43. London: Collins & Harvill Press, 1975.

———. "The Smatterers." In *From under the Rubble*, pp. 229–78. London: Collins & Harvill Press, 1975.

———. "As Breathing and Consciousness Return." In *From under the Rubble*, pp. 3–25. London: Collins & Harvill Press, 1975.

———. *"The Russian Question" at the End of the Twentieth Century*. New York: Farrar, Straus & Giroux, 1995.

Sperber, J. *The European Revolutions, 1848–1851*. Cambridge: Cambridge University Press, 1994.

Steele, J. *Eternal Russia: Yeltsin, Gorbachev, and the Mirage of Democracy*. London: Faber & Faber, 1994.

Stennik, Iu. V. "Ob istokakh slavianofilstva v russkoi literature XVIII veka." In *Slavianofil-stvo i Sovremennost*, edited by B. F. Yegorov, V. A. Kotelnikov, and Iu. V. Stennik, pp. 5–22. St. Petersburg: Nauka, 1994.

Steppun, F. "Nemetskii romantism i russkoe slavianofilstvo." In *Russkaia Mysl* (March, 1910).

Sugar, P., ed. *Eastern European Nationalism in the Twentieth Century*. Washington, DC: American University Press, 1995.

Szamuely, T. *The Russian Tradition*. Edited by R. Conquest. London: Secker & Warburg, 1974.

Thaden, E. C. "The Beginnings of Romantic Nationalism in Russia." *American Slavic and East European Review* 13, no. 4 (1954): 500–21.

Tilly, C., ed. *The Formation of National States in Western Europe*. Princeton: Princeton University Press, 1975.

Tompkins, S. "Vekhi and the Russian Intelligentsia." *Canadian Slavonic Papers* II (1957): 11–25.

Troitskii, I. *Shto Takoe Russkaia Sobornost?* Moscow: AKIRN, 1993.

Tsimbaev, N. I. *Slavianofilstvo: iz istorii russkoi obshchestvennoi-politicheskoi mysli XIX veka*. Moscow: Izdatelstvo Moskovskogo universiteta, 1986.

Tulaev, P. "Rossiia i Evropa." *Nash sovremennik*, no. 11 (1991): 156–62.

Venevitinov, D. *Polnoe sobranie sochinenii*. Moscow, 1934.

von Engelhardt, D. "Romanticism in Germany." In *Romanticism in National Context*, edited by R. Porter and M. Teich, pp. 109–33. Cambridge: Cambridge University Press, 1988.

von Haxthausen, A. *Studies on the Interior of Russia*. Chicago: University of Chicago Press, 1972.

Walicki A. *Legal Philosophies of Russian Liberalism*. Oxford: Clarendon, 1987.

———. *Philosophy and Romantic Nationalism: The Case of Poland*. Oxford: Clarendon, 1982.

———. *A History of Russian Thought from the Enlightenment to Marxism*. Stanford: Stanford University Press, 1979.

———. *The Slavophile Controversy*. Oxford: Clarendon, 1975.

Wirtschafter, E. *Social Identity in Imperial Russia*. Dekalb: Northern Illinois University Press, 1997.

Yack, B. "The Myth of the Civic Nation." In *Theorizing Nationalism*, edited by R. Beiner, pp. 103–18. Albany: State University of New York Press, 1999.

Yarmolinsky, A. *Road to Revolution. A Century of Russian Radicalism*. Princeton, NJ: Princeton University Press, 1986.

Yanov, A. *The Russian New Right: Right-Wing Ideologies in the Contemporary USSR.* Berkeley: University of California Press, 1978.

————. *The Russian Challenge and the Year 2000.* Oxford: Blackwell, 1987.

———— *The Origins of Autocracy: Ivan the Terrible in Russian History.* Berkeley: University of California Press, 1981.

Yoshino, K. *Cultural Nationalism in Contemporary Japan.* London: Routledge, 1992.

Zernov, N. *Three Russian Prophets, Khomiakov, Dostoevsky, Solovev.* London: S.C.M. Press, 1944.

Ziuganov, G. "Rossiia i sovremennyi mir." *Transition,* no. 11 (1996).

————. *Sovietskaia Rossiia* 19/3 (1996).

Index